The Diaspora Returns Home

Evangelical Missiological Society Monograph Series

Anthony Casey, Rochelle Scheuermann, and Edward L. Smither
SERIES EDITORS

A Project of the Evangelical Missiological Society
www.emsweb.org

The EMS Monograph Series publishes the best book-length works of EMS members. The monographs may be reworked dissertations or original works based on missiological research focused on aspects of history, theology, culture, strategy, or spiritual formation all relating to the academic and practical nature of the missionary enterprise. EMS monographs are peer-reviewed and authors work with an editing team from Pickwick Publications (Wipf and Stock). Typically, 3–5 monographs are published each year.

The Diaspora Returns Home

An Exploration of Diaspora Missiology in the Context of
the Returning Protestant Christian Việt Kiều and Việt Nam

Bryan M. Woods

☙PICKWICK *Publications* • Eugene, Oregon

THE DIASPORA RETURNS HOME
An Exploration of Diaspora Missiology in the Context of the Returning Protestant Christian Việt Kiều and Việt Nam

Evangelical Missiological Society Monograph Series

Copyright © 2024 Bryan M. Woods. All rights reserved. Except for brief quotations in critical publications or reviews, no part of this book may be reproduced in any manner without prior written permission from the publisher. Write: Permissions, Wipf and Stock Publishers, 199 W. 8th Ave., Suite 3, Eugene, OR 97401.

Pickwick Publications
An Imprint of Wipf and Stock Publishers
199 W. 8th Ave., Suite 3
Eugene, OR 97401

www.wipfandstock.com

PAPERBACK ISBN: 978-1-7252-9236-9
HARDCOVER ISBN: 978-1-7252-9237-6
EBOOK ISBN: 978-1-7252-9238-3

Cataloguing-in-Publication data:

Names: Woods, Bryan M., author.r

Title: The diaspora returns home : an exploration of diaspora missiology in the context of the returning protestant Christian Việt Kiều and Việt Nam / Bryan M. Woods.

Description: Eugene, OR : Pickwick Publications, 2024 | Series: Evangelical Missiological Society Monograph Series | Includes bibliographical references.

Identifiers: ISBN 978-1-7252-9236-9 (paperback) | ISBN 978-1-7252-9237-6 (hardcover) | ISBN 978-1-7252-9238-3 (ebook)

Subjects: LCSH: Theological anthropology. | Emigration and immigration. | Missions—Theory. | Migrations of nations.

Classification: BV4470 .W66 2024 (paperback) | BV4470 .W66 (ebook)

03/12/24

Contents

Abstract | vii

Acknowledgments | ix

Abbreviations | xi

1. Research Focus | 1

2. Literature Review | 14

3. Methodology | 48

4. Việt Kiều Returnees: Investigating the Experiences of the Returnees | 56

5. On the Receiving End: Non-Migrant Protestant Christian Vietnamese Experiences of the Phenomenon of Return | 129

6. Summary, Missiological Implications, and Recommendations | 175

Appendix 1: Table of Interviewees | 195

Appendix 2: Interview Protocol: Vietnamese Diaspora | 199

Appendix 3: Interview Protocol: Vietnamese Local Leaders | 201

Appendix 4: Letter to Invite Project Participants | 202

Appendix 5: Protestant Christian Diaspora Returnees Pre-Interview Questionnaire | 204

Appendix 6: Letter of Informed Consent | 206

Bibliography | 209

Abstract

IN RECENT YEARS, THE Vietnamese diaspora, including some of whom are Protestant Christian Việt Kiều, have returned to their natal homeland of Vietnam in large numbers. This dissertation investigates the phenomenon of the Protestant Christian Việt Kiều who have returned and reestablished belonging in Vietnam with a missional purpose and the perspective of non-migrant local Protestant Christian leaders as a case study of diaspora missiology.

Thirty-one semi-structured qualitative interviews were conducted with returnees and local leaders in Vietnam to enhance understanding of the lived experience of these transnational carriers of religion and the impacts in homeland spaces. This study discovered that three overarching categories describe the returnees' stance towards return: those who always wanted to return, those who never wanted to return, and those who returned from a neutral starting point. Furthermore, returnees articulated three crucial motivations for coming back: the philanthropist motivation, the explicit religious motivation, and kinship bonds. These three salient motivations served as core impetuses towards return for project respondents. Furthermore, the ministries of the Protestant Christian Việt Kiều are characterized by three primary ministry clusters or common avenues of ministry engagement. The ministry foci are discipleship-centric ministries, community development-centric ministries, and business as mission-centric ministries. The local Christian leaders are generally positive toward the phenomenon. They express stances that welcome back returnees and appreciation for the hearts of the returnees and their contributions. They affirm that the returnees are engaging in many tasks which largely correlate with the primary ministry foci expressed by the returnees.

As this study demonstrates, the Protestant Christian Vietnamese diaspora community is returning and reestablishing belonging in Vietnam. Evidence is seen for ministry by the diaspora to their kinsmen (through

ABSTRACT

the diaspora) and beyond ethnic boundaries as they return to Vietnam (by and beyond the diaspora). However, questions arise as to how far diaspora as a framework can carry us. Ministry by this diaspora community is far from the dynamic picture of excitement, boundary-blurring, and karios opportunity, that dominates the literature. The return journey is a road layered with complexities, contradictions, opportunities, and unique challenges. The act of migration has changed people and their relationship to their homeland people and places. Returnees are viewed as neither foreign nor local. Deep questions of identity surfaced for most returnees as part of the return journey. Among other implications is that ministry in the natal homeland is a cross-cultural exchange for the diaspora. Dynamics of economic and social remittance play out in a myriad of situations, adding layers of complexity to the encounter. This study demonstrates that the relationship between money and missions is even more complicated when you add long-established transnational remittance patterns into the equation.

Acknowledgments

THE WORK OF THIS manuscript has been supported by the work of many. First, I want to thank my professors at Trinity Evangelical Divinity School. Their wisdom, encouragement, and instruction have molded, challenged, and inspired me along the journey. I particularly want to thank Dr. Craig Ott and Dr. Harold Netland. Their expertise and guidance along the way has been invaluable.

I am thankful to the many Vietnamese who contributed to this research project. Their stories have inspired me and serve as the basis for this dissertation. Many in Vietnam made this research possible. I have enjoyed many cups of coffee, delicious meals, and wonderful conversations. Thank you for your warm hospitality, courageous sharing, and encouragement.

My wife, Selena, has been steadfast in her support throughout the many long years of study. I am grateful to have you at my side during this entire process, including our time in Vietnam. It would not have been possible without your sacrifices and encouragement. My parents have been a source of support over the years. Your encouragement inspired me to start asking questions and seek discovery. My children, Ava and Ian. You have been a source of great joy and a reminder of the bigger picture. Their encouragement and sacrifice will never be forgotten.

Most importantly, all glory, honor, and praise to Almighty God, who loved me, called me, and has allowed me the privilege to both serve him and study. This dissertation is because of him and for him.

Abbreviations

ECVN	Evangelical Church of Việt Nam
BAM	Business as Mission
NGO	Non-Governmental Organization
RQ	Research Question
STM	Short-Term Mission
OBT	Oral Bible Training

CHAPTER 1
Research Focus

Background Context of the Study

GLOBALIZATION HAS BEEN A complex multifaceted discourse that has fascinated many throughout the years. Academics representing a diversity of disciplines seek to understand our "global village"; this shared reality of a "global coexistence altered by transnational commerce, migration, and culture."[1] These multiple layers of global interconnectedness shape, define, and continually redefine, our shared experience as global citizens in the twenty-first century.

Migration, the mass movement of people in our modern world, has long captured the attention of a wide range of scholars exploring attributes of globalization. The overarching concept of migration studies and the more narrowly defined concepts of diaspora and transnationalism are considered in many places in the academy. These social processes are seen as highly interesting for social analysis and powerful tools for understanding contemporary social experience. Missiologists have also turned their attention to this phenomenon in recent years. Leading missiologists rightly notice the scope and impact of migration in our modern world and contribute the theological lens of examination to this complex phenomenon. As Nguyen states, "on the highways and byways of every continent, hundreds of millions of immigrants are constantly on the move."[2] The challenge for missiologists is to ascertain how God is presently at work in our epoch with our own challenges and opportunities that reverberate around the globe. Therefore, the discipline labors to extrapolate missiological praxis based on current global characteristics and theological sensitivity.

---

1. Lee, "World," 502.
2. Nguyen and Prior, *God's People*, xi.

Diaspora Missiology is a missiological discipline that has emerged with great excitement in recent years. As an emerging discipline it takes seriously the global context of mass migration with the theological lens that asserts that God is at work as the "master conductor of the global diasporas."[3] As Tira maintains, "contemporary migrations are within the sovereign missional purpose of God."[4] For advocates of diaspora missiology, God is redemptively at work through the twenty-first-century phenomenon of mass migration. The challenge is to innovate and agilely respond to our global context so that we can faithfully follow the Great Commission in our day and age.

The analysis of diaspora missiology is best undertaken by examining the complexities of specific occurrences. The context of modern Vietnam and the return of the Việt Kiều (Overseas Vietnamese) after forty years, presents a dynamic and evolving case study of missions undertaken by a diaspora community.[5] Recent years have witnessed a growing phenomenon of the return of this diaspora community to their natal homeland. This development has not gone unnoticed by scholars who have launched research projects to explore various dimensions of this transnational movement and outcomes.[6] While their studies are of great value, they have often neglected the domain of religion and specifically the Christian faith experience and missional motivation for return. Plentiful personal business opportunities[7] and durable family ties are not all that brings people home.

The most commonly cited number is that as of 2011, 500,000 Việt Kiều[8] are returning to Vietnam each year.[9] This is a significant number and

---

3. Im and Yong, *Global Diasporas*, 1.

4. Tira, "Diaspora Missiology and Lausanne Movement," 226.

5. Diaspora missiology literature is overwhelmingly focused on theory and examples of ministry to the diaspora. Very little empirical evidence is given to ministry by and beyond the diaspora. This study contributes to this knowledge gap.

6. E.g., Carruthers, "Saigon"; Koh, "You Can Come Home Again"; Ngo, *New Way*; Nguyen-Akbar, "Finding the American Dream Abroad?"; Pham, "Returning Diaspora"; Reed-Danahay, "Like a Foreigner"; Small, *Currencies of Imagination*

7.. As Bui unpacks, the economic impact of the diaspora in Vietnam is unmistakable as researchers point out that "the 4.5 million Vietnamese living abroad accounted for nearly 70 percent of all foreign investment in Vietnam since 1991, this capital is used primarily for business." Bui, *Returns of War*, 186. Moreover, "for the South Vietnamese who left, many have returned to Vietnam to find better opportunities in their former homeland." Bui, *Returns of War*, 187.

8. Nguyen, "Vietnam and Its Diaspora," 248.

9. It is important to note that this number simply attempts to count members of the

the ripple effects of such a mass return are being felt in the natal homeland in a variety of spaces. This includes the domain of the vibrant tapestry of religious life that is experiencing a nascent flourishing in the Doi Moi era.[10] Likewise, the Protestant Church is impacted as Protestant Christian Việt Kiều return among this wave of diaspora returnees. However, the experiences of the Christian returnees, their motivations, transnational networks, experiences and challenges in ministry, places of impact, and contributions to the growth of Protestant Christianity in Vietnam is little understood. This study explores and analyzes the experiences of the Vietnamese diaspora that have returned to Vietnam in recent years with a missional purpose among other reasons. This is an important knowledge gap that this dissertation will seek to speak into.

Research Concern

The purpose of this study is to explore a case study of diaspora missiology through the context of the returning Protestant Christian Việt Kiều to Vietnam. In what ways does the experience of Protestant Christian Việt Kiều inform diaspora missiology strategies? In recent years, the Vietnamese diaspora, including Protestant Christian Việt Kiều, have returned to their natal homeland in large numbers. However, the return of Protestant Christian Việt Kiều as transnational carriers of religion has not previously been studied. This study is concerned with those that have returned and reestablished belonging in Vietnam either as residents in Vietnam or transnational citizens and how local Protestant Christian Vietnamese leaders are experiencing this phenomenon.

Significance of the Research

This study is expected to help fill a knowledge gap in both missiological research and twenty-first-century missions practice. The context of the

---

Vietnamese diaspora entering Vietnam through a port of entry in a given year. The Vietnamese government does not attempt to differentiate between those that are traveling to Vietnam for a short holiday and those that are returning to live or live transnational lives and would fit established transnational criteria. This study is concerned with those that have returned and reestablished belonging in Vietnam either as residents in Vietnam or transnational citizens.

10. E.g., Taylor, *Modernity and Re-Enchantment*; Hoang, *New Religions*.

twenty-first century demands a responsive and innovative practice of faithful Christian mission and new research that helps us to see, understand, and faithfully respond in light of changing global realities.[11] As such, in recent years, missiologists have joined with scholars from a wide range of disciplines in expanding and sharpening our understanding of the complex changes reverberating around the globe today. However, the fruitful discussion that has developed in recent years bound together by the theories of migration, globalization and the shift of the church to the global South is a young discussion.[12] This dissertation will interact with key social processes in our contemporary world and provide a window of insight into the lived experiences of those for whom living missionally conscious transnational lives is an everyday reality.

While the rhetoric of missiologists celebrates the potential of new avenues for ministry as "kairos opportunities,"[13] the need to ground the phenomenon in robust research remains high. Empirical research on cross-cultural missions by diaspora communities has lagged behind the exuberant optimism for this twenty-first-century missiology. As such, the call for further research into the theory has emerged.[14]

Additionally, secular scholars conceptualize religion in the modern world as being in motion;[15] as an "aspect of contemporary social life that operates across borders."[16] The construct of social remittances has been employed within the discipline of sociology by scholars such as Levitt and Ngo as a productive tool of analysis for understanding religion on the move and transnational religious links in our contemporary world. The conceptualization of social remittances offers an intriguing tool for analysis when applied to this study. Furthermore, while focusing on Hmong in Vietnam and

---

11. Bellofatto and Johnson, "Christianity in Its Global Context."

12. George, "Diaspora"; Tira, *Filipino Kingdom Workers*; Wan, *Diaspora Missiology*.

13. Tira, "Diaspora Missiology and the Lausanne Movement," 217.

14. E.g., Downes, "Mission by and beyond the Diaspora," 88; Krabill and Norton, "New Wine," 449.

15. Levitt introduces the framework of transnational optic to understand this movement. She writes that a "transnational optic helps identify actors, ideas, and technologies that are the carriers of religion. It calls our attention to the real and imagined, past and present geographies through which religion travels and the pathways and networks that guide the elements circulating within them. Finally, it produces a clearer picture of how and why religious assemblages are created at these sites of encounter." Levitt, "Religion on the Move," 163.

16. Levitt, "Religion on the Move," 162.

diaspora Hmong, Ngo correctly noted the need to conduct further research on "missions carried out in the context of postcolonial and contemporary societies."[17] This dissertation seeks to contribute to filling in this knowledge gap with the case study of the returning Protestant Christian Việt Kiều as transnational carriers of religion working in the context of a postcolonial society. Therefore, this is a micro-level study of transnational relations that seeks to elucidate these experiences and pathways.[18]

Definition of Terms

Certain terms will be defined for clarity of reading. Additionally, I will briefly provide an overview of the contemporary landscape of Protestant Christianity in Vietnam.

Diaspora Missiology

Diaspora Missiology has been coined by Enoch Wan (2011) and further developed and heavily promoted by influential missiologists such as Sadiri Tira in multiple publications through the Lausanne network channels. Diaspora ministry, ministry to and through people on the move, is seen as a "karios opportunity."[19] In his seminal publication, Enoch Wan defines diaspora missions as "Christians' participation in God's redemptive mission to evangelize their kinsmen on the move, and through them to reach out to natives in their homeland and beyond."[20] This is delineated in three types of diaspora missions: missions to the diaspora, missions through the diaspora, and missions by and beyond the diaspora.[21] Missions through the diaspora is defined as "diaspora Christians reaching out to their kinsmen, though networks of friendship and kinship in host countries, their homelands, and abroad."[22] Mission by and beyond the diaspora is defined as

---

17. Ngo, *Protestantism and the Hmong*, 64.
18. Biney, "Transnational Religious Networks," 286.
19. Tira and Yamamori, *Scattered and Gathered*, 87.
20. Wan, *Diaspora Missiology*, 5.
21. Wan, *Diaspora Missiology*, 5.
22. Wan, *Diaspora Missiology*, 5.

"motivating and mobilizing diaspora Christians for cross-cultural missions to other ethnic groups in their host countries, homelands, and abroad."[23]

Mission

Mission, as used in this dissertation, is an expansive concept that encompasses both evangelism and social action. As John Stott articulated, "mission describes rather everything the church is sent into the world to do."[24] Christian mission therefore, includes both "evangelism and social responsibility, since both are authentic expressions of the love which longs to serve man in his need."[25] The Great Commission (Matt 28:19–20) and the Great Commandment (Matt 22:37–38) work together to holistically form the guiding vision and practice of Christian Mission. Christian mission is simply purposefully using ones God given resources and talents to be a blessing and participate as a sent one into the world to do everything the church is sent to do. A plurality of expressions of Christian love, directed towards serving people in Vietnam, captures the operational outlook at the center of many different activities collectively labeled Christian mission that the Việt Kiều undertake as they return to Vietnam.

Transnationalism

Transnationalism refers to the

> sustained linkages and ongoing exchanges among non-state actors based across national borders—businesses, non-government organizations, and individuals sharing the same interest (by way of criteria such as religious beliefs, common cultural and geographic origins)—we can differentiate these as 'transnational' practices and groups (referring to their links functioning across nation-states). The collective attributes of such connections, their processes of formation and maintenance, and their wider implications are referred to broadly as 'transnationalism'[26]

---

23. Wan, *Diaspora Missiology*, 5.
24. Stott, *Christian Mission*, 48.
25. Stott, *Christian Mission*, 55.
26. Vertovec, *Transnationalism*, 3.

These relationships have been "globally intensified" and are "planet-spanning" and exist "despite great distances and notwithstanding the presence of international borders (and all the laws, regulations and national narratives they represent)."[27] Transnational dynamics of religion are expected to be seen in this study as religion is an "aspect of contemporary social life that operates across borders."[28] This study explores the dynamic of religion moving along transnational pathways among people on the move and those in the homeland and inform the "ideas, behaviors, identities, and social capital that flows from host to sending country communities."[29] What is the relationship between homeland actors and diaspora citizens who have returned and reestablished belonging in their natal homeland? Therefore, the dynamic of social remittance in the process of mission through and by and beyond the diaspora is expected to be seen and will serve as a tool to help frame the study.

Việt Kiều

There are also terms specifically related to Vietnam, the Vietnamese diaspora, and Vietnamese Protestant Christians that will be used in this dissertation. First, the term for the Vietnamese diaspora I will be using in this dissertation is Việt Kiều.[30] This term is frequently used to designate to the Overseas Vietnamese. Specifically, it refers to ethnically Vietnamese people that were born in Vietnam and emigrated from Vietnam at one point in time (1st generation) and their children born outside of Vietnam (2nd generation), and have established belonging and citizenship outside of Vietnam in a new homeland. At the same time, they retain an identity as Vietnamese, connection and association with other Overseas Vietnamese, and their historic homeland of Vietnam. As such, international workers, international students, and others who are living outside of Vietnam on a temporary basis are not counted among the Việt Kiều. However, the terminology is not universally adapted by all who fit this profile. As such,

27. Vertovec, *Transnationalism*, 3.
28. Levitt, "Religion on the Move," 162.
29. Levitt, *Transnational Villagers*, 54.
30. See Koh for a detailed discussion on the etymology of the term, ongoing meaning construction and shifting connotations associated with the term, and acceptance and/or persistent rejection of the term by the Vietnamese global diaspora. Koh, "You Can Come Home Again," 182–84.

some who participated in this research project prefer terminology such as Vietnamese-American. Where possible, I use the precise language of the interviewee. Nevertheless, Việt Kiều is a useful descriptive term for the Overseas Vietnamese diaspora and will be utilized in this work.

Vietnamese Protestant Christians

It is helpful to provide the reader with a basic mapping of the landscape of Protestant Christianity in contemporary Vietnam. Protestantism in Vietnam has historic roots in the twentieth-century missionary work of the Christian & Missionary Alliance (CMA). Protestantism came to Vietnam in 1911. The CMA established an indigenous church, the Hội Thánh Tin Lành Việt Nam (Evangelical Church of Vietnam, ECVN), the first and to this day largest denomination in the country. Later, other Protestant denominations such as the Southern Baptist Church and the Mennonite Church entered South Vietnam during the war years. Starting in the 1980s, house (or home) churches appeared and grew quickly. Many of these home churches follow the theological perspectives of the ECVN.[31] Moreover, most of the key leaders of these churches were descended from the ECVN.[32] The Protestant Church remains structurally partitioned between the North and the South. As such, respondents will reference working with the ECVN South or ECVN North, etc. At times, Protestantism as an officially recognized religion in Vietnam is simply referred to by both believers and non-believers in Vietnam as Tin Lanh churches.[33] This term literally means Good News. In this usage, the term does not designate a specific denomination (i.e. the ECVN), but rather Protestant Christianity, sometimes to differentiate Protestant Christianity from Catholic Christianity, which has its own lengthy history in Vietnam. This dissertation employed purposeful sampling to gather data from respondents that identify with registered Protestant denominations and house churches that are all under

---

31. Truong, "Vietnamese Theology of Mission," 3.

32. Truong, "Vietnamese Theology of Mission," provides a detailed overview of the history and theological development of Protestant Christianity in Vietnam; Lê, *Short History*, is an excellent and often cited resource for understanding the first fifty years of the ECVN.

33. Le notes that the 2009 Vietnamese government census designates Protestantism as Tin Lanh. This census report found that one percent of the population identifies as Tin Lanh. Le, "Pentecostal Movements," 181. Although ministry leaders put the figure up closer to two percent of the population by some accounts. Kelly, *On the Edge*, 89.

the umbrella of Protestant Christianity in both the North and the South. Whenever possible, the term the respondent uses for their specific ministry affiliation is utilized.

Research Focus

This research will explore and analyze the experiences of Protestant Christian Việt Kiều that are returning to Vietnam with a stated missional intent and the impact and outcomes of their activities on the homeland Christian spaces. Particular focus will be given to motivations for return, ministry experiences as they return to their natal homeland with the intention of participating in missions, the exchange dynamics of social remittances along the transnational networks as they navigate their return, and how local non-migrant Vietnamese experience the phenomenon of return.

Research Questions

The research questions (RQs) for this project are thus as follows:
1. RQ Number 1: What are the motivating factors of Protestant Christian Việt Kiều returning to Vietnam for mission related purposes?

    a. Sub RQ1: Are the Christian Việt Kiều working in Vietnam, being commissioned, trained and sent by Vietnamese diaspora churches or other missions organizations? If so, what does that transnational link look like for these churches and ministry networks?

    b. Sub RQ2: What specific ministry goals did they have for returning?

2. RQ Number 2: What has been the experience in ministry of the returning Protestant Christian Việt Kiều regarding mission related reasons for returning?

    a. Sub RQ1: What have been unexpected positives and challenges to the return experience as it relates to life and ministry in Vietnam?

    b. Sub RQ2: Who do the returning Protestant Việt Kiều minister to?

c. Sub RQ3: How do the Việt Kiều perceive the fruitfulness of their return ministry?

d. Sub RQ4: How have the Việt Kiều themselves been personally impacted by their experience?

3. RQ Number 3: How have the non-migrants experienced the phenomenon of return?

a. Sub RQ1: How do the non-migrants perceive the missionary impact of the Việt Kiều?

b. Sub RQ2: How has the Vietnamese church practices and normative structures changed with the return of the overseas Vietnamese?

c. Sub RQ3: How do non-migrant church leaders experience power dynamics (e.g. decision making, resource sharing) in relationship to the ministry of Việt Kiều?

d. Sub RQ4: To what extent do Vietnamese Christians accept the returnees as insiders and with solidarity as brothers and sisters in the faith?

Limitations of the Study

The scope of this study is limited to diaspora Protestant Christian Vietnamese from the West, intentional engaged in Christian ministry in Vietnam as a part of their life as a returnee or transnational migrant in Vietnam and local Christian non-migrant leaders.[34] There are two major limitations to this study. First, the researcher was not able to travel throughout all locations around the country where returnees could potentially be found. The researcher could not for safety and security reasons conduct interviews outside of urban areas in Vietnam. Some rural provinces still require special permission to enter and all foreigners are closely monitored once you leave the major cities. Keeping this in mind, purposeful sampling was employed to include respondents (both Việt Kiều and local Christian non-migrants) from the North, Central, and Southern regions of Vietnam. However, all interviews that were conducted in Vietnam were

---

34. These would be people that "exhibit a transnational way of being . . . and also express a transnational way of belonging." Levitt, "Transnationalism," 42. Or demonstrate the evidence of "sustained linkages and ongoing exchanges among non-state actors based across national borders." Vertovec, *Transnationalism*, 3.

conducted in an urban context. Furthermore, given security concerns, most interviews occurred in neutral non-ministry spaces. This limited the ability of the researcher to conduct participant observation. Based on interview criteria, it might be possible to find people living and working in rural provinces.[35] However, any interviews with such persons would have had to occur while they were in America.

Second, the researcher was limited by time and travel demands. Some who would have participated in this study were not able to participate due to conflicting travel and ministry schedules. As much as possible was coordinated ahead of time to mitigate conflicting schedules. The researcher attempted to fit travel timing around the schedules of the potential participants. Even still, not every interested contact was able to participate. Furthermore, trust had to be quickly established for respondents to choose to participate. Trust was largely gained via introductions from trusted people within their active networks.

Delimitations of the Study

Based on these limitations the study has five major delimitations. First, only those individuals who fit the criteria as someone who identifies as Protestant Christian Việt Kiều and has returned with a missional intention were included in this study. This excluded many returnees who are exclusively back for other purposes such as employment opportunities, family visitation, holiday, or participation in a Short-term Mission trip.[36] It also limited the local non-migrant Christians. These respondents needed to have personal experience in some capacity with missional returnees. Many returnees were excluded that did not demonstrate a Christian missional intention for return. Others were excluded that did not demonstrate the necessary transnational "sustained linkages and ongoing exchanges."[37] This was primarily ascertained by an individual's own self-identification. In other words, in pre-questionnaires, if the respondents identify themselves

---

35. While all interviews occurred in major urban centers or via Zoom, not all participants worked in these urban centers.

36. An individual who is traveling to Vietnam for a short-term mission trip would not be able to identify "sustained linkages" Vertovec, *Transnationalism*, 3, or cultivate a sense of "belonging and being" Levitt, "Transnationalism," 42, in Vietnam. However, an individual that makes regular trips, even if the duration of each trip is short, can justifiably demonstrate the formation of "sustained linkages." Vertovec, *Transnationalism*, 3.

37. Vertovec, *Transnationalism*, 3.

as having established a sense of being and belonging in Vietnam through their transnational experience, or return and relocation to Vietnam, they qualified for this project. An individual's self-identification takes primacy for identifying respondents rather than a fixed time back in Vietnam or fixed number of trips to identity research participants.

Second, all interviews were conducted in English. While all the Việt Kiều that participated have a high level of English language competency, this limitation might hinder some of the local ministry partners who might otherwise have participated. Some might not have felt confident to speak to a foreigner in English. Some interviews with local non-migrants used some translation aids for key terms or to help express themselves. A few had translation assistance from other participants for expressing complex thoughts.

Third, contemporary Vietnam is a multiethnic, multicultural nation.[38] Many Protestant Christians are to be found among the various minority ethnic groups. However, this study cannot take into account the historical and contemporary, cultural, and theological differences between the various groups. Therefore, participants were limited to people from the majority ethnic group (Kinh also known as the Viet ethnic group). The Kinh make up approximately 85 percent of the population of Vietnam. Additionally, many ethnic minorities live in the highlands and other rural communities. Keeping travel and security restrictions in mind, the researcher was limited to the urban context. As such, while it might be possible to extrapolate insights to various ethnic minority communities residing in Vietnam such as the Hmong or Dao, and beyond to other nations in South-East Asia this study is focused on one country and the ethnically Kinh diaspora people with a unique and complex history and contemporary experience.

Fourth, Catholic Vietnamese, while making up the majority of Christians in Vietnam, and in and of themselves a fascinating movement with many ministry outlets and rich transnational links, will not be included in this study. It would simply become unmanageable to include both the Catholic Christians and Protestant Christians in Vietnam in this one study.

Fifth, the researcher focused on the motivations and experiences especially as these relate to Christian ministry work as one returns to Vietnam. The many comprehensive narratives shared during field research are

---

38. Vince Le references the 2009 census which reports that Vietnam has "more than fifty other ethnic minority groups that make up 14 percent of the population." Le, "Petecostal Movemement," 181.

intriguing and rich. Respondents touched on many topics in the course of conversations that are tangential to the research focus. While a component to the story, details pertaining to topics such as the leaving of Vietnam or life in the diaspora are not reported in this study. While highly informative, and relevant to the life journey, this research focuses on the return dynamics rather than a whole life story of an individual.

CHAPTER 2
Literature Review

VIETNAM HAS LONG CAPTURED the attention of a wide number of scholars exploring the intricacy of the subject matter. Multiple disciplines stake out their own territory, exploring questions of interest to their fields of inquiry. As Mandy Thomas noted in her 1999 study, "Since before the Vietnam War ended there has been a continuous scholarly interest in Vietnam. Since doi moi, the Vietnamese government's policy of economic renovation and reform, was introduced in 1986 there has been a virtual efflorescence of academic studies."[1] This has only accelerated in the twenty years since her rich study. Literature on Vietnam is booming. A basic library search reveals some 1300 works published in the last five years alone with Vietnam as the subject matter. This reveals a widespread and sustained fascination with Vietnam and the legacies of the conflict some forty-six years after the reunification event(s) that marked the advent of a new era for Vietnam and the genesis of the largest wave(s) of Vietnamese diaspora.

This literature review is organized around four major topics of research to frame the theoretical backdrop of this research project: diaspora missiology, an exploration of sociological literature that forms the core building blocks of the theory, academic studies of the Vietnamese diaspora with a narrow focus on studies exploring the evolving transnational dynamics of the diaspora and the homeland, and finally literature that locates this study within the particular Vietnamese church ecosystem with its own history, established theological traditions and relevant missiological questions. As such, an overview of the Protestant Church in Vietnam today and current theological works will be introduced.

---

1. Thomas, *Dreams in the Shadows*, xv.

Diaspora Missiology

Diaspora Missiology has emerged as a prominent topic within the field of missions studies today. There has been an explosion of research and rhetoric in the past decade that has reflected on migration, globalization, and the shift of the church to the global South. Enoch Wan and Sadiri Tira are visionary pioneers who have been central in developing and promoting the theory of Diaspora Missiology. Enoch Wan introduced the precursor to diaspora missiology as early as 2004.[2] Wan's 2011 work, *Diaspora Missiology: Theory, Methodology, and Practice*, marks a watershed moment in the development of this emerging theory. Within this work, Wan sets the stage for his theory by presenting the twin phenomena of mass migration in the twenty-first century and the shift of the church to the global South. According to Wan, "the changing landscape of the 21st century, namely the global phenomena of large-scale diaspora and Christendom's shifting center of gravity, requires serious reflections on the missiological conceptualizations and strategies for Christian missions."[3] As such, Wan attempts to argue for diaspora missiology as a new missiological approach to supplement traditional missiology.[4] Wan coins the term "diaspora missiology" to define and conceptualize this alternative twenty-first-century missiology (see Wan's definition in chapter one).

Enoch Wan has been widely influential in disseminating this construct into current missiological vernacular through his leadership roles in the Evangelical Missiological Society, work with the Lausanne Movement, and mentorship of scholars who have taken up the cause such as his mentee, Sadiri Joy Tira. Tira has successfully utilized his leadership platform within the Lausanne Movement to widely distribute and advocate for the new paradigm through the prolific publication of works engaging the topic of diaspora missiology.[5] Tira is a passionate ambassador for diaspora missiology. The general pattern of his publications is to recount the development of the concept and demonstrate how it is gaining momentum, while inviting others to join in the movement. These are inspirational articles that are rhetoric rich, but empirically weak.

---

2. Wan, "Phenomenon of Diaspora," 103–21.

3. Wan, *Diaspora Missiology*, 3.

4. Wan, *Diaspora Missiology*, 4.

5. E.g., Wan and Tira, "Diaspora Missiology," 27–54; Tira, *Human Tidal Wave*; Tira, "Diaspora Missiology and Lausanne Movement," 214–27. In this article, Tira notes that "Cape Town 2010 changed the terminology within the Lausanne Movement from referring to diaspora peoples as "diasporas." They are referred to as "scattered peoples": Tira, "Diaspora Missiology and Lausanne Movement," 215. While the terminology changed, the concept remains similar. Hence the name of the 2016 volume, Tira and Yamamori, *Scattered and Gathered*.

Tira has also contributed his own work of original empirical research to this emerging body of literature. His 2008 dissertation, *Filipino Kingdom Workers: An Ethnographic Study in Diaspora Missiology*, was published by the Evangelical Missiological Society Dissertation Series in 2011. This dissertation is one of the first scholarly attempts to employ the emerging theory in an ethnographic study. Additionally, this case study has been cited as evidence for the validity of diaspora missiology in future publications by Wan, Tira and other proponents of the theory and presented as a case study for inspiring other diaspora communities to capture God's purposes for their scattering. Within this dissertation, Tira provides clear evidence that Filipinos are scattered globally. What is less clear from the study, is how they are successfully living missional lives and reaching out beyond their diaspora group. Simply because one is scattered from a homeland does not necessarily mean they should be labeled as kingdom workers or jump to the conclusion that they are reaching out beyond the diaspora. The evidence presented by Tira does not appear to match the rhetoric and invites further empirical research.

The statistical data on global migration patterns presented by Wan, Tira, Sam George, and others, as a foundation for the theory are impressive. Furthermore, as a missiological theory, diaspora missiology draws from a robust theological lens to advocate for the paradigm. The theological foundation for diaspora missiology is credibly developed by several theologian practitioners.[6] These theologians have taken up the task of presenting a theological foundation for diaspora missiology which establishes the Biblical pattern linking missions and migration. It is perceived that God worked to bring about his plan of salvation through people on the move in the Biblical record such as Priscilla and Aquila (Acts 18).[7] Moreover, it is observed that the theme of human migration runs throughout the Biblical narrative. There is a "spirit of migration that permeates the biblical record and defines biblical religion."[8]

As missiologists, Tira and associates go beyond simply describing the scope and patterns of the vast people movements reverberating around the globe in the twenty-first century and the optic that sees the link between

---

6. E.g., Van Engen, "Biblical Perspectives"; Walls, *Crossing Cultural Frontiers*; Santos, "Exploring the Major Dispersion Terms"; Ott, "Diaspora and Witness"; Caldwell, "Diaspora Ministry"; Carroll, "Biblical Perspectives on Migration"; Senior, "Beloved Aliens and Exiles."

7. Ott, "Diaspora and Witness," 82–84.

8. Hanciles, *Beyond Christendom*, 139.

migration and God's redemptive work in human history as recorded in the Biblical narrative. Most importantly, this has profound present day missional praxis implications. Tira uses the terminology of "kairos movement"[9] and "karios opportunity"[10] in another publication to portray the theological dimension behind the numbers that demonstrates the present day divine missional opportunity. For diaspora missiology advocates, God is at work as the "master conductor of the global diasporas. God has devised and orchestrated the scattering and gathering of individuals and people groups. . . . Global diasporas and migration have been and will continue to be a significant and indispensable means by which God accomplishes his redemptive purposes in this world through Jesus Christ."[11] Or as Tira contends, "contemporary migrations are within the sovereign missional purpose of God."[12] God is redemptively at work through the twenty-first-century phenomenon of mass migration. In Tira's assessment, this is a divine opportunity to fulfill the Great Commission. As God worked in the scriptures through migratory movements; God is at work in our epoch to bring about his redemptive purposes. However, empirical research needs to be conducted that ascertains how this is unfolding and allows missions practitioners to best be agile and responsive to our context.

This dissertation will utilize this theoretical framework to examine the experiences of the returning Vietnamese diaspora as a case study of diaspora missiology. While the theological foundation is robust, the empirical research that supports these bold claims or demonstrates how this is happening amid the people doing diaspora missiology is scarce. It is simply assumed that because people are scattered in great numbers, it is an actualized and effective divine opportunity to participate in what God is doing to "evangelize their kinsmen on the move, and through them to reach out to natives in their homeland and beyond."[13] Empirical research that sheds light on how diaspora peoples live out the modes of ministry through and by and beyond the diaspora is called for so that we can better assess the validity of the theory, where the gaps are, and what questions ought to be asked as we contemplate missions in the twenty-first century.

---

9. Tira, "Diaspora Missiology and the Lausanne Movement," 215.
10. Tira and Yamamori, *Scattered and Gathered*, 87.
11. Im and Yong, *Global Diasporas*, 1.
12. Tira, "Diaspora Missiology and the Lausanne Movement," 226.
13. Wan, *Diaspora Missiology*, 5.

Scott Sunquist, in writing about the challenges and opportunities of missions and migration, places the focus squarely on the Western context and migration to the West. It is assumed that we, the Western church, need to revise our mission theology to embrace what God is doing in our day and age as the mission field comes to us. Sunquist reminds us that "migration is the normal Christian way of existing,"[14] and that we need to develop a "mission theology that is focused on people moving away from their home region or country."[15] According to Sunquist, "the development of a mission theology that embraces both individual missionaries going out and migration coming to us has not been done before."[16] Western Christians are "missing the missionary opportunity at their doorstep because they lack an understanding of migration as mission."[17] Sunquist goes onto articulate that,

> the nations are coming to the Christian nations and to Christian contexts. . . . In all contexts where there are Christian communities, the arrival of migrants should be seen as a sign and opportunity from God. More importantly, the nations are coming to the cities of the world, so a robust theology of the missional nature of the city is important for us today. Missiologically, we can say that migration can be seen as God's providential movement of people to encounter his kingdom on earth, as it is in heaven. The churches' responsibility, is thus, to actually and thoroughly be the church completing God's purpose for the nations.[18]

For Sunquist, the view of migration and missions is primarily restricted to Wan's category of missions to the diaspora. Migrants are coming to the West (conceptually imagined as a location retaining its identity as Christian nations), and they need to be ministered to and brought into a knowledge of Christ.

In his 2014 Doctorate of Ministry thesis,[19] Thanh Trung Le focused on understanding the Protestant Vietnamese diaspora in their adopted homelands and details the implementation of a "non-formal lay leadership training program in Canada, Australia and Taiwan."[20] This study is

---

14. Sunquist, *Explorations in Asian Christianity*, 242.
15. Sunquist, *Explorations in Asian Christianity*, 242.
16. Sunquist, *Explorations in Asian Christianity*, 242.
17. Sunquist, *Explorations in Asian Christianity*, 242.
18. Sunquist, *Explorations in Asian Christianity*, 244.
19. Le completed his doctorate under the supervision of Enoch Wan.
20. Wan and Le, *Mobilizing Vietnamese Diaspora*, 168.

primarily concerned with ministry to the diaspora. Le does not attempt to imagine the Vietnamese diaspora as a case study for missions by or beyond the diaspora. Le conceptualizes the Vietnamese diaspora church as needing to be ministered to and equipped, hence the case study implementing this lay leadership program. For Le, the operative framework for engaging with the Vietnamese diaspora falls into the territory Krabill and Norton's astute critique of the theory.[21] There is a glaring omission of any substantial mention of missional outreach activities undertaken by Vietnamese diaspora believers either in the lands in which they reside or back to Vietnam.

Some scholars, such as Jehu Hanciles, have expanded the scope of the conversation. Hanciles explores the nexus of global migration and Christian missions in his 2008 work, *Beyond Christendom: Globalization, African Migration, and the Transformation of the West*.[22] This study, while noteworthy for credibly establishing the connection between migration and the spread of Christian faith historically, invites a degree of scrutiny and further research when it comes to the contemporary experience of reverse missions, or in Wan's terminology, missions through the diaspora. Hanciles is primarily concerned with African migration to the West as a form of reverse missions. However, while he finds the African diaspora to be intentional, creative and exuberant in their outreach, the Nigerians did not succeed in evangelizing local Americans.[23]

Ajani arrives at a similar conclusion as he studied the missionary outcomes of the Jesus House Chicago church for his 2015 PhD dissertation. Ajani discovered that this Nigerian church demonstrated an intentional missional engagement. This missional engagement has impacted "Hispanics and African Americans though the provision of important services. However, such engagements have not impacted White Americans. Moreover, no significant spiritual assimilation of these subcultures in the life of JHC has occurred. Some of the major challenges the group faces in her missional engagements beyond its ethnic subcultures, include racial stereotyping, and lack of assimilation into the socialcultural norm of the American society."[24]

---

21. Krabill and Norton criticize some of the basic assumptions of the theory that sees the diaspora primarily as "passive and in need of help in the LOP 55." Krabill and Norton, "New Wine," 449, among other critiques.

22. Hanciles has released a 2021 work *Migration and the Making of Global Christianity*. This work was not in circulation at the time of writing this literature review section.

23. Hanciles, *Beyond Christendom*.

24. Ajani, "Migration and Mission," v.

Stan Downes employed Wan's diaspora missiology framework in his 2015 study included in the EMS edited volume, *Diaspora Missions: Reflections on Reaching the Scattered Peoples of the World*.[25] This article represents one of the first attempts to empirically study missions by and beyond the diaspora.[26] Within this short study, Downes raises several observations and provides reflections on pragmatic tools for diaspora believers and churches in diaspora.[27] As a rationale for his study, Downes observes that there is a noticeable literature gap when it comes to examples of diaspora Christians reaching out beyond the diaspora and reaching members of the host society. As Downes observes, "Enoch Wan includes eight case studies in his book Diaspora Missiology, all but one of them deal primarily with missions to or through the diaspora."[28] His study is an attempt to remedy this gap. In this attempt, the study fell flat. The Romanians diaspora as a case study in this article, failed to produce a good example to add to the conversation. In fact, Downes concludes that, "as we have seen, it can be quite a challenge for diaspora believers to make a spiritual impact on the local people among whom they live."[29]

Moreover, Downes seems to articulate an argument that undermines the diaspora missiology paradigm and could be cause to dampen the enthusiasm. Downes concludes that

> great opportunities are found with later generations: the first generation to move to a new place will always have the hardest time

---

25. This work published papers presented at the EMS national conference based on the EMS annual theme of Diaspora Missiology. The work was edited by Pocock and Wan. Pocock contributed his own article to this volume.

26. Ybarrola considered the case of the Brazilian diaspora in his 2012 article. He found that "when I spoke with one of these Brazilian pastors/missionaries, he told me that he was not there just to minister to the Brazilians in diaspora, but also to reach out to the broader society. However, like many of the 'reverse mission' churches in the U.S., so far this church has not had much of a local impact beyond the Brazilian diaspora." Ybarrola, "Anthropology, Diasporas, and Mission," 89.

27. Downes, the assistant area director for One Challenge in Europe, turns to his Romanian context to "explore the potential for and experience of diaspora Christians impacting people of other ethnic groups for Christ" (Downes, "Mission by and beyond the Diaspora," 78). This is largely based on firsthand observations and anecdotal accounts from his "experience as a missionary in Romania from 1996 to 2008 with OC International, and my role as OC's Europe area director since that time." Downes, "Mission by and beyond the Diaspora," 78.

28. Downes, "Mission by and beyond the Diaspora," 88.

29. Downes, "Mission by and beyond the Diaspora," 88.

adjusting and may have a harder time having a spiritual impact on the local people. The situation is quite different for later generations. As children grow up in the new environment and go to school, they become proficient in the local language and much more in tune with the host society. They are then better equipped to minister to the people around them.[30]

For Downes, the later generations are bicultural and this is seen as being advantageous to ministry in the host context. This may in fact be a more accurate representation of the picture of ministry by and beyond the diaspora. However, mission through later generations is a radically different ministry paradigm than the concept that Tira exuberantly promotes as he writes of the potential missionary impact of the groups such as the Overseas Filipino Workers in his dissertation. It also raises the question of the distinct contribution of the theory as immigrant churches have its own literature. Nevertheless, Downes is optimistic even in this discovery. He calls for more research to be published that fills in this gap and encourages the many diaspora churches.

Krabill and Norton advance a critical appraisal of diaspora missiology in their 2015 article. They readily acknowledge the helpful insights that the discipline provides. The main point of critique has to do with the manner in which Enoch Wan sets up diaspora missiology as a distinct discipline in contrast to his characterization of traditional missiology. They also point out a rather limited engagement with the explosion of literature in migration studies and missiological discourse on migration studies,[31] and some of the basic assumptions regarding the agency of the diaspora.[32] They provide counternarratives within the literature that would challenge this basic assumption.

Krabill and Norton have much to say about the basic assumptions that comprise Wan's defining of traditional missiology. They note that, "the elements that comprise Wan's traditional missiology do not accurately represent the last twenty-five years of missiological thinking."[33] Furthermore, they raise several questions on Wan's categories of comparison between traditional missiology and diaspora missiology. In each category, Wan's characterization of traditional missiology raises several questions that beg

---

30. Downes, "Mission by and beyond the Diaspora," 85.
31. Krabill and Norton, "New Wine," 447.
32. Krabill and Norton, "New Wine," 448.
33. Krabill and Norton, "New Wine," 445.

for clarity and "implicitly links the diaspora missiology framework to a missiological discourse of an era that no longer exists."[34] Wan is accused of developing a "caricature of missiological themes of a bygone era."[35] As such, this calls into question the distinct contribution of the theory. In conclusion, the authors agree with the basic diaspora missiology premise. "Yet, the way diaspora missiology is often described and strategically presented represents a narrow understanding of the significance of migration for missiological reflection and praxis."[36]

All in all, while rich in optimism, the theory is lacking in robust empirical research to support the ambitious claims. Krabill and Norton[37] and Downes[38] both are correct in noting the noticeably few examples of missions by or beyond the diaspora. Empirical research is needed to support the passionate rhetoric of this "karios opportunity,"[39] especially as it pertains to missions through and by and beyond the diaspora. As the field matures, more literature needs to be generated that produces robust studies of these Kingdom workers experiences as they engage in mission through and beyond the diaspora. This current study is one such attempt.

Sociological Foundations of Diaspora Missiology: Migration Studies, Diaspora, and Transnationalism

As a conceptual framework for analysis, diaspora missiology draws from an interdisciplinary foundation of theological reflection and sociological insight. This section of the literature review will interact with a selection of the relevant insights drawn from the sociological building block of diaspora missiology. There has been a considerable amount of robust research in the disciplines of migration studies, diaspora, and transnationalism in the past thirty years. The vast scope and depth of this research attests to the prolonged expanse and increasing significance of migration in our contemporary world.[40]

---

34. Krabill and Norton, "New Wine," 446.
35. Krabill and Norton, "New Wine," 447.
36. Krabill and Norton, "New Wine," 452.
37. Krabill and Norton, "New Wine," 449.
38. Downes, "Mission by and beyond the Diaspora," 88.
39. Tira and Yamamori, "Scattered and Gathered," 87.
40. Peter Phan observes that "as a social institution, the church is unavoidably influenced by events, factors, movements, and trends in the secular society, and this is

Transnationalism was defined in chapter one. It is a research lens that is primarily concerned with unraveling the complexities of "sustained linkages and ongoing exchanges among non-state actors based across national borders."[41] As a research lens the term can be considered as related to, yet distinct from, the term diaspora.

> Although both terms refer to cross-border processes, diaspora has been often used to denote religious or national groups living outside an (imagined) homeland, whereas transnationalism is often used both more narrowly—to refer to migrants' durable ties across countries—and, more widely, to capture not only communities, but all sorts of social formations, such as transnationally active networks, groups and organizations. Moreover, while diaspora and transnationalism are sometimes used interchangeably, the two terms reflect different intellectual genealogies. The revival of the notion of diaspora and the advent of transnational approaches can be used productively to study central questions of social and political change and transformation.[42]

Diaspora is the older of the two terms. The concept suggests the imagery of scattering from a particular location. "Where immigration connotes travel from one country to another, diaspora is the scattering throughout the world from one geographic location."[43] Furthermore, the term has the characteristics of a "splitting in the sense of home. A fundamental ambivalence is embedded in the term diaspora: a dual ontology in which the diasporic subject is seen to look in two directions — towards an historical cultural identity on one hand, and the society of relocation on the other"[44] and "exile." "In this sense the term retains the meaning from the original

---

especially true in matters concerning migration, which has enormous impact on all aspects of life in the countries as well as the churches of origin and destination. Except for explicitly religious purposes such as missionizing, Christians voluntarily migrate, or are forced to do so, for the same reasons, undergo the same migration dynamics, and are governed by the same migration policies as other migrants, religious and otherwise. Consequently, to understand Christian migration, it is necessary to place it within the larger context of global migration in general." Phan, "Christianity as an Institutional Migrant," 10. Hence, the larger body of scholarship informs the theory of diaspora missiology and the specific experiences of the returning Protestant Christian diaspora in this study.

41. Vertovec, "Transnationalism," 3.
42. Faist, "Diaspora and Transnationalism," 9.
43. Ashcroft et al., "Part Sixteen—Diaspora," 425.
44. Ashcroft et al., "Part Sixteen—Diaspora," 425.

text of Deut 28, verse 25 in which dispersion is a punishment. In many respects the experience of diaspora retains these characteristics."[45]

Additionally, the term connotes meaning and identity construction. As Ashcroft emphasizes, "diasporic identity demonstrates the extent to which identity itself must be constructed and reconstructed by individuals in their everyday life."[46] Robin Cohen, in his seminal work, transcends the classic diaspora definition[47] by adding a focus that recognizes the "positive virtues of retaining a diasporic identity."[48] For Cohen, "the tension between an ethnic, a national and a transnational identity is often a creative, enriching one."[49] For Ashcroft, the creativity comes through travel as "diaspora highlights the global trend of creating, constructing, and reconstructing identity, not by identifying with some ancestral place, but through travelling itself. While the diasporic subject travels, so does culture. A travelling culture means a culture that changes, develops and transforms itself according to the various influences it encounters in different places."[50] Creativity and a traveling culture that develops and transforms among diaspora provides insight for the experiences and identity construction questions that surface in this current study.

While there is overlap, migration, diaspora, and transnationalism are not equivalent, interchangeable words in a technical sense.[51] Some,

---

45. Ashcroft et al., "Part Sixteen—Diaspora," 425.

46. Ashcroft et al., "Part Sixteen—Diaspora," 426.

47. Cohen's robust scholarship provides a very helpful summary of the classic notion of diaspora (the Jewish tradition) and transcends that for the twenty-first-century phenomenon. Cohen, *Global Diasporas*, 21. Cohen builds off the classic notion of Jewish diaspora and Safran's seminal 1991 article, to propose nine common features of diaspora. Cohen, *Global Diasporas*, 26.

48. Cohen, *Global Diasporas*, 24.

49. Cohen, *Global Diasporas*, 24.

50. Ashcroft et al., "Part Sixteen—Diaspora," 427.

51. See for example Castles and Miller. They conclude that the rapid growth of transnational theory has raised more questions than can be easily answered with the research findings at our disposal. They note that, the "degree to which migrants do actually engage in transnational behavior has not been adequately established. Nor do we know how salient such behavior is for receiving and sending societies, and for the relationships between them . . . the majority of migrants probably do not fit the transnational pattern. Temporary labor migrants who sojourn abroad for a few years, send back remittances, communicate with their family at home and visit them occasionally are not necessarily 'transmigrants'. Nor are permanent migrants who leave forever, and simply retain loose contact with their homeland. The key defining feature is that transnational activities are a central part of a person's life. Where this can be shown empirically to apply to a group of migrants, one can appropriately speak of a transnational community." Castles and Miller, *Age of Migration*, 32–33.

such as, Emma Wild-Wood muses that among some missiologists, "diaspora is applied loosely."[52] She argues that "while it is worthy of study, diaspora cannot be the overarching term for new theory and methods. The broader term of migration, to describe a variety of movement is more appropriate."[53] The terms migration, diaspora, and transnationalism can be considered as related, yet distinct research lenses. Each lens can be applied to the current study in useful ways.

The concept of migration studies is widely discussed by scholars representing many disciplines. Castles and Miller have coined the phrase the "age of migration"[54] in their discussion of this complex phenomenon. Castles and Miller stress that, "while movements of people across borders have shaped states and societies since time immemorial, what is distinctive in recent years is their global scope, their centrality to domestic and international politics and their enormous economic and social consequences."[55] They note that migration studies is an inherently interdisciplinary field of inquiry. This draws from disciplines such as history, political science, anthropology, sociology, economics, and cultural studies to shape our understanding of complex social dynamics.[56]

For Castles and Miller, "migration is a process which affects every dimension of social existence and which develops its own complex dynamics."[57] Individuals and their communities are forever changed by the migration process. Dimensions of social existence are forever changed as people leave, among those that stay, and further complicated by the dynamics of return. The domain of religion is one such space that is transformed by the processes of migration. This is true for the community that remains behind and those that migrate. The complex dynamics of migration are seen at work in migratory groups such as the Protestant Christian Việt Kiều. Exploration of some of these complex dynamics will help to inform the understanding of missions by and beyond the diaspora.

Many scholars have drawn fruitful insights as they explore various dimensions of the complex dynamics of the migratory process through the lens of the domain of religion. Sociologist, Peggy Levitt is one such

---

52. Wild-Wood, "Common Witness," 58.
53. Wild-Wood, "Common Witness," 60.
54. Castles and Miller, *Age of Migration*, 2.
55. Castles and Miller, *Age of Migration*, 3.
56. Castles and Miller, *Age of Migration*, 21.
57. Castles and Miller, *Age of Migration*, 21.

scholar that has focused much of her career on lived religion and the transnational links of migration. According to Levitt, "religion has become transnational."[58] She has provided a very helpful discussion on these complex dynamics with the robust exploration of the concept of "social remittances"[59] in her study of transnational links between the Miraflorenos community in Boston and back home in the Dominican Republic.

Social remittances are understood by Levitt to be the "ideas, behaviors, identities, and social capital that flow from host- to sending- country communities."[60] Levitt proposes that there are "at least three types of social remittances -normative structures, systems of practice, and social capital."[61] Her research explores the ways in which "ordinary people, at the local level, are also cultural creators and carriers. Migrants send or bring back the values and practices they have been exposed to and add these social remittances to the repertoire, both expanding and transforming it."[62] As migrants move back and forth between host and sending country these social remittances produce ongoing rounds of culture creation on the local level. "Social remittance exchanges occur when migrants return to live in or visit their communities of origin; when non-migrants visit those in the receiving country; or through exchanges of letters, videos, cassettes, e-mails, and telephone calls."[63] Notably these social remittances flow along "identifiable pathways," they are transmitted "systematically and intentionally," and they are usually "transmitted between individuals who know one another personally."[64]

Levitt introduces the conceptual framework of a "transnational optic"[65] in her later work. A transnational optic "helps identify the actors, ideas, and technologies that are the carriers of religion. It calls our attention to the real and imagined, past and present geographies through which religion travels and the pathways and networks that guide the elements circulated within them. Finally, it produces a clearer picture of how and why

---

58. Levitt, *Transnational Villagers*, 159.
59. Levitt, *Transnational Villagers*, 54.
60. Levitt, *Transnational Villagers*, 54.
61. Levitt, *Transnational Villagers*, 59.
62. Levitt, *Transnational Villagers*, 55.
63. Levitt, *Transnational Villagers*, 63.
64. Levitt, *Transnational Villagers*, 63–64.
65. Levitt, "Religion on the Move," 163.

religious assemblages are created at these sites of encounter."[66] Moreover, "most aspects of religious life are potentially mobile."[67] Furthermore, according to Levitt, "religion also strongly influences individuals' migratory journeys, including how they travel, what it means to be pious and respectable once they arrive, and how values and practices are transmitted and changed along the way."[68] The context of the returning Vietnamese diaspora is a fascinating location to study the mobile aspects of religious life and how these are being transmitted along transnational links.

Ebaugh and Chafetz' 2002 project explores transnational religious ties between members of Houston congregations and one New York congregation and individuals, groups, and communities in their sending communities.[69] This project was an outgrowth of their 2000 project among Houston-based immigrant congregations in which the researchers discovered and summarized issues of religious transnational linkages to be further explored under five key findings. Their second and third findings are the most salient issues of exploration for my research project. Namely, "2. Over time, immigrant congregations develop innovative religious structures and practices as adaptations to their new home. 3. Over time, the flow of material resources reverses, and the flow of religious personnel and innovation may reverse or at least become bilateral."[70] Further exploration of the issues revealed that "it was clear that religious beliefs and customs follow a circular path. Immigrants bring with them many religious practices from their home countries that they subsequently adapt to their lives in the United States. Likewise, they communicate with family and friends left behind in their homelands, they influence religious structures and practices there."[71]

One chapter in this project focuses on Houston's Vietnamese American community and how transnational links have developed over time. Ha builds off Levitt's theory to document ways in which Vietnamese Americans have built transnational ties at the institutional level with Catholic Churches and Buddhist temples in Vietnam in their desire to help the needy in Vietnam. In early years, transnational links "consisted

66. Levitt, "Religion on the Move," 163.
67. Levitt, "Religion on the Move," 163.
68. Levitt, "Religion on the Move," 163.
69. Ebaugh and Chafetz, *Religion across Borders*, 9.
70. Ebaugh and Chafetz, *Religion across Borders*, xvi.
71. Ebaugh and Chafetz, *Religion across Borders*, 6.

of micro-level family connections. Over time, they developed into community liaisons. These ties initially enabled Houston's Vietnamese to aid relatives and friends, but eventually they were able to help whole villages and communities, including temples and churches. Vietnamese religious bodies have become one of the most highly trusted conduits for channeling resources between Houston and Vietnam, a transnational linkage that enables the former community to increase its aid for the needy in the latter."[72] The transnational ties highlighted by Ha are primarily between individuals in the United States and religious institutions in Vietnam once the immediate family has been helped. This is a trust issue. The religious institutions are seen as most trustworthy and safest means to send remittance to those in Vietnam who actually need the help.

Steven Vertovec notes that "contemporary patterns and processes of migrant transnationalism also give rise to significant forms of religious transformation."[73] Vertovec notes the research gap when it comes to "research concerning religious links maintained between post migration communities and their origins."[74] He goes on to state that "enquiry into patterns of religious change surrounding this set of categories—migration and minority status, diaspora and transnationalism—will shine significant light on yet broader processes affecting religion in the world today."[75]

Paul Freston in his discussion on globalization and religion draws attention to the reality that "evangelicalism today is practically everywhere that it is permitted to be."[76] Of most significance is his nuancing of the discussion. Freston encourages scholarship to pay attention to not only diasporic globalization,[77] but also "conversionist globalization,"[78] noting that it

---

72. Ha, "Evolution of Remittances," 127.
73. Vertovec, *Transnationalism*, 145.
74. Vertovec, *Transnationalism*, 145.
75. Vertovec, *Transnationalism*, 148.
76. Freston, "Globalization, Religion, and Evangelical Christianity," 37.
77. For example, Hinduism has become globalized via diaspora. As a result the visible presence of religions hitherto associated only with other parts of the world, such as Hinduism in Britain. Freston notes the contrast between globalization of Hinduism which remains diasporic and Evangelical Christianity which is diasporic and conversionist globalization. For Freston "Christianity is different not only in scale (well over fifty countries) but also in type. There is, evidently, a diasporic evangelism . . . and its study is important; but its conversionist globalization is even more vital." Freston, "Globalization, Religion, and Evangelical Christianity," 37.
78. Freston, "Globalization, Religion, and Evangelical Christianity," 37.

is vital for scholars to "study the very different dynamics and implications of global missionary activity and conversion."[79] As he states, "we need to study the key missionary centers of evangelicalism and the key diasporic flows, in order to map out the characteristic channels of contemporary evangelicalism's multilateral networks."[80] This is because, "Third World missions are an important part of the current transformations of religion in an era of globalization."[81] The contemporary movement of Protestant Christian Vietnamese voluntarily moving back to their natal homeland is an informative overlooked contributor to the story of religion in an era of globalization. The Vietnamese story has received less attention than the South Korean, Chinese, Filipino, or Nigerian experiences as Christians in diaspora. Inquiry into the patterns of the Vietnamese diaspora as they return to Vietnam as a story of "conversionist globalization" will shine significant light on one facet of missions in the modern world.

Vietnamese Diaspora

There is a wealth of studies with different entrance points into topic of the Vietnamese diaspora. These include robust studies examining sociological works detailing various aspects of social life and meaning making in contemporary Vietnam, memory making[82] among various communities in Vietnam and the diaspora, identity formation, religion and ritual both historic and contemporary in the homeland and among the diaspora, economically focused studies exploring dimensions of trade, development and wealth creation in the contemporary globally connected Socialist Republic of Vietnam, gender studies focused on the lives of women in Vietnam and/or the Vietnamese diaspora, and memoirs[83] detailing personal experience.

---

79. Freston, "Globalization, Religion, and Evangelical Christianity," 37.
80. Freston, "Globalization, Religion, and Evangelical Christianity," 41.
81. Freston, "Globalization, Religion, and Evangelical Christianity," 41.
82. Memory making is one discourse that fascinates many in the academy as Vietnam provides the scholar with fertile and contested vantage points. Rivka Eisner's *Performing Remembering: Women's Memories of War in Vietnam* is one such work. Within this work, Eisner provides the reader with a helpful brief history of Vietnam sketching major historical events from the colonial era to the modern day to frame her study. Eisner, *Performing Remembering*, 10–16.
83. Some such as Andrew Lam's work, *Perfume Dreams: Reflections on the Vietnamese Diaspora* have been very well received, awarding winning works. These collection of personal essays also spawn many academic pieces within the academic field of literature.

The topic is rich, dynamic, and of keen interest to many in the academy and the general population. While informative, this vast web of literature serves primarily in the background of the current study.

An astonishing quantity of robust studies explore various aspect of the Second IndoChina War from different vantage points.[84] 2015 marked the fortieth year since the conclusion of the Vietnam conflict. This milestone has generated a fresh wave of scholarship devoted to the war era and immediate years of reunification. Books such as Michael Kort's 2018 work, The Vietnam War Reexamined, continue to feed the insatiable appetite for understanding this transformational time from the many different perspectives of all who were involved in the conflict. Kort writes for the student of history to undertake a serious investigation into the conflict and be able to come to their own informed options regarding what "revisions historians have to say about the Vietnam war" as well as "citing the historical record as presented by orthodox commentators."[85] Military histories showcasing perspectives from all sides involved in the conflict continue to be churned out. Time has moved forward, but the profound interest in the subject matter persists. War and its many lingering questions is actively contested territory. While substantial, war, the aftermath of war, and reexamined perspectives on the war is but one substantial discourse. This complex history, while not central to this dissertation, sheds important insight into contemporary experiences. One cannot understand the present, and most importantly, the Việt Kiều, without this historical sensitivity. For those who lived through the days of April 1975, reunification (the fall of Saigon), is forever seared in their memory. It remains fresh and poignant after all these years. Most importantly, for the purpose of this particular study, this optic informs the social background of the project respondents. They either lived through these turbulent times or they are the children of those that did.[86]

Chin-Ming Wang is one such scholar who writes concerning the "cultural politics of what I call the 'homecoming stories' of the Vietnamese diaspora." This is accomplished via the choice to "focus on the theme of physical return in Andrew Pham's *Catfish and Mandala* (1999) and Andrew Lam's *Perfume Dreams* (2005), in which dissimilar quests for reconciliation and disconnection emerge as critical concerns." Wang, "Politics of Return," 163. Scholars are fascinated with these semi-autobiographical memoirs. Memoirs have much to say regarding belonging in the diaspora, displacement, memories of the lost homeland, and transnational links.

84. See for example Bradley, *Vietnam at War*, for a perspective of Vietnamese people on all sides.

85. Kort, *Vietnam War Reexamined*, 5.

86. Laderman and Martini offer a collection of helpful articles examining the legacies.

As a field of inquiry, the Vietnamese diaspora residing in the West has fascinated many scholars over the decades. Avenues of inquiry into the Việt Kiều experiences, and especially questions of identity formation in diaspora, and questions of resettlement and assimilation, are considered by several authors.[87] Rutledge, provides careful documentation of the waves of Vietnamese refugee peoples, stories of the refugee journey and initial accounts of entrance into America and other nations in his frequently referenced 1992 work.[88]

Schwenkel joins with many in the academy by noticing the phenomenon of durable transnational ties between the United States and Vietnam. However, her focus is not restricted to the returning Vietnamese diaspora. Rather, she focuses on transnational healing and discovers that Vietnamese perspectives on healing and reconciliation are not the same as perspectives articulated by the mostly American veterans that return for these purposes. Different perspectives, motivations, and anticipated outcomes are seen in the encounter between Vietnamese and American actors even as they participate in joint projects and share new memory making experiences. As she writes,

> Healing, a concept that shapes return journeys and humanitarian work, was also complicated by my Vietnamese respondents who pointed to different cultural, historical, and economic meanings attached to the term. Vinh, who had been a student protestor in Saigon during the war, again alluded to desires for more prosperous futures: 'You Americans came here to fight, then left Vietnam suddenly. So you had no closure and now desire healing. But for the Vietnamese, [these projects] aren't about healing, but hope. What motivates people to reconcile is hope for the future'. The idea of economic betterment as a driving force behind reconciliation (as well as forgiveness) also surfaced when Tai reflected on usage of the term 'healing' in Vietnam: 'Healing is used occasionally, but not in the same way that Americans use it. The government might use 'healing' to refer to relations with the United States, but

---

As noted, "one of the most lasting transnational legacies of the war, of course, is the diaspora of millions of Vietnamese citizens and the complex cultural memory of the war and its legacies this diasporic process created." Laderman and Martini, *Four Decades On*, 8.

87. E.g., Louis-Jacques, "Defining the Overseas Vietnamese"; Louis-Jacques, "Politics, Kinship, and Ancestors"; Trinh Vo, "Vietnamese American Trajectories"; Chan and Christie, "Past, Present and Future"; Rutledge, *Vietnamese Experience*; Valverde, *Transnationalizing Viet Nam*; Vo, *Viet Kieu in America*.

88. Rutledge, *Vietnamese Experience*.

only if they are trying to attract investors. More often we use the phrase 'build friendship'. . . . Tai's observation on the selective use of American constructs by Vietnamese officials was confirmed in my own analysis of Vietnamese press discourse: while the English language Viet Nam News commonly employed stock phrases such as 'heal the wounds of war' and 'reconcile with the past' when referring to U.S.—Vietnamese relations, such terminology was rarely employed in Vietnamese-language newspapers unless quoting an American source.[89]

This quote highlights the way in which two communities linked by events in the past equate different meanings to joint activities undertaken in contemporary Vietnam. The returning Protestant Christian diaspora likewise, will encounter a plurality of perspectives and associated meanings as they engage in their natal homeland. Homeland actors and missional Việt Kiều jointly participate in many activities; sometimes the associated meanings and rational for participation will tightly correlate, at other times divergences will be seen.

Many scholars recognize the rich and durable transnational links to the homeland and explore research projects within this pathway of Vietnamese diaspora scholarship. Alexander Cannon argues for a new direction in Vietnamese diaspora studies with a collection of essays in the Journal of Vietnamese Studies.[90] He advises that modern scholarship "moves beyond narratives espoused by the state, reexamines the concepts of 'nation' and 'tradition' in relation to Vietnam and the Vietnamese diaspora, and debunks pervasive binaries."[91] This particular collection of essays "deal with the active and creative border-crossing moves of diasporic Vietnamese."[92] As he contends, "State narratives, simple binaries and outdated diaspora formulas cannot contain the fullness of what is transpiring."[93] There is a nuanced and highly complex dynamic to the returning diaspora that demands robust examination and occurs outside of State sanctioned purposes.

In recent years, academics have produced a wealth of enriching and insightful studies that embrace the call for modern scholarship advocated for by Cannon. Each study contributes a nuanced understanding and adds a

89. Schwenkel, *American War in Contemporary Vietnam*, 43.

90. This new direction is a critique in part of Louis-Jacques, "Politics, Kinship, and Ancestors."

91. Cannon, "Introduction: Epic Directions," 1.

92. Cannon, "Introduction: Epic Directions," 2.

93. Cannon, "Introduction: Epic Directions," 3.

layer to the complex tapestry of contemporary Vietnamese diaspora scholarship through robust exploration of the many subcomponents comprising the Vietnamese diaspora. Carruthers is one such scholar. Carruthers, explores the role of media, specifically how the various "movements of media performers, producers and texts between homeland and diaspora operate to determine the visual representation of transnational Vietnamese geographies and, above all, the imag(in)ing of the city of Saigon."[94] Likewise, Valverde, explores Vietnamese popular music in one of his case studies, as he considers the "transnational cultural flows and forms of collaboration and influence between Vietnamese Americans and Vietnamese music makers."[95] Music as a cultural product is a "good example of the deeply entrenched transnational process . . . individuals in Viet Nam and in diaspora created their own timeline for informal relations, avenues for cooperation, and venues for political discussion."[96] Valverde documents, among other things, the "staunch anticommunist element within the Vietnamese American community (that persists after thirty-five years) and uncovers how transnational connections go undetected by Vietnamese government officials, who may be unable to stop these flows of exchange even when the officials deploy extreme measures such as incarceration."[97]

Yuk Wah Chan has conducted innovative research on the experiences of the Việt Kiều returning to the homeland and the perceptions of the Vietnamese towards the Việt Kiều through the focus on the specific plight of the Chinese subcomponent of the diaspora. He unpacks their journey of how people that who were once exiled based on ethnic distinctiveness of being "Overseas Chinese" living in Vietnam have had that part of their identity erased by modern Hanoi discourse. They have been collectively lumped together into the same category as all the "Overseas Vietnamese" and urged to return to the homeland and rebuild the nation.[98] Homeland politics shape the identity and future of this subcomponent of the diaspora community at the same time that this once rejected group is acting as a change agent in generating changes in the homeland.

94. Carruthers, "Saigon from the Diaspora," 68.
95. Valverde, *Transnationalizing Viet Nam*, 23.
96. Valverde, *Transnationalizing Viet Nam*, 24.
97. Valverde, *Transnationalizing Viet Nam*, 147.
98. Chan, "Hybrid Diaspora," 526.

Several scholars have made fruitful contributions via the analyzation of the complex economic remittances dimension of the diaspora[99] and the Hanoi government's policy changes helping to fuel this trend.[100] Nation building via economic remittance is a key objective of state policy. State policy and official rhetoric have changed dramatically in the Doi Moi era to encourage the overseas Vietnamese to return.[101] Yet, as Small asserts, "return is an agential choice by those Việt Kiều living overseas, outside the purview of the Vietnamese state."[102] Indeed, these scholars provide an important perspective on the vast scope of this reverse diaspora and highlight the complexities of the exchange and the ways in which "remittance offer insight into the stories, behaviors and motivations of those actors, reveal the networks, and gesture toward even more."[103] Economic remittance and the public rhetoric that promotes this exchange is important to this current study even as Protestant Christian returnees have their own agency for return. The remittance of Christian faith happens in all the complexity of a society and state policies, not apart from it. As such, the economic story is relevant. How does the economic remittances factor into the Christian story? To what extent are the returning diaspora funding Christian ministries

---

99. E.g., Small, "Embodied Economies"; Small, *Currencies of Imagination*; Pham, "Returning Diaspora"; Anh, "Enhancing the Development Impact."

100. Small highlights the use of language strategically employed to welcome the overseas Vietnamese back to Vietnam. Việt Kiều are referred to as bridges and the term kiều bào was used to officially welcome the overseas community. The official use of the term kiều bào "suggests an agenda of constructing diasporic subjectivities intimately linked to with the womb, nation, or homeland. Overseas Vietnamese subjecthood is metaphorically constructed as a bridge always pulling them back (return) to the primordial origins, even in a globalized era of widespread mobility and emigration." Small, *Currencies of Imagination*, 130. Small notes that the immigration counter at the Saigon airport for the 2008 Lunar New Year displayed a banner which read "the homeland welcomes our overseas compatriots returning to celebrate the New Year." Small, *Currencies of Imagination*, 130.

101. The 2008 Law on Vietnamese Nationality among other policy changes that are opening the door for the returning Vietnamese. "Article 7. Policies toward persons of Vietnamese origin residing abroad: 1. The State of the Socialist Republic of Vietnam adopts policies to encourage and create favorable conditions for persons of Vietnamese origin residing abroad to maintain close relations with their families and homeland and contribute to the building of their homeland and country. 2. The State adopts policies to create favorable conditions for persons who have lost their Vietnamese nationality to restore Vietnamese nationality." These policies are in place to create a climate of "solidarity." Nguyen, "Vietnam and Its Diaspora," 248.

102. Small, *Currencies of Imagination*, 130.

103. Small, *Currencies of Imagination*, 138.

and other faith-based development projects and/or NGO's? If so, what is the impact of this influx of Western money on the church in Vietnam?

Thomas conducted ethnographic research exploring the interconnected multifaceted relationship between overseas Vietnamese and the homeland through ethnographic interviews with their families living in diaspora in Sydney and Canberra, Australia and their relatives that remain in Hanoi. This research "is a study of the experiences and perceptions of home of a small group of people born in Vietnam and now living in Australia, in relation to the social and political environment in which they live. . . . These families exhibit a range of migration experiences, and through the examination of memory and place, they all allowed me to see the connections that one place, Hanoi, had in their imagination."[104] Thomas discovers that "for many Vietnamese here, life in Australia is described as having two faces, one looking forward and one looking back."[105] Furthermore, "the pain of separation from home and family weighs heavily,"[106] "many people suffer a form of 'survival guilt,'"[107] and that "the majority of Vietnamese in Australia are deeply concerned about the economic and social conditions in Vietnam."[108] Her 1997 article concluded, that thus "a central question in the minds of many is thus 'did I (in escaping) do the right thing? This question is projected onto relatives back home in that in order to justify a life overseas, many feel that they must contribute to life in Vietnam."[109] Although dated, Thomas' findings present a strong rationale for the existing transnational links and phenomenon of return seen in contemporary Vietnam in the era of the open-door policy.

Nathalie Huynh Chau Nguyen explores the return journey through the lens of experience of Vietnamese diaspora women. She draws the conclusion that "these women's return journeys, whether real or imagined, were undertaken, in Andrew Lam's words, 'in order to take leave' (Lam, *Perfume Dreams*, 115). The return brings with it a double realization: the fact that they have truly lost the country they remember and that their lives now lie elsewhere. Their narratives explore plural truths, a mixture of

---

104. Thomas, *Dreams in the Shadows*, xix.
105. Thomas, *Dreams in the Shadows*, 186.
106. Thomas, *Dreams in the Shadows*, 186.
107. Thomas, *Dreams in the Shadows*, 188.
108. Thomas, *Dreams in the Shadows*, 188.
109. Thomas, "Crossing Over," 164.

experience, history, and perceptions."[110] Among these women, family is the primary motivator to return. Yet, in returning the women realize that their home is no longer home for them. As she articulates,

> their reconnection with a place that had once been familiar is characterized by ambiguity, as they detail the changes that they observe and struggle to adjust to the gap between their memories and the reality. Return narratives share a sense of grief and loss, as well as the regret engendered by lives lived far away from kin. . . . Overall, the women's narratives reveal two central factors: first, the predominance of family as the motivation for the journey home; and second, the women's acknowledgment that their lives now lie in their new country and that the Vietnam they remember is truly lost to them.[111]

Nguyen discovered that the narratives "illustrate their continued attachment to relatives in Vietnam, they also demonstrate that their lives are now based overseas. Even if women had been unsure of where 'home' truly was before their return journeys, the trip to their former homeland was to affirm their place in the diaspora and their adopted land as 'home.'"[112]

Similarly, for Long the diaspora returned to "establish a sense of place based on their own memories and experiences and to expand family relationships and kinship ties."[113] "Yet, those that returned also acknowledged the continuing ambiguities of space, time, and relationships in their lives. Citizenship and social and kinship ties were multi-layered."[114]

The concept of religion in Vietnam and amongst the Vietnamese diaspora is a domain of scholarship that has seen abundant productivity in recent years. Scholars exploring the phenomenon of religious life in contemporary Vietnam find common ground in agreeing that Vietnam has seen a remarkable explosion of religious expression in the Doi Moi era.[115] Religion is "thriving"[116] in modern Vietnam. As Hoang states, "renovation since 1986 paved the way for sociocultural and religious transformations

110. Nguyen, *Memory Is Another Country*, 160.
111. Nguyen, *Memory Is Another Country*, 142.
112. Nguyen, *Memory Is Another Country*, 145.
113. Long, "Viet Kieu Fast Track Back?," 87.
114. Long, "Viet Kieu Fast Track Back?," 88.
115. E.g., Taylor, "Modernity and Re-Enchantment"; Hoang, *New Religions*; Jellema, "Returning Home"; Schlecker, "Apparitions of Sapiocracy"; Bouquet, "Vietnamese Party-State."
116. Taylor, "Modernity and Re-Enchantment," 1.

in Vietnam."[117] Moreover, renovation has seen a major ideological shift as a series of Party resolutions have paved the way for a new relationship with religion in the secular Party-State.[118] Furthermore, religion has seen a "blurring of the boundaries between state and non-state institutions"[119] and a "decentering."[120] This decentering has magnified existing tensions and exposed new rifts between the party and religious participants. As such, religion is "domain of constant negotiation."[121]

This constant negotiation occurs among religious participants and adherents of the many faiths that are seen in contemporary Vietnam. However, negotiation of the role of religion in the context of religious growth has particular implications for Christians and hence the missional returnees. This is seen in the various decrees that the Vietnamese State has implemented in recent years. One Vietnam observer writing about the 2013 Decree ND-92, draws the

> conclusion that Decree ND-92 is much more designed to be a tool for the management control of religion than a step toward religious

---

117. Hoang, *New Religions*, 41.

118. Renovation has seen a major ideological shift as a series of Party resolutions have paved the way for a new relationship with religion in the secular Party-State. The 1999 resolution No. 24-NA/TW implemented by the sixth congress of the Vietnamese Communist Party marks an important milestone. This resolution states, "belief and religion are spiritual needs of a segment of the population. These needs exist and will continue to co-exist with the nation during the process of building socialism in Vietnam." Bouquet, "Vietnamese Party-State," 92. Furthermore, a series of laws and statements passed by the Vietnamese congress have gone well beyond the 1999 resolution and are being widely implemented in modern Vietnam. Notably, the 2009 amendments and supplements to the articles of the Law on Cultural Heritages (No. 32/2009/QH12) passed by the national assembly represent a crucial development. Article 17 declares that, "the State protects and promotes the values of intangible cultural heritages through the following measure" (The National Assembly, No. 32/2009/QH12). The article details five ways that the State engages in this practice including providing finances. Of particular importance is measure 2, in which the State will act "to transmit, disseminate, publish, perform and revive intangible cultural heritages" (The National Assembly, No. 32/2009/QH12). Measure 3 of the amendment to article 25 is in a similar trajectory of intention, stating that the secular Party state will "selectively revive rites of traditional festivals" (National Assembly, No. 32/2009/QH12). These sweeping changes in policy have been widely enforced so that in modern Vietnam, the secular Party state is seen championing explicitly religious platforms as they embrace specific messages and religious rituals that have been deemed positive aspects of traditional culture.

119. Hannah, "Mutual Colonization," 86.

120. Taylor, "Modernity and Re-Enchantment," 50.

121. Taylor, "Modernity and Re-Enchantment," 51.

freedom. The Party's and the government's deep suspicion of religion and religious people remains clearly on display. The decree appears to unmask the real purpose and attitude behind Vietnam's 2004 Ordinance on Religion and Belief which is mostly meant to manage, control and contain religious groups.[122]

Specifically, if "strongly implemented the degree will mean more deep intrusion into religion's affairs. It would clearly and immediately render illegal hundreds of house churches in a movement begun 25 years ago."[123] The returning diaspora is entering into a society undergoing a religious effloresce and one in which this decentering is negotiated though many interactions on the local levels as the State no longer holds a monopoly on religious life. At the same time, the State remains determined to exercise authority, manage, and hopefully contain religion. This has many layers of implications and legal ramifications for the returnees as they navigate life and ministry back in their natal homeland.

Moreover, the Party State has promoted what is seen as positive and unifying aspects of traditional culture in recent years in the milieu of rapid globalization. The State has issued significant and sweeping statements concerning religious rituals in recent years that is directed to those in the homeland as well as the diaspora. As Jellema discusses:

> In a February 2005 statement meant to diffuse ethnic and religious tensions in the highlands, the Vietnamese government reported: 'in Vietnam, the worship of ancestors—the most popular form of belief—is practiced virtually by the entire population.' If convinced of the claim that all Vietnamese worship their ancestors, it is perhaps not far-fetched to argue that to worship the ancestors is to be Vietnamese . . . this position allows the state to impute a cultural nationalism not only to the Kinh majority but also to ethnic minorities, Catholics and overseas Vietnamese. At the same time, ancestor worship as an ancient, shared belief can act as a bulwark against the impending tide of globalization . . . the Doi Moi state hopes to capitalize on the potential for ancestor worship and associated 'returns to origins' activities to counteract the fragmentation of the increasingly global and globalized Vietnamese populace by pulling wayward Vietnamese back home.[124]

---

122. Veteran Vietnam Observer, "Two Steps Back?," 3.
123. Veteran Vietnam Observer, "Two Steps Back?," 1.
124. Jellema, "Returning Home," 72.

This positive aspect of traditional culture, namely the construct that to be Vietnamese is to worship one's ancestors, has been embraced and advocated in recent years by the State. In modern Vietnam, you see self-declared atheist ranking party members (to be a party member, one has to declare that they are atheist) participating in and leading rituals of ancestor worship and encouraging good citizens to do likewise. This idea of cultural nationalism of ancestor worship has been linked to the 'return to origins' movement which is simultaneously aimed at both the Việt Kiều and citizens of the homeland.

Tam T. T. Ngo scrutinizes the wide spread and rapid conversion to Christianity of the Hmong in Vietnam. Ngo gives special attention to the transnational characteristics of Christianity as a world religion in her scholarship to understand this phenomenon through the lens of the underground American Hmong missionaries returning as missionaries to reach their fellow Hmong people in Asia.[125] She pays close attention to the transnational religious networks of the Hmong converts in Vietnam and overseas Hmong missionaries,[126] and the changes that result from the encounter for both the Hmong converts and overseas Hmong missionaries.[127]

Ngo draws from Peggy Levitt's social remittances framework to "suggest that the evangelical mission carried out by the Hmong diasporas to Christianize the Hmong in Vietnam and elsewhere in Asia can be seen as a type of social remittance, in particular as a 'remittance of faith and modernity.'"[128] Furthermore, Ngo describes a situation in which "becoming a missionary, for many Hmong Americans, is one of the solutions to the contradictions they experience in their lives. Evangelism to their Asian Hmong ethnic fellows is an act of paying one's dues to one's kinsmen elsewhere as well as an act of remitting modernity."[129] American Hmong missionaries are seen as a remittance of modernity in the sense that "there are impulses to both recapture a lost past and modernize and improve it."[130] Ngo discovered that, "some of the Hmong missionaries . . . emphasized the humanitarian side of their work and saw themselves as development

---

125. Ngo, *New Way*, 64.
126. Ngo, "Ethnic and Transnational Dimensions," 333.
127. Ngo, "Ethnic and Transnational Dimensions," 339.
128. Ngo, "Ethnic and Transnational Dimensions," 341.
129. Ngo, *New Way*, 82.
130. Ngo, *New Way*, 81.

agents"[131] as they assist their Vietnamese brethren in breaking with the past and progressing towards a better future. The irony for Ngo is that this remittance of modernity is "double-edged." "Not only did it transform Hmong society in Vietnam via massive conversion, and by doing so it effectively causes disappearance of traditional culture for which American Hmong have a longing."[132] Additionally, Ngo points out the orientation that the transnational mobility of return is present in the encounter. For the contemporary Hmong Americans, unlike colonial era Protestant missions,[133] "contemporary missionaries do not see going to Asia as a lifetime commitment, but rather more of an extended trip abroad."[134] The Hmong are one of the largest ethnic minority groups in Vietnam. To what extent do the findings on Hmong-American missional activity and motivations hold true for the Vietnamese Kinh diaspora that have returned in recent years?

Research Related to the Vietnamese Evangelical Church

The rich tapestry of studies on contemporary Vietnam and the Vietnamese diaspora, by and large, ignore the Protestant Christian community, and hence miss an important dimension of Vietnamese studies and global Christianity. While quality literature focused on the Vietnamese church and Christian movement in Vietnam is not as developed as the other bodies of literature, there are several important sources to mention here to frame this current study.

Any well-informed study of this nature must begin with understanding the past. One cannot understand the Vietnamese church today and contemporary experiences of returning Christian Vietnamese, without understanding the foundation built in the pre-diaspora years. Tradition carries heavy weight in the present in the Vietnamese church. One good source of data comes from missionary bibliographies.[135] These accounts provide key windows of insight into the foundations of the church practices,

---

131. Ngo, *New Way*, 81.

132. Ngo, *New Way*, 82.

133. Ngo notes that contemporary Hmong missionaries share some obvious similarities with colonial era missions. Namely, "both share the conviction that they have a moral obligation to bring the truth of the Gospel to those who have not yet heard it (and) their missionary zeal has its roots in their own conversion." Ngo, *New Way*, 65.

134. Ngo, *New Way*, 65.

135. E.g., Stebbins and Stebbins, *Pioneering with Christ*; Stemple, *My Vietnam*.

culture and theological and political positions from the pioneering generation of the Protestant movement in Vietnam.

Of most utility is H. P. Lê's exhaustive account.[136] It remains the definitive text telling the story of development of the church from its inception to the war of reunification. More recently, a former missionary and researcher who has remained deeply involved in Vietnam, Reg Reimer, published an account that documents what happened behind the bamboo curtain. It is a slim but important overview of the Protestant Church behind the bamboo curtain. His knowledgeable insights can be built upon to flesh out one side of the research.

Of keen importance to this particular study are the accounts of what happened in the tumultuous days of April 1975. Events of those days cast a long shadow over the Christian diaspora community and are documented by several firsthand accounts.[137] These accounts fill in a picture of those chaotic final days before and immediately after reunification from the vantage point of Christian Vietnamese. Cowles provides a rare eye witness account of what happened on location in the immediate months after reunification through the firsthand account of Earl Martin, a Mennonite Central Committee volunteer, who stayed behind in Vietnam until July 28, 1975. His description of proceedings from the first Tin Lanh (ECVN South) annual conference after reunification is highly informative. As Cowles writes, "At the church conference many Christians felt those who had attempted to leave were not worthy to continue their offices of leadership. Those who actually fled[138] were officially removed from office."[139]

Hostetter draws a similar conclusion as he writes about the situation in 1977. Hostetter records that "about 35 of the approximately 200 Vietnamese Protestant pastors, however, left at the encouragement of American missionaries just prior to the revolution. Numerous other clergy, including several prominent Protestant leaders, were permanently discredited in the eyes of their fellow citizens when they tried unsuccessfully to leave at the end of the war."[140] Hostetter does not specify denominational affiliation (i.e.

136. Lê, *Short History*.

137. E.g., Cowles, *Operation Heartbeat*; Roeck, "Vietnam, Cambodia and Laos"; Hostetter, "After the Debris."

138. Some of these that "fled," or their children (pastor's kids), are now returning and these decisions are not historical footnotes, but present day realities. Some that "fled" have been pastors and Christian leaders in the West for up to forty years.

139. Cowles, *Operation Heartbeat*, 140.

140. Hostetter, "After the Debris," 21.

Mennonite, ECVN, etc.) for this number. The article implies all Protestants as a group. This is contrasted with the stance of the Catholic Church. "The Vatican encouraged all Vietnamese Catholic leaders[141] to remain . . . not one Vietnamese Catholic bishop was among the more than 300,000 Vietnamese who left at the collapse of Saigon."[142] He went onto quote a former unnamed missionary that voiced regret for what unfolded. "The flight of these pastors, some of them key leaders, bitterly disappointed many Vietnamese Christians who felt abandoned by their shepherds. It also gave the new authorities ammunition for their accusations that the Protestants were directly attached to the fleeing Americans."[143] Additionally, according to Hostetter, "there were more than 50 American Christian mission programs or relief agencies in south Vietnam prior to the end of the war, all of which claimed to serve without regard to political considerations. However, when the American military presence was removed, all except the Mennonites and Quakers discontinued their programs."[144]

In an honor/shame culture the use of the term discredited carries heavy weight. The importance of what are described as "discrediting actions" at the close of the war era remains a potentially significant variable informing present day relationships. The extent that that attitude has been preserved and institutionalized needs to be fleshed out. Do Việt Kiều return hoping to rectify the shame that was acquired by fleeing during the war chaos? To what extent are present day ministry opportunities, experiences, and networks shaped by the turmoil of forty years ago? Does mistrust (going in either direction) manifest itself in the contemporary transnational relationships? Does the Christian diaspora community agree that they should be discredited for events that happened forty years ago? The Hanoi government has changed the terminology concerning the diaspora. Negative characterizations and labels have been officially erased and a unifying discourse has been put into effect. To what extent has a changing discourse been enacted among the Christian community?

Recent years have witnessed Christian theologian-practitioner practicing the craft of theology and producing writings from the diaspora that

---

141. While this might have been the official Vatican position, it is worth noting that one of my respondents escaped on a boat with his uncle, a Catholic priest in 1984. His uncle has served as a priest in the United States since that time.

142. Hostetter, "After the Debris," 22.

143. Hostetter, "After the Debris," 21.

144. Hostetter, "After the Debris," 20.

articulate a framework towards a contextual paradigm of Vietnamese theology among other concerns.[145] A more recent development has been the publication of indigenous theology by Vietnamese theologians who have earned advanced degrees in the West and returned to serve in Vietnam. These pastoral theologians have produced contextual theology for their church context in Vietnam.[146]

Tu Thien Van Truong's 2009 PhD dissertation proposes a Vietnamese theology of mission through the "contextual understanding of the justice of God (Troi) in order to enable Vietnamese Protestants to engage in mission in two dimensions simultaneously: evangelism and work for social justice."[147] Truong lays out a position that rejects the isolationist position of the ECVN in which one should not get involved in worldly affairs. For Truong, "this isolationist attitude is responsible for many of the problems that the ECVN is now facing. The church is poor both financially and intellectually . . . as a result, the church is in the midst of a leadership crisis."[148] A carefully constructed contextual exploration of the concept of Missio Dei, scriptural readings that inform a correct understanding of God's justice, and insights from traditional Vietnamese people as well as insights from a few theologians[149] leads Truong to a new twofold understanding of the nature and role of the church. Christians "are called to do evangelism which includes the proclamation of what God has done in Jesus for the whole world and the healing of the brokenness of their society by their life, their work for social justice. God's good news includes both of these. That means that true evangelism cannot only hold the proclamation and leave the work for social justice behind. They must be done together."[150] This contextualized understanding of Missio Dei in light of Vietnamese understandings of justice and responsibility in the world and a correct understanding of God's justice in scriptures fundamentally changes the way a Christian ought to live out Christian love in the world when Christians see the suffering of Vietnamese people and engage in loving actions that better the world.

---

145. E.g., Le, "Bamboo Cross"; Phan, "Dragon and the Eagle."

146. Truong, "Vietnamese Theology of Mission"; Nguyen, "Contextualized Model for Small Groups"; Le, *Vietnamese Evangelicals and Pentecostalism*.

147. Truong, "Vietnamese Theology of Mission," 5.

148. Truong, "Vietnamese Theology of Mission," 3.

149. Truong, "Vietnamese Theology of Mission," 247.

150. Truong, "Vietnamese Theology of Mission," 265.

Writing for his Doctorate of Ministry thesis, Nguyen is concerned with addressing root causes of the "several major obstacles that hinder the growth of the church."[151] As such, a contextualized case study is undertaken through the formation of a holistic small group ministry situated in the author's home church. Nguyen hopes that the development of contextual small group ministry model will addresses an essential weakness of the "traditional church."[152] These obstacles include the lack of "understanding of spiritual warfare and the power of the gifts of the Holy Spirit," the pervasive knowledge gap in which "most pastors in Vietnam have not been taught nor have they taken the risk to learn this deeper truth," and the spiritual maturity crisis brewing over in the traditional church as "there is little room for people to become spiritually mature because of the lack of discipleship."[153] For Nguyen, the existing ecclesiology does not readily foster an environment that produces mature disciples. Indeed, "because of the lack of discipleship and authentic relationships, people cannot easily share their deep hurts and receive spiritual or inner healing for them."[154] To this end, the author designed a study to "answer the question: what should constitute a contextualized model for holistic small groups that will foster spiritual renewal and awakening in the ECD (Evangelical Church Danang) in Vietnam in a way that will lead to increased growth in the future?"[155] "The specific purpose of this ministry project is to develop and introduce a holistic small group model inside the ECD, which is the first Protestant church in Vietnam."[156] This model would then be able to be multiplied beyond the ECD.[157]

151. Nguyen, "Contextualized Model for Small Groups," 4.
152. Nguyen, "Contextualized Model for Small Groups," 7.
153. Nguyen, "Contextualized Model for Small Groups," 7.
154. Nguyen, "Contextualized Model for Small Groups," 10.
155. Nguyen, "Contextualized Model for Small Groups," 6.
156. Nguyen, "Contextualized Model for Small Groups," 18.
157. This holistic small group is modeled after the small groups called Covenant Communities of the I-61 Ministries. Therefore, in the following the author would like to design an effectiveness study to test how this model can be contextualized with the goal of training young adults as small group leaders in the context of Vietnam so that subsequent new small groups could be multiplied. Nguyen, "Contextualized Model for Small Groups," 130. Methodologically, the process of building up this model involves four different phases. The first phase is to select leaders to form a core group. The second phase is to train these leaders through the four ministry distinctive: spiritual warfare and deliverance, emotional healing, exercising gifts of the Holy Spirit and discipleship growth. The third phase is to encourage these leaders as they go out to make disciples

Vince Le frames his 2016 study with the important observation that speaks to the picture of the composition of the Protestant Church in Vietnam. Le writes,

> As of today, about one-third to one-half of Vietnamese evangelicals (and counting) associate themselves with Pentecostalism. A closer look at the contemporary Vietnamese evangelical demographic also reveals an important fact: evangelicalism grows mainly among the country's ethnic minorities. Such minorities make up 14 percent of the Vietnamese population, yet they account for three-quarters of all the evangelicals in the county. The average Vietnamese evangelical is a person belonging to an ethnic minority group living in the highlands, centered in providences indicted by the World Bank as having the highest poverty headcount in the country and far away from its commercial hubs. This typical contemporary Vietnamese evangelical is usually a woman who speaks her native language. She may or may not be able to communicate in Vietnamese, the language of the Viet people and the official language of the State. Also, by virtue of living in one of the country's poorest providences, she has less economic power and less access to economic development opportunities than the average Vietnamese individual does[158]

Le provides a very helpful examination of this stream of Pentecostal movement, the relationship between the movement and the party state, and proposes compelling rationale why it is enjoying robust growth. Within the study, Le "make(s) the case for a general interpretation that the Pentecostal belief in divine intervention grows as it offers meaning to an underprivileged segment within contemporary Vietnamese evangelicalism. The claim, however, is far from being straightforward, since the long-held evangelical ethos that gives rise to this focus on divine intervention also and at the same time shows itself at an impasse — one that questions its ability to engage and respond efficiently to the inevitable challenges of modernity

---

themselves, applying the same principles and tools, beginning with deliverance. The fourth phase happens when more people (i.e., the new disciples) join in a Covenant Community, which results from the reaching out of the original small group leaders. That is, the personal spiritual growth that will take place will necessitate that groups will grow organically, forcing them to split into two or more new groups, each group having both new and old members in each group. Nguyen, "Contextualized Model for Small Groups," 130.

158. Le, *Vietnamese Evangelicals and Pentecostalism*, 3.

in a communist society."[159] It is a movement that addressed the realities that one faces in daily life as "the Pentecostal movement adds concern for the underprivileged at the top of Vietnamese evangelicalism's social agenda and constitutes a particular grassroots approach that seeks to enhance the life of the underprivileged in the face of the challenges of modernity in a communist society."[160] It is also a movement which can be seen as

> a public statement that sovereignty, salvation, and history do not belong to the State. Accordingly, the mass conversion to evangelicalism by the ethnic minorities in the mountainous areas of the North and Central Highlands of Vietnam can be viewed as a movement seeking to reject the broad claims of a state[161] that fails to deliver societal betterment and, instead, marginalizes (by withdrawing or impeding social opportunity); oppresses (through the dispossession of personal property and the establishment of laws and social customs that institutionalize the marginalization of targeted groups); and abuses (through, for example, unfair compensation and public humiliation) the members of ethnic minority groups.[162]

Le concludes his work with three astute observations[163] that are helpful for Vietnamese evangelical theological discourse and informative to the experiences of the returning diaspora as they engage in Christian ministry in their natal homeland. Theologians such as Le, provide valuable insights into the Vietnamese evangelical conceptualizations of how the church understands their sociocultural reality and an intriguing thesis for the rapid growth of the church in recent years.

Finally, it is important to remember that Protestants do not hold a monopoly on the Christian experience in Vietnam. In fact, the Catholic Church has been working in Vietnam for almost four-hundred years and

---

159. Le, *Vietnamese Evangelicals and Pentecostalism*, 7.

160. Le, *Vietnamese Evangelicals and Pentecostalism*, 149.

161. "In contemporary Vietnam, the state-party relies for the most part on the argument that it, as an institution is the most knowledgeable, capable, and philanthropic entity for leading the country in a salvific manner; thus the state-party buttresses its claim to retain power. . . . Marxist thinking . . . has been used in contemporary times as an ideology to build a belief system to protect the State's right to rule." Le, *Vietnamese Evangelicals and Pentecostalism*, 132. The mass conversion and declaration that Jesus is Lord is a rejection of this claim.

162. Le, *Vietnamese Evangelicals and Pentecostalism*, 132–33.

163. Le, *Vietnamese Evangelicals and Pentecostalism*, 154–55.

has produced more scholarly research and writings than the Evangelical community. Catholic scholars[164] describe the interplay between State laws and the modern Catholic Church and experiences of the Catholic Church in the reunification era. Phan makes a keen observation regarding the application of the Vietnamese constitution that is applicable to both Catholic and Protestant Christianity as they practice their faith:

> The 1992 Constitution of the Socialist Republic of Vietnam, amended on 15 December 2001, stipulates that: citizens have the right to freedom of belief and religion, and may practice or not practice any religion. All religions are equal before the law. Public places of religious worship are protected by law. No one has the right to infringe on the freedom of faith and relation or take advantage of the latter to violate State laws and policies. (Article 70) Basic to the VCP's stance toward religious freedom is the distinction between religion as faith and belief (tin nguong) and religion as religious organization and activities (ton giao). For the former, there is a guarantee for complete freedom of believing and not believing; for the latter, there are restrictions, especially to protect 'national security.'[165]

In particular, "the practice of government control and oversight of religious institutions and their activities. It requires registration and government approval for matters that are universally regarded as routine and internal to religious institutions such as the establishment of seminaries, enrollment of candidates to the priesthood, and activities outside church buildings"[166] Parallels to the Protestant church can be drawn from these careful works, particularly the writings of Phan.

---

164. E.g., Hansen, "Vietnamese State, Catholic Church"; Phan, "Vietnam, Cambodia, Laos"; Phan, "Christianity in Vietnam Today"

165. Phan, "Christianity in Vietnam Today," 10.

166. Phan, "Christianity in Vietnam Today," 11–12.

CHAPTER 3
Methodology

THIS RESEARCH UTILIZED A qualitative research approach to answer the research questions. The purpose of a basic qualitative study is to "understand how people make sense of their lives and their experiences."[1] A qualitative study utilizing semi-structured, in-depth interviews, therefore, is more appropriate for this project, as it allows for the gathering of rich data in order to see perspective of the respondents. As Maxwell describes, the qualitative approach then helps the researcher to understand "(1) the meanings and perspectives of the people you study—seeing the world from their point of view, rather than simply from your own; (2) how these perspectives are shaped by, and shape, their physical, social, and cultural contexts; and (3) the specific processes that are involved in maintaining or altering these phenomenon and relationships."[2] These three features of qualitative inquiry produce an approach to research that is inductive, open-ended, and works towards a "primary goal of particular understanding rather than generalizations across persons and settings."[3]

This approach allowed for eliciting narrative stories which illuminate the experiences of the returning Protestant Christian Việt Kiều to help make sense of their lives as missional agents. This approach is best suited for this study as it discovers valuable insight regarding the lived experiences, joys, challenges, opportunities, and impacts for these individuals and their communities as the Protestant Christian Việt Kiều return and reestablishing belonging in their natal homeland with the purpose of participating in Christian missions among other reasons for return. Furthermore, this analysis is undertaken primarily at the "micro level," the level focused on "individuals and persons or couples directly involved in relevant religious

---

1. Merriam and Tisdell, *Qualitative Research*, 24.
2. Maxwell, *Qualitative Research Design*, viii.
3. Maxwell, *Qualitative Research Design*, viii.

networks,"[4] as this is the level which best elucidates how people involved in transnational religious networks make sense of their lives and experiences. This is the level of analysis performed for this current study as it is primarily concerned with individuals directly involved in religious work in Vietnam, and their relevant personal religious networks in Vietnam, rather than religious organizations (meso level) that are engaged in transnational networks at a corporate level, or international religious bodies (macro level).[5]

Research Participant Selection

I conducted interviews in Vietnam in July and August of 2019. A small number of interviews were conducted via Zoom in April and May of 2019 for interviewees that were deemed more conducive to this modality. Eight interviews were conducted in this modality. The rest were in-person meetings that occurred in Vietnam. RQ 1, and RQ 2 are answered through semi-structured interviews with Protestant diaspora returnees or transnational migrants. RQ 3 is answered through interviews with non-migrant Protestant Christian Vietnamese that have direct experience with returnees.[6] A total of thirty-one semi-structured interviews were conducted with adults. This included twenty-four returnees and seven non-migrant local Christian leaders. Refer to appendix 1 for table of interview respondent pseudonyms and group identifiers. The interview protocol for the Protestant Christian Việt Kiều returnees is included in appendix 2. The interview protocol for non-migrant Protestant Christian Vietnamese interviews is included in appendix 3. The interview questions began broadly and generally followed the interview protocol based on informant responses. All interviews were conducted in English. All returnees were fluent in English. The local non-migrant Christians had a high degree of English fluency as well. Three of the interviewees possessed high intermediate English fluency. These interviewees were conducted in pairs and the other interviewee was able to assist with minimal translation when necessary.

4. Biney, "Transnational Religious Networks," 286.
5. Biney, "Transnational Religious Networks," 286.
6. RQ 1: "What are the motivating factors of Protestant Christian Việt Kiều returning to Vietnam for mission related purposes?" RQ 2: "What has been the experience in ministry of the returning Protestant Christian Việt Kiều regarding mission related reasons for returning?" RQ 3: "How have the non-migrants experienced the phenomenon of return?"

Purposeful sampling was employed in the data collection. Informants were selected based upon the number of qualifications. This was ascertained in communication with potential project participants prior to the interview. Most potential participants were first identified through the researcher's contacts in Vietnam. This included the author's personal contacts with foreign missionaries and national colleagues and associates in Vietnam, and from among the diaspora. These contacts were instrumental in identifying excellent participants and the establishment of trust for the researcher. Most of the interviewees were not personally known to the researcher prior to the contact bridged by the mutual contact. A small number of the interviewees were personally known to the researcher. Once identified, invitational letters were sent to potential project participants. The letter is included in appendix 4.

Once communication and project interest were established, most potential Việt Kiều interviewees were sent a preliminary questionnaire. The preliminary questionnaire used in this study is included in the Appendix 5. This questionnaire confirmed key interviewee criteria were met and gathered some of the basic demographic information. Namely, that the interviewee identified as a member of the Vietnamese diaspora community and a Vietnamese returnee or as a transnational migrant. Secondly, the interviewee self-identified as Protestant Christian and as intentionally engaging in Christian ministry or explicitly state that they have a missionary motive as a part of their return experience. A snowball approach was also utilized to identify potential respondents, with those interviewed being asked if they could refer me to others within their networks that would be a good candidate for this research.[7]

Data Collection and Analysis

Intentionality was taken to ensure an appropriate diversity of interviewees involved in diaspora missions to Vietnam. Diversity in geographic location, primary ministry focus, denominational affiliation, age, and gender were all intentionally sought for this interview project. Therefore, the interviewer traveled to major urban centers in the North, Central, and South of Vietnam in order to achieve the desired respondent diversity. However, as stated in the limitations, my personal travel in Vietnam was restricted to

---

7. Merriam and Tisdell, *Qualitative Research*, 98.

the major cities. This chart shows the geographical breakdown of where the interviewees are based.

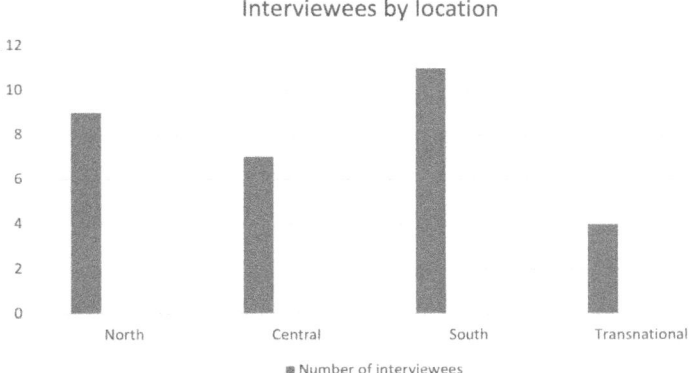

Both men and women have returned to Vietnam with a missional purpose. Therefore, I wanted to achieve a representative sample of men and women. This was achieved with a near equal representation as the pie chart demonstrates.

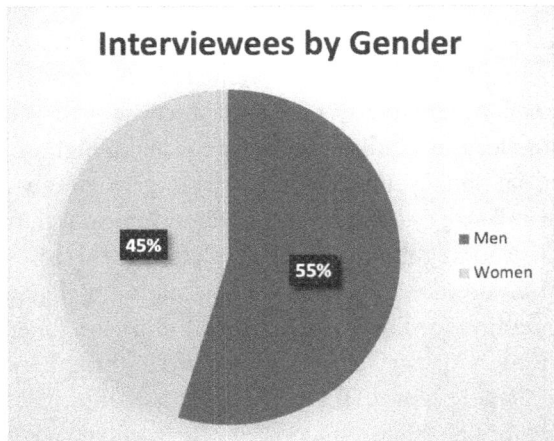

Similarly, intentionality was taken to ensure the selection of a diversity of Vietnamese national interviewees for this project. Informants were selected based upon a number of qualifications. Namely, that the interviewee identified as a Vietnamese national Protestant Christian leader and as someone that had direct personal experience working in some capacity with Protestant Christian Vietnamese returnees that are involved in diaspora missions to Vietnam.

Purposeful sampling was employed in the data collection among Vietnamese nationals. Diversity in geographic location, primary ministry focus, denominational affiliation (specifically ECVN and house church leaders), and gender were all intentionally sought for this interview project. Two of the interviewees are members and leaders within the ECVN, three are leaders in house church ministry networks, and two are regional leaders in an international faith-based missions organization. In total, three of the interviewees were not known prior to the contact bridged by the mutual contact. Four of the seven interviewees were personally known to the researcher.

A few obstacles were encountered in interviewing Vietnamese national leaders. First, a limited number of national leaders that I had been in contact prior to the research trip through mutual contacts declined the interview once in country. Most commonly, this was due to the variable of incompatible travel schedules.[8] In this one specific case, once it became clear that I was requesting to interview the national leader and house church pastors in this ministry network, rather than simply visit a ministry site, the tone of the email conversation changed drastically. Suddenly, the once enthusiastic leaders were no longer available and the offer for help in logistically tasks such as transportation and housing evaporated. Second, there were a handful of potential interviews that did not occur due to the language barrier. As previously noted, all interviews were conducted in English and the local non-migrant Christians had a high or intermediate degree of English fluency. Interviewees were largely comfortable conversing in English and able to express themselves well. However, this limitation sidelined some who might have been considered for this research project.

Vietnam is considered a creative access nation. Religious worker visas are not an option for the vast majority of returnees. Likewise, some of the national leaders that were interviewed serve in ministries that operate outside of State approval. Therefore, confidentiality was important to protect the identity of the respondent and their ministry networks. Most interviews took place at a neutral location chosen by the interviewee, such as a local public coffee shop or restaurant. Some interviews occurred at the researcher's rented apartment. A few took place at the interviewees' ministry site or residency. Before the formal interview took place, respondents

---

8. This was a potential difficulty for interviews with returnees as well. The month-long research trip in Vietnam was intentionally structured to capture opportunities to meet with as many potential interviewees as possible. However, I was not able to meet with all of the potential interviewees that I had been in contact with prior to the research trip.

were informed that their personal information would not be shared and that a generic code would be used to identify each individual (F1 for female number one, F2 for female number two, M1 for male number one, etc.).[9] This identifying code was used during the interview itself to enhance anonymity for interviews that occurred in Vietnam.

The establishment of trust was essential. For many interviewees, trust was established as contact was bridged by a mutually trusted individual. Trust was further established through casual conversation that occurred before the formal interview started. I often shared a little of my personal background working in Vietnam. Following this, ten to fifteen minutes were used to discuss the purpose and method of the interview, establish that the respondent met the selection criteria, discuss confidentiality, and gain consent for the interview. The letter of informed consent was read by each participant prior to starting the interview. Participants gave verbal consent to participate. The Letter of Informed Consent is attached as appendix 6. I explained that I was not looking for a "right or wrong" answer or to prove or disprove anything about their ministry or the missionary enterprise, or about the Church in Vietnam or among the diaspora. Rather, I was interested in hearing their personal perspectives and experiences, based on their individual thoughts and experiences. This approach follows Bernard's advice in beginning interviews, "first of all, assure people of anonymity and confidentiality. Explain that you simply want to know what they think, and what their observations are."[10]

After this, the formal interview began and was recorded using a digital recorder. Interviewees orally and on the recording, stated their agreement with the informed consent, but were not requested to sign a physical copy as this would build a paper trail that could be viewed as a safety liability. Recorded interviewees typically lasted one hour and fifteen minutes. Recordings were uploaded to a secure Dropbox and deleted from the recording device after the interview. Field notes were typed up and uploaded to Dropbox as well.

After data collection, interviewees were transcribed verbatim by the researcher and with the assistance of Rev.com, a professional transcription service. NVivo, which is software that assists in analyzing qualitative data, was used to code and analyze transcribed interviews. This process of categorizing the data was critical to "provide an overview of large amounts

---

9. This was the method utilized by Greenham, *Muslim Conversions to Christ*, 139.
10. Bernard, *Research Methods in Anthropology*, 215.

of transcripts and facilitate comparisons."[11] Analysis identified emergent patterns in the interviews that related directly to the RQs and sub RQ's. These codes were assigned by the researcher based on what was observed in the data and from the exact words of interviewees in some cases. This started with large descriptive codes such as motivations for return, ministry highlights, disappointments in ministry, self-identity, and who the Việt Kiều are ministering to in Vietnam among others. Data within codes was further analyzed in the process of "axial coding"[12] with an emphasis "focusing on patterns and insights related to your purpose and questions and guided by your theoretical framework."[13] This followed Merriam's advice to continue analysis until a sense of saturation is achieved during the process of "movement from inductive to deductive."[14] This process facilitated the organization and presentation of data presented in the findings chapters. The non-migrant national Vietnamese leader data was separately analyzed and compared with their own emergent descriptive categories such as highlights in working with diaspora missionaries, lessons for the Việt Kiều as seen by the non-migrants, impressions of the returnees, contributions of the Việt Kiều, and areas of misunderstandings with Việt Kiều as experienced by the non-migrants. Additionally, I developed an informant chart to help facilitate respondent comparison. This chart included essential data pieces such as the interview name or generic code and assigned pseudonym, primary ministry and national partners, number of years serving in Vietnam, informant age, age when they migrated from Vietnam to the West, and if they were sent by an organization or supporting church(es).

Validity

Maxwell encourages researchers to address the validity threats of researcher bias and reactivity.[15] Both of these are potential significant to this study. As a researcher, I was mindful that I have spent three years work in Vietnam and have formed some preconceived ideas about the returning diaspora from prior interactions and observations from traveling around Vietnam. I also am well aware that reactivity is significant challenge to qualitative

11. Brinkmann and Kvale, *Doing Interviews*, 122.
12. Merriam and Tisdell, *Qualitative Research*, 208.
13. Merriam and Tisdell, *Qualitative Research*, 208.
14. Merriam and Tisdell, *Qualitative Research*, 210.
15. Maxwell, *Qualitative Research Design*, 124–25.

research among Vietnamese. Christian Vietnamese might attempt to provide the answer they think I as a Western Christian might want to hear. They might be inclined to paint an overly rosy picture of situations and experiences rather than share data that might bring perceived shame to themselves, their national partners, or certain ministries.

To ensure the validity and reliability of this research, I was guided by the following verification strategies. Maxwell lists several methods for verification strategies, several of which were implemented in the research process. First, I gathered "rich data" through thorough interviews with verbatim transcripts. Questions were frequently reworded and worked into the interview to enhance the gathering of rich data. This enabled the collection of detailed data that "provides a full and revealing picture of what is going on."[16] Moreover, interviews were conducted until a level of data saturation was reached where no new information of themes seemed to arise. Second, my data is "triangulated" and "comparison" is employed by interviewing non-migrants and a diverse range of Việt Kiều returnees. I also gathered and analyzed documents such as ministry updates and prayer letters from the returnees when appropriate.[17] A limited amount of participant observation was achievable for this project. Furthermore, by traveling on location in Vietnam, the interviewer was able to have several informative conversations with many cross-cultural missionaries, expats working in Vietnam and national Christians in Vietnam, as well as, diaspora Việt Kiều in the Chicagoland area.[18] These conversations did not meet all the criteria for a formal interview, but were nevertheless conversations that helped to add texture to the picture of the local ministry context. Third, I was attentive to "search for discrepant evidence and negative cases" as I coded and analyzed data. As an additional factor of validity, an expert panel, namely my dissertation committee has been utilized.

---

16. Maxwell, *Qualitative Research Design*, 126.

17. Maxwell, *Qualitative Research Design*, 126–29.

18. These are conversations with actors informed on Christian missions and the Church in Vietnam. For example, some of these conversations were with the American spouses of female interviewees. Two of the women that participated in the interviewees are married to white American men. One was with a local Christian leader who did not sit for an official interview but nevertheless contributed valuable reflections. Yet another was with a diaspora Việt Kiều who might become a transnational in time, but is not yet.

CHAPTER 4
Việt Kiều Returnees

Investigating the Experiences of the Returnees

Chapter Introduction

THE PHENOMENON OF THE returning Việt Kiều reveals a fascinating case study of cross-cultural missions in our contemporary interconnected global village in the context of a postcolonial society. These are remarkable narratives as members of this diaspora community undertake to carry the Christian gospel back to their natal homeland. The core research question framing this study seeks to discover how the experience of the Protestant Christian Việt Kiều returnees inform diaspora missiology theory and strategy by providing insight into the current practice of Christian missions undertaken by a diaspora community. Answers to this question are found in the information provided by Việt Kiều respondents in this chapter. The following chapter will provide the perspective of non-migrant Vietnamese local Christians that are serving with the returnees.

The Việt Kiều hold their own unique story of diaspora sojourn, motivation to return, ministry experiences, joys and disappointments, and lessons learned along the way. This chapter will provide a thick description of the Việt Kiều that have returned to Vietnam with a missional purpose. This chapter dives into the data focused on RQ 1 and RQ 2. Namely (RQ 1), what are the motivating factors of Protestant Christian Việt Kiều returning to Vietnam for missions related purposes? Second (RQ 2), what has been the experience in ministry of the returning Protestant Việt Kiều regarding missions related reasons for returning? This chapter will be organized around the answers provided by the respondents as they engage the questions.

Why Return to the Natal Homeland?

In this first section, I will investigate the stated motivations that serve to pull the Overseas Vietnamese back to their natal homeland. The Việt Kiều share common bonds of diaspora sojourn and themes of immigrant experiences that help to define the community. Yet at the same time, the Việt Kiều are far from a monolithic one-size-fits-all story. The story becomes increasingly nuanced the more the lens of examination is zoomed in. There are multiple waves of emigration from Vietnam, specific refugee experiences in leaving, pre-emigration social status and experience, and life experiences in the West, among other variables that help to shape the individuals that form the collective group whole. All of these variables factor into the community DNA. There is diversity within the group. Reflecting this, the Protestant Christian Việt Kiều that participated in this research project each have their own unique journey of return, motivations for return, and experiences back in the homeland as this chapter will unpack. Yet at the same time, one's uniquely personal journey share elements of commonality with other interviewees along with the places of divergence unique to each individual. There are common themes of motivation that emerge from the narratives as this section will demonstrate.

The Unfolding Journey of Return: The Impetus of Intention

One of the striking aspects of the experiences of the returning Việt Kiều is that the majority of participants described a journey or unfolding process in their return experience and development of a missional vision. Stories of the diaspora reveal that there was a journey to leave Vietnam and resettle in a new homeland for many. Likewise, there is a journey of return; a process that leads people to return and reestablish belonging in their natal homeland. Movement towards return and reestablishing belonging in Vietnam is series of deliberate choices that unfolds over time for many of the project participants.

In fact, a majority of the interviewees (72 percent) specifically describe having taken multiple short trips back to Vietnam before they decided to return and reestablish belonging. These trips were discussed as being influential towards the formation and actualization of their eventual return and missional activity.[1] These are meaningful trips that were taken in response

---

1. This is not to definitively state that the other project respondents did not visit

to the unextinguished ties to the natal homeland. Some people reported returning to visit extended family and/or old friends that remained behind, introduce a new spouse to the physical place one was born, for a holiday, or even a secular company work assignment. However, for most, they were simply a temporary return visit. They were undertaken without a sense or intention that return visits would become regular occurrences or that one would eventually move back to Vietnam. Additionally, these early trips often did not include any ministry-related intentions. The community went first for other reasons. These trips were eventful in and of themselves. Yet, for these respondents, these early trips were not the culmination. Rather, they clearly mark the beginning of a return journey that culminated in the re-establishment of belonging back in the homeland.

Once back in Vietnam, this temporary act of visiting their natal homeland sparked a growing vision that eventually pulled them back to reestablish belonging in Vietnam. This is true whether someone always wanted to return or had minimal to no interest in returning to live in Vietnam. Indeed, respondents articulated a limited range of stances regarding return when they started the journey. The majority of participants had strong feelings one way or the other. Some did not. Regarding motivation, returnees fit into three groups as I will unpack in the following pages.

Those Who Always Wanted to Return

First, there were project respondents who articulated that they always wanted to return. They established belonging and lives in the West, but the pain of loss, separation from the homeland and friends and family that stayed behind weighed heavily. They made it out, but maintained a mindset of looking back and wanting to return if or when the time was right. Thomas discovered that many within the Vietnamese community in Australia, describe life in the West as "having two faces, one looking forward and one looking back."[2] Furthermore, Thomas found that many in the diaspora report that they "feel that they must contribute to life in Vietnam."[3] Though dated, this finding would aptly describe a group of returnees that expressed

---

Vietnam prior to their move back. Rather, they did not comment on this area as a specific factor contributing to their eventual return.

2. Thomas, *Dreams in the Shadows*, 186.
3. Thomas, "Crossing Over," 164.

a desire or hope to return when or if the time was right. They were never really at home in their adopted homelands.

Two participants in this project are international adoptees. Both of whom describe always wanting to return when the time was right. As Cau articulated, "so I first visited Vietnam in 1997. Context, background, I was part of the boat people immigrate to the States in 1984, but my family brothers and siblings and everyone, was here in Vietnam.[4] So I live [sic] with a foster family in the States. So, the first time I came back with some 1997 at that time Vietnam was really a poor country, still developing. And my first reaction was, wow, I have to come back to Vietnam eventually to do something." This statement is almost verbatim to Thomas's finding. Cau had made it out; yet he was always looking back. He expressed longing to cultivate a relationship with his birth family, learn of his heritage, and contribute to Vietnam. While he first visited in 1997, it was not until 2008 that he able to return and realize that vision. There is the element of a process towards return shown in this story. During his years living, being educated, and working in the West, he was never fully at ease in his adopted homeland.

Likewise, Dao, who was adopted as a young child, reported a similar unwavering pull towards return, to reconnect with his biological family, and discover his heritage. As he describes, "When I grew up, I always wondered, 'Where did I come from? I'm living with these people that don't look like me.'" He eventual made his way back to Vietnam. An additional similarity with Cau is the missional motivation that finds its expression in the practice of business as mission (BAM).[5] Both articulated a vision to start business enterprises that achieve a kingdom value while also functioning to improve the economic condition for their family among others. The

---

4. Cau left as a boat refugee in 1984 and lived with a foster family in the States as his immediate family remained in Vietnam. He went to the States with his uncle. However, he was not able to stay with his uncle in the States and lived with a foster family.

5. Discussion on BAM can be found in many places. One movement that has done a substantial amount of work in this space is the Lausanne Movement. Lausanne discusses BAM stating that "Business, done well, is glorifying to God and has enormous potential to do good in society. Business has an innate God-given power to create dignified jobs, to multiply resources, to provide for families and communities, and to push forward innovation and development." Business as mission has four identifying characteristics: 1. Profitable and sustainable businesses. 2. Intentional about kingdom of God purpose and impact on people and nations. 3. Focused on holistic transformation and the multiple bottom lines of economic, social, environmental, and spiritual outcomes. 4. Concerned about the world's poorest and least evangelized peoples." Lausanne Movement, "Business as Mission."

motivating pull of business is not simply a personal opportunity, but a tool to contribute to the flourish of life in Vietnam.

For some returnees, it is a matter of holding firm to a conviction to return and intentionally organizing life so that the vision to return could be actualized when the time was right. Tuan was born in a Western nation, but spent some of his formative years as a missionary kid in the northern part of Vietnam. God used this time to help spark his own vision for return. As he says,

> my family came back in the 90s at first because my dad was doing missionary work. That was some really formative years for me, and then I really felt like I guess you could say a calling that I wanted to be back here, even after going back to Canada for high school, university, and my goal through all of that was to get back here. It's hard to maybe describe maybe one single thing, but I've just felt like that's where I needed to be, and where God was moving for me to be. So that's kind of just basically doing everything to get back here.

Tuan completed his education his Western homeland, all the while holding firm to the goal of returning to Vietnam and taking decisive actions while living in the West that would position himself to return.

Similarly, Van, held firm to a conviction to return and he eventually returned with his family. Life in the West was arranged in such a way that he could return one day. On the surface it is simple; one keeps the commitment to return alive until the time is right to actualize the vision. As he says, "I think my reason to come back very simple. I just kept my commitment to come back after my study." However, Van's story provides insight into the complexity of the decision to return even for a Việt Kiều that always wanted to return. Return is not simple. Along the way he married, started his family and worked in the U.S. He watched as many of his friends in the diaspora established deep roots in the West. As he experienced, "along the way most of the friends, they decided to stay in the U.S., some intentionally did that, but some others it happened just naturally. They got married for example, they want to have children, and then no thought of going back anymore." Milestone life events happened, roots of belonging deepened that resulted in people putting down roots in the diaspora and erasing the determination to return. Van was very intentional to not go down that pathway. Over the years, he was very intentional to "not to let things happen in a way that I could not move back someday."

VIỆT KIỀU RETURNEES

Even though Van has returned with his family and they are engaged in vocational ministry, it was not an easy onetime decision to leave their life in the States behind. Within the same nuclear family, you might see a range of emotions and positions towards return, as in the case with Van's family. This was not uncommon for project participants. For Van, it was very hard for his wife to move back. Van eventually returned without his family living a transnational missionary life for four years before his family joined him and they fully returned as a family unit[6] in 2013. It was very hard for his wife as

> she was also a refugee. She grew up in Vietnam . . . and she knew what was in Vietnam. The situation back home, and actually, I don't think many people once they have a residential permission in the U.S wanted to come back to live in Vietnam, unless they have some kind of mission, or history. And the reason that help me keep my commitment to move back, because I think that the need for education both in church and in society is really huge in Vietnam. And I think I can contribute in some way to that.

Van remained committed and perceived a clear purpose in returning. He saw a way that he could personally contribute. This helped him to keep the plan for return alive over the slowly unfolding multiyear process of return.

At times, one may always want to return, but the desire might go dormant for a season as in the case of the transnational Việt Kiều, Liem. His is an inspiring and extraordinary story. He grew up a pastor's son in Central Vietnam during the war years and was inspired by the preaching of an American GI turned evangelist that had been invited to share at a school assembly by his father. Liem ended up fleeing, spending almost a month on a boat seeking his freedom in the aftermath of the war's conclusion. He eventually settled in the States, pursued his education, got married, and developed a very successful career. His life was good and he had everything he needed. The refugee was living the American dream when his company

---

6. Van's wife eventually caught the vision for return and they are back in Vietnam serving as a family. This was not the case for all the project participants. Transnational Viet Kieu, Kiet has engaged in an evangelism ministry for many years and maintains a desire to fully relocate back to Vietnam. God answered his prayer on his first trip when he met local Christians that would become long-term ministry partners. While he is engaged in ongoing ministry in Vietnam after this initial holiday trip, he remains living in the West as his Việt Kiều wife does not share the vision to return and live in Vietnam. His vision to return and stay in Vietnam as a full-time missionary remains unfulfilled at the time of the interview. Unlike Van, Kiet has remained transnational. His family supports a transnational ministry, but not a relocation back to Vietnam.

transferred him to different branch in a new city. The office happened to be across the street from the ministry center of the GI evangelist he had meet in 1974, nearly twenty years earlier in Vietnam. In the context of this unexpected reunion, Liem shared his heart burden that "I need to bring the gospel back after my people in my country." This unexpected, God ordained meeting, launched the return of Liem to Vietnam[7] and his bivocational ministry which eventually shifted gears into full-time cross-cultural ministry. In this narrative, faithfulness found fertile soil that needed many years to incubate. However, the burden to return and bring the gospel to his natal homeland never left and at the right time, God brought this seed to life growing a vibrant multi-nation ministry that has now been working in Vietnam for twenty-six years at the time of the interview.

Those Who Never Wanted to Return

A sizable number of participants articulated positions that would lend compelling credibility to Van's assessment that not "many people once they have a residential permission in the U.S wanted to come back to live in Vietnam." Steps towards return can be uncomfortable, create family disharmony, and resistance. Indeed, return to the natal homeland tends to evoke strong emotions among the diaspora even after all these years.

There is a nuancing of the stance as participates spoke of the early days of their journey. Some of the Việt Kiều that participated in this project reported no desire to return whatsoever under any circumstance. They

---

7. Like others, Liem shared mixed emotions and hesitancy to initially return to Vietnam even as he deeply desired to bring the gospel back to Vietnam. This first return and the launch of the ministry in Vietnam occurred in the 1990s prior to normalization of Vietnam American relationships. Return has become a very common event. This was not the case for those that first returned in the 1990s or even the early 2000s. Stories and rumors quickly make the rounds in the diaspora community of things such as tales of some Việt Kiều being denied entrance upon arrival and held until it was time for their return flight or large bribes. Courage was demonstrated in going despite the rumors that circulated. As Liem describes he spent a harrowing twenty-seven-day journey leaving Vietnam in which he "almost lost my life on the way, looking for freedom and now you're coming back to the big monster, the what I call it, the big monster, what you tried to run away, now you're coming back, not the easy. But this is what the GI said, 'Liem, you care about your people, don't think about the government, don't think who run the government, think about your people.'" Different expressions are used by different Việt Kiều to describe the Hanoi regime. Often the diaspora remains deeply distrustful of Hanoi government. Courage is demonstrated as they return despite the hesitations of returning to a homeland still under the Hanoi regimen.

expressed wanting to avoid returning at all costs even for a temporary excursion. For others, they expressed slight curiosity regarding the natal homeland and/or a small degree of openness to consider visiting for a temporary nostalgic holiday or to see family that remained in the homeland. In any case, the nuancing of this stance speaks to the degree of openness for consideration of returning to Vietnam for a temporary visit. The idea that one would personally return and live once again in Vietnam engaging in ministry was not on the radar in any capacity as these respondents spoke of the genesis of their journey. For these participants, the journey towards a life of living back in Vietnam and engaging in ministry started from a place of resistance or outright opposition to return.

Respondents made a variety of statements that demonstrated their opposition to return. Many statements were pointed. For instance, Quyen stated, "I had no intention of coming back." Ha used stronger language to convey her personal perspective regarding how the diaspora community really feels about the question of return. She stated, "so let us just say that and anyone who leave Vietnam, I hate Vietnamese, I hate Vietnam. Honestly, that is very common sense of Vietnamese-American." For Ha, not only does she personally feel these feelings, but from her perspective, her opposition is normative among the diaspora community.

Some such as Mai, a second generation Vietnamese-German, perceived a calling to global missions as she was exploring career options, but did not want to go to Vietnam. She was less oppositional in her resistance towards return than Ha or Quyen. Mai's pathway was one in which God closed doors in such a way that she was directed to Vietnam. Despite her resistance, she ended up coming initially to Vietnam for a one-year exploratory trip that eventually developed into a long-term career assignment. As she says, "I didn't like the Vietnamese culture so much because of my parents, the way they educated me was very different to the way how German parents educate their children. So I've never dreamt of going back to Vietnam because I was born in Germany." Her stance was softer. Nevertheless, she wanted to go elsewhere; return was not on her radar.

A process of return is seen in many of the respondents. One such returnee is Ha. She experienced a great reversal that moved her from hating Vietnam to feeling love and following God's leading to return to the land of her birth. This happened in an unexpected set of experiences that redirected her life trajectory. At a certain point in her life, Ha remembered her childhood dream of being a missionary, and was in a two-year season of developing a deeper passion for mission as she earnestly prayed for God's leading. During this season her feeling was firm that "I had the passion for mission, but I don't want to go back to Vietnam, I want to be a missionary in Africa." It was at this key moment, that Ha and her Việt Kiều husband, Bing, undertook a trip that changed their life trajectory and set them on a path to return to Vietnam.

They were sent by their American church to visit and evaluate church sponsored missionaries serving in Asia. They received approval to make a side trip during this travel time and stop by Vietnam to visit Bing's mother, who was sick at the time. Two key occurrences happened in quick succession. As Ha describes, they discovered that a missionary couple on the field were still struggling to learn the language after being there for ten years to the point that it was even causing their work to stop. This was an eye-opening discovery for Ha as "when I think about the couple learning the language is really long time, and God has put in my heart that well, he really not mistake to make me Vietnamese." This is followed by the stop in Vietnam which God used in a deep way to reach out and soften their hearts for returning.

> We stop by in Vietnam the first time for twenty years, I haven't come back to Vietnam. When I landed in the airport, I saw a lot of young people walking in the dark. It's really strange picture because I said, well this is a lot of young people walking in the darkness and I feel love. The love that God put in my heart is really tremendous and I feel really love them. . . . But for me, from that time God put in my heart for the love of Vietnam, what is I don't like Vietnamese seriously. I think that's love God is confirming my heart to come back to this country along with the conversation with the couple learning the language. I feel like God really confirmed for me back to Vietnam and through that love, I think that God has put us for the last ten years to stay in here, but that's really difficult in this country if we don't have the love for the lost.

She powerfully sensed the vision of the people in darkness and felt love replacing the hatred and hurt. This unexpected experience of love motivated them to return and has acted as an anchor keeping them in Vietnam over the ups and downs of their missionary career.

Likewise, Nhan reported that "the truth of the matter is I never wanted to come back." She had perceived and was exploring a call to global missions engagement and was starting to act upon the interest in serving as an overseas missionary, but had no interest in actualizing that calling to Vietnamese people or in Vietnam. However, as she describes, "so they talked about Vietnam. I mean, I thought, well that might be an interest, but then I really don't want to go back. I think that some part of me wanting to figure out who am I really, what is my identity. Where do I fit in in this whole, I guess they call us like the half-generation. Yeah. But then on the other hand, I really don't want to go back to Vietnam. We fled the country for a reason. I don't have a good feeling about it. I don't really care to go back." Her answer illuminates a sentiment perhaps shared by many in the diaspora. Namely, the diaspora fled for a reason. By and large, this was a painful involuntary migration. The weight of the history can make it hard to desire to return. There are wounds from the trauma suffered as people were thrust into the diaspora. The distrust runs deep as the Hanoi regime is still in place. As Ha articulated, from her perspective, the common sentiment among the Vietnamese-Americans is to hate Vietnam and/or the Vietnamese. Why would one return to the place from which they fled?

Those That Have Returned from a Neutral Starting Point

The majority of respondents started the return journey from a place of strong feelings towards return. Either they never wanted to return like Ha, Nhan, or Quyen or they always had a desire to return such as Cau and Liem. Participants in either category have diametrically opposed, but often equally strong feelings towards return. Regardless of the original strong feelings towards return, both groups expressed commonality in the way that there is frequently an unfolding definitive journey towards return. This often unfolds over a period of years with multiple short trips and culminates in returning to live once again in Vietnam.

There is a third category of returnees for whom passion towards or against Vietnam and return would not aptly characterize their stance towards return. There are those that began the return journey back from a more emotionally neutral starting point. They neither reported feeling passionate nor hostility or disinterest towards return. Like many others, participants with this starting point often shared the common experience of the long unfolding journey towards return and an interest that deepened over the course of multiple experiences in the homeland.

As a diaspora community it is common and natural to have some level of interest in the natal homeland. Their connections to Vietnam as diaspora members afforded them opportunities to visit. A seed was planted.

The experience of a journey towards living in Vietnam with a missional purpose started with a short visit and unfolded over time. One visit turned into multiple visits, which turned into reestablishing belonging in Vietnam. Vy's narrative illustrates this journey. Vy was living her life in California when she was able to return to visit old friends in Vietnam in 2009. This was her first trip to Vietnam since her journey leaving the nation in 1979. She had a positive trip simply as a visitor. However, as she attests, "I don't think about to go back to Vietnam again." Vy had no plans to return beyond that one trip. Nevertheless, a small seed was planted. The positive experience of returning to visit friends had fertilized the soil, so that when her non-denominational home church presented the opportunity to return with a STM trip she leaped at the opportunity. This trip led to another the following summer, transnational ministry engagement, and hatched a still in progress plan to relocate.

Similarly, Lan, illustrate the sense of the lengthy unfolding journey that starts from a neutral position with slight inclination that led to a missional return. As she described, "actually was a ten years plan. It was a ten-years praying and asking the Lord for direction. We came back to Vietnam two, three times just to visit. And then that's when God's just started to put in our hearts." For Lan, it was a ten-year journey of visits, seeking the Lord for direction and growing sense of missing Vietnam. Over a period of many years, she experienced more pronounced times of missing Vietnam that could simply not be ignored. Eventually she took her American husband back to Vietnam to visit her "hometown just to see where I was living, where I grew up, that kind of thing. And it's just birth the desire to want to move back. And he was on board with it." The seed was planted, took root, and could not be ignored. It was a seed that started from a more emotionally neutral starting point and grew into a burden to return and engage in ministry in the natal homeland.

Still for few others in this project, the primary driver of return was not their desire to return to their natal homeland and trips taken to Vietnam, but obedience to accept an overseas ministry assignment. Their respective mission organizations made the decision for them. They reported being open to anywhere, neither for nor against a return to Vietnam. Rather, being part of the Vietnamese diaspora, their mission organizations saw them as good fits for the ministry assignment in Vietnam.

Returnees such as Anh Dung and Dieu have been faithfully serving in Vietnam for over two decades. Yet, it was not an intentional choice to return to his natal homeland that facilitated the missional return. They neither reported strong feelings towards or against return to Vietnam. As he says, "Actually, I never chose to go back to Vietnam. I was more interested in overseas ministry. . . . At that time, the Lord called me into the ministry, and so I signed up with the [denomination]. I was open for anywhere. I didn't particularly choose Vietnam at that time." They went through the missionary sending process and were sent by the denomination to Vietnam.

Suong and Bach are similar in their return journey. They went where their mission organization placed them. Initially this was not in Vietnam, but in another South-East Asian nation where they were assigned to work among Vietnamese migrant workers. These respondents reported a sense of calling to overseas missions. They joined a missions organization and accepted an overseas ministry assignment. They reported a sense of calling and openness to going anywhere and the mission organization they are serving with assigned them to Vietnam. Some of these respondents wanted to go to other nations initially. However, they choose in obedience to accept the ministry assignment. Their primary motivation to return is not from a sense of kinship and connection to their natal homeland. Rather, it is in acceptance of a ministry assignment from their sending organization.

Key Attributable Motivations for Return

I now turn my attention from the three overarching categories that describe the returnees stances towards return to focus on specific motivations. This section will explore the way in which kinship contributed and did not contribute to the return experience, the philanthropist motivation to bestow charitable goodwill, and the explicit religious motivation. These three salient motivations serve as core impetus towards return for project respondents. These motivations are not mutually exclusive. Most respondents described a combination of all three working to pull them back to return and reestablish belonging in Vietnam.

Motivation of Kin or Kinship Networks in Vietnam

Diaspora missiology theory suggests an importance of kin or kinship networks as gospel bridges. The idea is enshrined in Enoch Wan's definition of missions through the diaspora. This is defined as "diaspora Christians reaching out to their kinsmen, though networks of *friendship* and *kinship* (italics added) in host countries, their homelands, and abroad."[8] For the Vietnamese diaspora in this case study, it is noteworthy that biological family and existing kinship networks in Vietnam are of minimal importance for the majority of the respondents as it pertains to motivation to relocate to their natal homeland and establish belonging back in Vietnam. Nor are kinship networks a strategic advantage or ministry platform for the majority of the project respondents as the diaspora missiology paradigm suggests. This is not to say that family in Vietnam did not contribute into the return journey. Family was more of an initial motivation rather than a sustaining motivation that contributed to relocation. As such, family is an important part of the journey for many. For some of the respondents, visiting family that remained behind in Vietnam was a motivation for an initial visit to the home city/village. As noted above, this initial action helped set people off on a return journey. However, it was of minimal or even no importance for most of the respondents in terms of their decision to return after the initial visit(s).

The Vietnamese diaspora community is well established in the West. For many in the diaspora, they have lived outside of Vietnam for the majority of their lives. For others, they are the children of the refugees. They have only known Vietnam through the stories and memories of the older generation. After such a lengthy sojourn, existing kinship networks are not durable enough for most returnees to motivate them to return and reestablish belonging in Vietnam. In fact, many of the respondents that participated in this project, do not have any kin left in Vietnam. For others such as Tuan, he had some family when he first returned. However, contact was minimal and existing family has passed. Remaining family are not relationally close and live-in different cities. This is common for those that report still having kin in Vietnam. Therefore, a majority of respondents have not reintegrated with kinship networks that remained in Vietnam.[9]

In fact, 93 percent of returnees interviewed did not return to their home village/city or providence. Respondents such as Lan are living and

---

8. Wan, *Diaspora Missiology*, 5.

9. This might be a somewhat unique feature of the Vietnamese as a diaspora community engaging in missions. Extended family bonds and connection to specific locations (people and place) in a nation-state might be found to be stronger with diaspora communities that are earlier in their diaspora sojourn. Nevertheless, the nuancing of the diaspora missiology conversation to ask questions of who the specific diaspora group is and how this impacts relationships with the homeland (people and places) are worth exploration. Each diaspora is unique, yet the literature tends to paint with broad strokes.

working in the Central region, yet she is originally from the South. Others are living and working in the North, yet they are originally from the South. Ministry needs and perceived opportunities rather than family ties is the stronger motivator. For example, Anh Dung is based in the North. He commented, "well, strategically we wanted to be in the north because, as you know, with the war in Vietnam, the country got divided in 1954 in the North and South. Even though the communists took over the whole country now, we felt that the church in the North needed more help to rebuild. That's why I chose the North." The agency to choose a region of the country is selected by perceived spiritual need rather than a memory of the past and a desire to live again in the ancestral lands for most that participated in this project.

Still others work in the South though they are from the Central or North. Nhan, originally from the Central is a good representative of the respondents and the journey that can unfold. Nhan, describes an initial trip back where she reconnected with family that remained. "I went back to [Central city]. That's where I was born to meet my grandmother for the first time, my aunt and my uncle for the first time after thirty-seven years. To them I'm like a stranger. To me, they are a stranger too. There's no relationship, but it was just trying to reconnect. Yeah. Reconnecting the relationship, reconnecting with the family that you left behind. But I think in that trip, it was actually finding healing. Yeah. Because I think there were bitterness, there were anger as far as why we had to leave the country, you know the that war that separated the Vietnamese and the Vietnamese-American. So that was a little bit of healing." That trip was meaningful. However, when Nhan and her American husband returned to live and minister in Vietnam (they also took multiple STM trips during the movement towards return), the extended family was not a factor in the decision. She has had "no contact" with the family since they have moved back. Again, vocational ministry calling rather than family is the primary driver of return. As Nhan says, "I didn't feel called to come back here to minister to my family here in Vietnam." Upon return on a permanent basis, this family does not even know she is back and they are ministering in a different region of the country. The opportunity to visit family was a motivation for initial visit and this act of visiting contributed to a journey of return. However, family is not a motivation for relocation nor a ministry bridge into Vietnam. For many returnees like Nhan, kinship networks in Vietnam plays little to no part in their current lives or ministry back in their natal homeland.

A handful of the project participants are outliers as it concerns family as a motivation for return. For a small number of project participants, family reconnection was an important motivator for return and plays an active part of their lives back in Vietnam. For these returnees family carries equal and/or essential motivational weight to other return motivations. For instance, reconnection with family was an intentionally stated key motivation for both Cau and Dao. As Cau stated, he had three purposes in returning. One was to reconnect with his family. By his own appraisal, this has been accomplished. At the same time, it is worth noting that while family reconnection was a salient motivation for relocation, neither respondent returned to their home village where their family lives(ed). This is largely economically related. The village is not suitable for business initiatives. Nevertheless, family relationships are important and influence ministry philosophy for both of these respondents. They are motivated to establish kingdom business ventures that will serendipitously benefit their extended families.

Likewise, family was a core motivator for Ping. For Ping, she was motivated to reconnect with her father who had returned some twenty years earlier. As she says, "I felt like God wanted me to reconcile with my dad because for twenty years, I didn't have a relationship with him and that was a challenge, but it's almost like part of my journey was the inner healing and whatever needed to be dealt with in Vietnam can only happen in Vietnam." This could only happen back in Vietnam. However, while family (specifically her father) contributed a strong rational for return and she does live back in her hometown, family does not inform her ministry practice in Vietnam. Her ministerial identity is largely compartmentalized from her family. Furthermore, ministry related motivations are described as a part of her return journey and are essential to keeping her in Vietnam in times of trial and frustration. Family reconnection and inner healing helped to get her to Vietnam. However, it is ministry and the burden of the salvation motivation that keeps her in Vietnam.

Quyen is unique among the participants. For Quyen, strong extended family bonds both motivated her to return and have informed her ministerial identity. Quyen had visited her large extended family several times prior to deciding to move back. The desire to share the gospel message directly with her family clan was a compelling decisive motivating factor in her return and has helped to keep her in Vietnam over the last decade. Her family clan has also helped to inform her ministry strategies. In fact, she is deliberately living in her home village on her father's plot of land that she left behind when she migrated with her family as an eight-year-old to the United States. As she describes, "so 2002 was my first short-term mission trip to Vietnam . . . with the intention of taking care of their soul. When that start happening, then the Lord started showing me more needs, in especially my own family members, because none of my family members are saved. So, then I started just going back more frequent, and then the Lord was revealing to me what was needed, what were the weaknesses in the Christian church in Vietnam, what were the issues with normal everyday people, that they are not willing to accept Christ. My family had a big part in that." The salvation motivation is explicit for Quyen and intentionally aimed to her extended family among others. As Quyen has stated in relationship to her family, "I am here to give you a message, and I have to give you that message, and I will not leave until I give you that message, or that I feel like you understand the message. It's not just me giving the message, but that you really understand the message. Then if you decide one way or the other, it's okay." Furthermore, her family are farmers. This helped Quyen to see the large number of Vietnamese that still live as farmers even with the rapid increase in urbanization and perceive a BAM strategy that accompanies her discipleship ministry.

Among the transnational Việt Kiều, respondents provided a few examples of kinship networks being strategic ministry doors. This is of particular importance for early trips before they were well established back in Vietnam. One transnational returnee has utilized robust kinship networks for effective evangelism and church planting. Vien was pastoring a Vietnamese church in an East Coast American city when he discovered that a sizable number of congregants were originally from a certain area in Vietnam that had no Protestant church. In this specific case, the connection opened doors to establish relationships, share the gospel, and is the basis of an ongoing ministry strategy. As he says, "we want to use our family members and friends. So we don't have to go and up and set up a tent and middle anywhere and go for it, just to the family member. So we went to every single family members of our church . . . family members became believers, and even disciples after seven years." Vietnamese became believers during the initial trip and subsequent trips, and new home churches were formed. His non-migrant Aunt and cousin are both believers and function as local ministry partners/pastors (along with one other local pastor) for these newly formed faith communities. In recently years, he has helped with theological education for his aunt and support her as a local pastor for newly formed Christian community.

However, for the majority of the transnational Việt Kiều (75 percent), kinship networks did not demonstrate evidence of robust bridges for ministry. For example, Kiet works primarily with a local Vietnamese evangelist. This person is not kin. The relationship was formed with the local ministry partner during his first exploratory holiday trip to Vietnam. Vy is perhaps the most representative of transnational Việt Kiều. She works primarily with three locations in Vietnam, none of which are established through kinship connections. One location utilizes a friendship connection. She works with a pastor's wife that she met on one of her first trips, the local ministry partner that coordinated one of her STM trips, and finally, a Vietnamese doctor friend from her Vietnamese high school days that lets her know of various needs among the community. These experiences demonstrate that while in some situations kinship networks served as a natural and effective gospel bridge, it is not to be considered normative or an essential variable for a robust transnational ministry.

The examples of the returnees and transnational Việt Kiều suggest that kinship networks can be strategic ministry bridges for a small number of the Việt Kiều. However, the evidence from these respondents suggests that kinship need not be elevated as key for ministry through the diaspora or as an essential motivation for returning. Other variables are stronger for most. Transnational kinship ties are not durable after this length of time. A more generalized motivation for ministry in one's natal homeland proves stronger and more strategic than family.

Charitable Motivations: The Perception of Humanitarian Need in the Homeland

A salient motivation for many participants was the internalized perception of need back in Vietnam. Perception of need is multifaceted and manifest in many social spaces and relationships. The humanitarian concern weighs heavily for many that have returned. The Việt Kiều see the contrast between their life and opportunities in the West and the condition of some, or many, in their natal homeland. For many, they see their homeland as underdeveloped, or people and communities that they care about, as underresourced. They have experienced what they describe as quality education. They want to give back. People want to help. Jesus's teaching that "from everyone who has been given much, much will be demanded; and from the one who has been entrusted with much, much more will be asked" (Luke 12:48b), is not an abstract theological concept. Rather, this is descriptive of their life journey and personally speaks to the motivation to return for some. The concept that there is a perception of need, and that one can personally contribute is a powerful motivator for return. Respondents spoke of wanting a legacy that betters the living conditions in the homeland. This Christian charitable motivation is a powerful ingredient into the emerging motivations that lead one to return to Vietnam with a missional intention. As Van says, "I think I can contribute in some way to that."

The perception of need is expressed through economic and educational lenses for most respondents. This sense of seeing need weighed heavily for many participants as they reflected upon motivations for return. As Ping states, "You saw the need of the country and that was my home country." Nhan describes, "you know what, let me go back to saying like part of why I wanted to come back too, I almost feel like this country, the way it is, you can elaborate more on that really need the Lord and we feel that only God can change this nation because the condition that is very corrupted. It is very ungodly. I mean there's a big need in Vietnam. Yeah. There's a huge need." The need is spiritual and material as Nhan sees it.[10] They often are linked together. There is a moral bankruptcy that contributes to the material bankruptcy. Likewise, Lan and her American husband state, "As we were traveled here. We just saw so much need and it's just a different environment as far as. . . . Need is different here, it's a miracle. They have no safety nets. And it was just so much more need here. We just felt like we could be more useful here." Seeing the need motivated action. Respondents simply could not ignore the need they saw in their homeland and among their kinsmen and continue their lives in the global West. This conviction of the need in Vietnam often grew for the respondents as they moved closer to relocating reinforcing the path they were taking.

Quyen's story reflects elements of many respondent stories. Quyen expressed that she had no intention of returning to Vietnam. It was circumstances within a crisis in her formative years that lead to her returning to visit extended family in Vietnam. This visit had unexpected life trajectory changing ramifications. As she describes her experience

---

10. The perception of the country as being morally corrupt is a common sentiment among the Viet Kieu.

During that trip, there were two major things that the Lord spoke to me about. One was I had two cousins who were my age . . . that I met on that trip who their lifestyle was just totally different from mine. That was my second or third year in college, and I was on my second car by then and spending $150 on dinner, and didn't blink. But their family of nine were living in a hut, and they were also in school like me, but they had two outfits to their name, riding bicycles. The floor of their housing was just clay, and the sides were wood, and it was falling down from termites and stuff. So, just the contrast between my life and theirs was so huge. So, I asked the Lord, 'Why did you, Lord, allow me to go to the US and have the life that I have with. . . . I'm on my second car and spending this kind of money, and here they are in this life?' So, the response that I got wasn't an answer, but a question. So, I heard the Lord say to me, 'So, what are you going to do about it?'

The contrast was obvious and unsettling. Secondly, during that trip, Quyen experienced a clear almost audible sense of calling to return. As she recounts, "I went back to visit my dad's old property that we had grew up on, and as I was walking out, I heard an almost audible voice that said, 'One day, you're going to have a plantation here.'" This clear almost audio sense of calling fused with the unsettling question changed the trajectory of her life and eventually, after many years and many STM, led her to relocate. She is doing something about it as she is engaged in business and discipleship ministries.

Many respondents shared the theme of being deeply unsettled by what they saw during visits to the homeland. For some returnees, these pivotal experiences also contribute to forming ministry strategies as they engage with the homeland. Conviction leads to life changing action. For instance, Cau describes the eye-opening visit in 1997 in which he witnessed the rampant poverty in Vietnam. His means of doing something developed into the BAM work that eventually brought him back in 2008. BAM is more than a legal means of entry into the nation. It is Cau's primary means of earning a livelihood (he has also worked in other sectors for seasons). More than that, BAM is entered into in anticipation of the hope that the business will contribute to the betterment of society through the creation of economic activity and employment. It is his way to use his training and passions to do something to help.

Likewise, the conspicuous sights of economic suffering and vast societal disparities motivates the transnational Việt Kiều, Vy. Her return visit broke her heart for those left out of the economic revitalization in Vietnam and serves as motivation to return on additional STM and desire to relocate. She did not start out with a plan to return regularly and engage in Christian ministry back in Vietnam. However, as she says, "because I see the poor. I see the orphanage, I see the children they poor and they family can't support them go to school so I wish I will have something to help them for one year two years or through their schooling. So that is my wish that's why I want to go there again and again." Seeing motivates action and the formation of her transnational ministry.

This perception of need in the natal homeland drives people to action. For the Việt Kiều that participated in this project, it may not be their direct extended family they are driven to help, yet people and places are not without bonds of connection (even if it is only imagined). There is an intersection of shared history and a lifetime of memories that tie the individual to the natal homeland. These bonds strike at a deeper cord. They made it out and have established belonging in the West. Yet, as they look back, they are unable to blissfully ignore the material needs they see in their natal homeland. They want to do something positive that improves the everyday lives of their kinsmen in the homeland. They are motivated to remit certain aspects of the developed modern life that they have enjoyed in the West in the forms of education, health care, care for the poor, etc., in a way that breaks from the past and helps their fellows in Vietnam move toward a more stable flourishing future. This motivation shares similarities with the findings of Ngo and her findings with the Hmong-American returnees whom she describes in a contradiction of bringing a remittance of modernity to the Hmong in the Vietnamese highlands.[11] The Việt Kiều are bringing a remittance of charitable action.

The Salvation Motivation

The humanitarian concerns were powerful motivators for many. An equal, if not more compelling rational for return for many, is the explicit salvation motivation. Specifically, motivational phrases that relayed the sense of religious need in Vietnam were frequently discussed in conversations. This has a twofold manifestation. First, this included statements directed towards the society as a whole that emphasized the low number of Christians in Vietnam. Respondents are well aware of the low number of Protestant

11. Ngo, *New Way*, 81.

Christians in Vietnam. Percentages and demographic breakdowns were cited as compelling motivation to return. This including citing influential Evangelical missions thinking. Namely, the Vietnamese are categorized as an unreached people group. This designation weighed heavily on the hearts for many returnees.

For example, Ping says, "we have a two percentage of Christian community in Vietnam, that's the whole country, and so where I am is like once I realized I'm here for that reason versus just for my work life, or just to have a normal life, then I think I became more committed to this." For Ping, the low percentage of the population that is Christian was both a motivation to return and a fact that keeps her committed to the task at hand while the going has sometimes been rough. There is no going back to her normal life in the States when the salvation need is so profound in Vietnam. Similarly, Kiet stated, "it's always been my heart to share the gospel with anyone, but especially I have the heart to get back to Vietnam because I need to, percentage there is very small, the Christian there is very small." Likewise, Vien always had a heart for ministry reaching out to the Vietnamese diaspora in the States. A powerful religious experience left him convinced that he must missionally invest in his natal homeland as there "is a lot of Vietnamese, the people I came from, 90 millions, basically 89 millions are unsaved. [At] that moment, I realized that I said, I need to go back to Vietnam quickly, to begin the work with Vietnam." God put this salvation burden in his heart that he must act upon. This motivation of the perceived need for the gospel in Vietnam was expressed by most of the respondents.

Sometimes this salvation need motivated the return to Vietnam in general; other times it motivated specific ministry strategies and ministry locations. Thuc echoes this sentiment and describes their strategically chosen home base in religious terms that utilize the popular missions terminology. As he says, "the biggest thing, especially here in the north is, there's still a lot of unreached people. So that's probably one of our big deciders, is to go where the unreached, little or no church. Here, even though there are a lot of churches in [city] but just outside these provinces. There's still many people groups that have very little believers and little gatherings or groups. That's probably our biggest motivation to come back and specific choose here in the north. I'm actually not from up here, so there's a lot of questioning, why are you moving up there?" Thuc is in the North in response to going to the part of the country that is perceived as having the greater salvation need even though his family is originally from the South.

Again, ministry need/opportunity takes precedent over family ties or ties to a former hometown.

Secondly, the salvation motivation is addressed to the existing church. Many respondents expressed the compelling motivation to return specifically to help the existing Protestant Church grow in maturity. Returning Việt Kiều are well aware that Protestant Christianity has a long history in Vietnam. Most expressed intentions to work with the existing church in some capacity. They do not desire to reinvent the wheel or do their own thing. However, fair or not, the overall sentiment is that the existing Protestant Christian Church has ample room to grow in maturity. As such, the religious motivation is both evangelistic and discipleship oriented. As Mai stated, "they (the local pastors) are doing a great job in evangelizing and doing courses, but that's their job. And we will do the other part, we will disciple the people who are new believers." Many of the returnees are passionate about disciple-making. Returnees are motivated to equip the local believers and local leaders through the investment in discipleship ministries that will help the existing local church to flourish.

Like the charity motivation, this is an area in which many expressed being captured by the need and seeing that they can personally contribute. Simply put, there is this explicit religious motivation for return and remaining in the natal homeland among the majority of my respondents that frequently came up in the conversations. There is a perceived salvation need in comparison to living life in the West. As Kiet states, "the field is very ripe." There is a sense projected that one can be more kingdom impactful working where the field is ripe for the harvest among an unreached people group. Motivated by the realization of the extent of the salvation need in their natal homeland and one's sense of personal missionary responsibility to engage in the task of bringing the good news of salvation back to Vietnam is a powerful motivator for many returnees.

What Are People Doing in Ministry—Experiences and Perspectives from the Returning Diaspora

I interviewed participants in the North, Central, and South regions of Vietnam to gain a picture of how the returning Việt Kiều are engaging in ministry, how they are influencing the growth and development of Christianity in a particular region, and what we can learn from this sample of the missionary population.

First, as has already been demonstrated in the motivation section, the Việt Kiều returnees in and of themselves are a diverse group. Purposeful sampling was followed to represent this diversity in the data collection. This group of respondents represented a collected 190 plus years of ministry experience in Vietnam. Some are on the front-end of their ministry career having only been back a few years. Others have been in Vietnam for twenty plus years. Naturally, what people are doing changes over such a lengthy ministry career. Also, as many participants noted, the country itself has changed greatly during their time of service. They have largely proven adaptable and flexed to the ever-changing realities on the ground. The Vietnam of 1999 is different from the Vietnam of 2006 and the Vietnam of 2016. Ministry experience reflects this ever-changing reality on the ground. Many of the Việt Kiều demonstrate high levels of creative adaptability as they faithfully engage in their natal homeland. This in and of itself is a finding that ought not to be glossed over.

Among respondents, some returned with very clear ministry visions. They either had intentional equipping or life experience that they wanted to remit to the homeland in their ministerial identity. Formal training, vocational, ministry and life experiences in the West inform and shape the nature of the work they are doing in their natal homeland. This includes respondents such as Lan. Her motivating ministry vision was shaped in part from their life and ministry experiences in the States. As she describes, "we adopted four children and through that adoption is kind of birthed in vision of wanting to implement foster care in Vietnam and adoption because adoption is a foreign language, for Vietnamese people." This ministry vision has guided their efforts in Vietnam. Many have had business training and are operating BAM centric ministries. Some have had theological equipping and are engaged in discipleship centric ministries that utilize passions and compelling motivations to return.

Still others returned in faith with only limited conceptualization of what they would be doing back in their natal homeland. They simply were compelled to go and they went. They have persevered and established life and ministry rhythm over time. As Tuan described, "basically it was just learn Vietnamese and then figure out how I can be useful to the kingdom here. I didn't have any kind of grand, master plan. It was kind of like I feel my callings to be here, but I don't have a specific." The plan has unfolded over time for Tuan and others such as Ping. Ping returned in faith with a high level of commitment and a low degree of concrete plans. As she states, "so I didn't have a plan." It was not easy for her at the beginning. Her resolve to return and remain carried her through. As she says, "I saw myself as coming here, committed, and not having a return date."

Overall, respondents were fairly split on this category. Project respondents from both groups demonstrate times of flourishing ministry and the lows that can come with cross-cultural missionary service. A clearly articulated ministry vision is not a necessary motivating variable to return and sustain the return over the course of the experience. Furthermore, it is worth noting that having a clear ministry vision ought not be confused with actual experience in ministry. Put another way, on the ground ministry realities trumps motivating vision. This was one of the common lessons that the respondents shared. Expectations need to be held loosely for Việt Kiều thinking of returning. Your lived experience will rarely align neatly with the expectation. This is even true for some that had taken multiple STM prior to relocation and thought they knew what they were getting in for.

Ministries and the Ministry Clusters of the Việt Kiều

If you sample thirty people from a diverse group you discover thirty rich and nuanced lived experiences. Indeed, the Việt Kiều are engaged in a wide variety of ministries within Vietnam. However, core ministry clusters emerge from the participant answers.

Core ministries are not mutually exclusive or permanent. The scope of ministry is fluid and flexible with many variables that contribute to experience. This is both by intentional choice by the Việt Kiều, and others that are put upon the Việt Kiều, by dynamics specific to living and working in the local context.[12] For the returnees, a wide skill set is often drawn upon and honed over time through experience. Often one person is involved in many different ministries at different points in time as they have creatively engaged in the homeland. Sometimes primary ministries overlap; sometimes they might be contained to different seasons over the course of their missionary career. Amongst diversity, there is a commonality of experiences.

There are three primary ministry clusters or common avenues of ministry engagement that characterize the ministries of the Protestant

---

12. People will make different choices on a range of issues, such as to register or not to register that set in motion a series of potential outcomes. Nevertheless, many of the choices that confront returnees would be familiar for most of the respondents.

Christian Việt Kiều. The ministry foci are: discipleship centric ministries, community development centric ministries, and BAM centric ministries.

Discipleship Centric Ministries

Discipleship centric ministries correlate with the high levels of salvation motivation to return to Vietnam. These ministries are lived out in many expressions that intentionally engage the wider society as kingdom witnesses and seek to foster discipleship that strengthen and equip the existing Christian community. Works that fall under the umbrella of discipleship are seen by many as a key way that they can positively contribute.

Mai provides a good example of a discipleship centric ministry that fuses the outreach burden with Christian discipleship within the ministry context of working closely yet distinctly from a local church. Mai and her team are focused on building community that equips and empowers university age students (both Christian and non-Christian) who will become the next generation of leaders.[13] This particular ministry is done in relationship with a local church, but distinct from the local church. As Mai says, "we are members of that church, some of us work in teams, groups, youth group but we do not work for the church here. So [name of place] is not part of the church. Sometimes the leaders of the church wish that [name of place] was, but it's not." There has been some negotiation of roles along the way as they have learned to complement each other. For Mai and her team, their discipleship focused vision is actualized primarily through a certain location that has classes, conversation spaces, sports, and social projects selected by the community for the benefit of the local community. It is a place built for building relationships and empowering. "[Name of place] is a place where we meet people, where we gather people and where we get to know people." This really goes to the heart of the concern for Mai that brought her back. As she says, "I felt God wants to use me as an encourager for Vietnamese young ladies. That's why I went back." This encouragement is given though a lot of time investment and listening. "I often approach people by asking a lot of questions about their life and listening. I'm trying to feel what they feel and to cry with them, to laugh with them, to spend time with them, and to love them the way they are and to accept them. And to let them know

---

13. Mai is on a team with four Việt Kiều and other foreign workers. She was the only one in country at the time of the research trip. The others were out of the country attending a cross-cultural training course.

that we all have failures but still we are all loved." Discipleship happens in the context of listening and participating in this community. Friendships are formed, people are discipled, conversations happen, healing happens in the small group discussions, and people are empowered as they flourish in the community.

Suong and Bach have a discipleship centric ministry that is responsive to the trends of globalization. They were first sent to serve in a South-East Asian nation, ministering among the ethnic minority Vietnamese migrant workers working abroad in this nation. Eventually, the tide turned, and the bulk of these migrant workers returned to Vietnam. At this point, they moved back to Vietnam with this community. As they describe, "I say we are working with those that believer [sic] that come back from [South-East Asian nation], our goal is to continue to support them to train them and help them reach out to their own people. Those . . . who accept Christ in [South-East Asian nation] majority of them are a minority people group. They are not the national group they are a tribal group." They are ministering to an ethnic minority population. In Wan's delineation, this is a case of ministry by and beyond the diaspora. Like many missionaries, they have engaged in many different forms of ministry with seasons of success and frustrations along the way. More of that will be detailed in 2b. At the heart of it all is a burden for reproducing discipleship. As they state their overarching purpose, "we are still focused on discipleship. We live among the tribal people so we hope we are looking to disciple them and help to reach out to them." Recently, they have launched a creative discipleship model. They have "open up a farm as a training center so we receive any student willing to be discipled, we will receive them and they can move into our farm and stay with us." It is not a formal program or classroom teaching content-based approach. It is living and working together, intentional conversations, Bible study and immediate application. They are attempting to do life together for periods of time as a tool for discipleship. This is responsive to what they see as the real need among the rural Christians they are working among and from the lessons they learned from times of frustration.

Some of the Việt Kiều that participated in this research project are theologically trained, come to Vietnam with vocational ministry experience, and have discipleship centric ministries that flow from these ministry competencies. For example, Hung was a church planter in the West before he took the leap to return to Vietnam. He draws upon these years of ministry experience as he disciples potential leaders and pastors a church plant. It is on the ground, hands on living life, doing ministry together kind of discipleship. As he says, "I believe in churches which creates disciples, reach out and place disciples." Within the church plant that he leads, they have various evangelism activities that draw non-Christians into the faith community and is a training grounds for discipleship that develops suitable people as ministry apprentices in preparation for formal theological education and vocational ministry. As he describes, we

> want . . . to reach out to non-Christians, and we have small groups. We have three small groups, and about five groups with different houses. And we just study the Bible, they come to my place for dinner, and then we share and all that. Then now we have one-to-one discipleship which means I'm training a number of people with the aim that they may want to apprentice with us. So, I've got what's called a seven-step discipleship program. So, only one Christian, then across young toddler, teenager, young adult, mature adult and training in ministry. So, I try see where everyone is at that then one-to-one. So, there's a new Christian training, mature Christians to meet one-to-one with them. I disciple people, and I train people, and also step seven is to train apprentices, I have a two-year program where I find suitable people, who are gifted, who have leadership abilities and can teach the Bible to apprentice with me for two years and then send them over to overseas to study.

This is a comprehensive discipleship model. It is also a clear example of social remittance. The ministry apprenticeship model was practiced in his context in the West and has been remitted to the Vietnamese context.[14] Discipleship is the heartbeat of his ministry. It is practiced in a way that comes from Hung's training and prior experience.

Likewise, Thuc is also theologically trained and engages in a discipleship centric ministry. However, each returnee takes their own missional approach. Thuc is based in a major urban center as a strategic ministry home base. However, it is not this city, nor is inhabitants, that are the primary ministry target in the long-run. This is not unusual for my respondents. Where one lives is not always directly correlated to one's geographical ministry focus. For Thuc, his specific ministry aspirations focus on igniting a

---

14. "In [Western city], we call it MTS, Ministry Training Strategy, here it is called Apprenticeship Ministry. Then, they get paid a salary for working two years, and they get to do church stuff, they run small groups, they meet people one-to-one, they disciple, they organize evangelistic ministries and all that."

church reproducing discipleship movement among two minority groups that live in the providences near the urban area. In this way, we see an example of aiming to engage in ministry by and beyond the diaspora. However, that is really a long-term goal and one that is delicate to achieve. The location makes access a challenge. Currently, government restrictions keep him from engaging with that group on their home turf. Even though he is Việt Kiều, he does not have permission to travel freely to these regions and work openly with these populations. As many Việt Kiều note, being Việt Kiều does not give you a free pass from government oversight. However, the city is a hub and people can find ways to travel into the city and partake in ministry related activities. There is also the now and not yet aspect of their ministry. What their day-to-day life looks like now is a focus on language and cultural acquisition language, ministry exploration, and discipleship. Like many who are in the earlier years of ministry engagement, he is "praying that the Lord will just kind of direct us to what He's already doing, to what doors He's opening to, access to people. But right now, my focus is on discipleship." In this way, Thuc is much like many of the Việt Kiều that return. They are still on the front end of their ministry and are exploring the lay of the land to find the right ministry door to fulfill the ministry vision to make progress on their motivating and long-term missional objectives. Discipleship is both a current ministry priority and a long-term ministry vision.

Respondents engaged in discipleship centric ministries frequently demonstrate high levels of patience, creativity, and grit as they remain engaged in what is often a challenging ministry context. Commonly, this results in ministries that are conduits of social remittance, showcase missionary work by and beyond the diaspora, and complex and nuanced relationships with the local church systems. I will briefly mention two examples here. Van has established a three-year theological education training program for pastors and church leaders taught at their educational level. It is a high school equivalency Theological Education by Extension program (TEE) tailored to the educational needs of the students. A majority of students are Hmong and other ethnic minorities. Classes are organized in the villages rather than having students come into city. He is able to multiply his effectiveness as he is invested heavily in training the teachers and developing the contextual curriculum. He also runs an American curriculum English language homeschool for local Vietnamese to bless society. This praxis comes from his missional conviction and times of training in the

West. He is a theologian by training, and his convictions have led him to missionary praxis on societal engagement with the largely non-Christian society. This ministry, along with the TEE program being intentionally non-denominational, has strained his good relationship with his ECVN upbringing.

Quyen runs an oral Bible training (OBT) program that has taken her throughout Vietnam. She has a disciple-maker's heart. As she says, "the OBT program has been the most fruitful, and I think the most beneficial, because that's our ultimate goal here. I mean, everything else, like the farming and the business, they're practical helps for the people, but ultimately, it's about. . . . My skill set is in discipling . . . discipling comes naturally to me, and that's where my strength is." Her ministry is another example of ministry by and beyond the diaspora as she counts leading the program for "eighteen different ethnicities now, and I've done workshops outside of Vietnam." Much could be said positively about this ministry. While it is a tool fine-tuned for discipleship, it is also part of a larger comprehensive ministry strategy, a program that has been the vehicle for local ministry partnerships, and an example of social remittance.

As the discipleship tool it is part of a comprehensive strategy with a farming and BAM component for the largely agrarian population that participate in the program. This is one means that Quyen hopes will have many layers of benefits locally including helping to avoid dependency for the local church and fund ongoing OBT training. A national program of this nature has many layers of local ministry partnership. The program is done in partnership with national workers who have taken over the teaching of the program. The program can live on and thrive if or when she leaves Vietnam. She has been very intentional about wanting to raise up local national leaders that can take over the leadership of the program. This has been slow, but successful transition as she hands the reins over to national leadership and they take on increased decision making for the program.

Secondly, Quyen offers an interesting anecdote that speaks to the concerns of social remittance. The OBT program in and of itself is an example of social remittance. It is a discipleship program written by someone else for a different national context. The program has gone international and has been brought into Vietnam by my respondent. This is a familiar story in contemporary Vietnam. Many programs are being brought into Vietnam by many different agents, including the returning Việt Kiều, as the once closed nation has opened the window to allow the possibility of such exposure (a smaller number of programs are being written on site specifically for the ministry context as the Van example shows). Quyen made a crucial observation concerning some of the program assumptions behind this specific discipleship program that would undoubtedly be applicable to more than just this one program. The person who wrote the program operated from the mindset that worldview does not matter, it is Biblical culture that matters. The operative assumption was that the program was transmitting a pure Biblical worldview in the story form. However, as Quyen taught the program she came to realize that actually the program "was written from definitely a Western world view" and that

> when I started teaching it, I took on whatever 'M' taught me, which is worldview doesn't matter. I'm going to just teach you the biblical word and the Bible worldview. Well, in the first two years that I was teaching it, when I didn't open myself up to the possibility of worldview affecting how people learn, or worldview affecting what people learn from the same Bible passage, it made the learning process for the students more difficult because I didn't adjust. I was set in my way, my thinking, and I thought, who cares what their worldview is? Their worldview is wrong. We just need to get them to think about the biblical worldview."

This is a part of her experience of the journey of working in Vietnam. She learned that this program does in fact have an operative worldview and that worldview assumptions matter. Worldview assumptions are not something that can be taken off and removed from the communication exchange.

Even while recognizing the validity of worldview and making communication adjustments, the program remains a vehicle for social remittance. One of the worldview values that is remitting back to Vietnam though this discipleship program is critical or creative thinking and the value of choice. Creative thinking is a value that many of the Việt Kiều prize and deliberately desire to remit to the homeland. Quyen articulates sentiments that came up in many of the interviews as she outlines part of her approach and a lesson learned along the journey. As Quyen outlines, "my assumption and the way we do things in the US is the most valuable thing you can give to somebody is choice, or their right to choose. So, then you present all the information, and you ask them to make a choice. I used to do that in our training." This could be for unimportant things such as which restaurant to eat or more significant discipleship area. She came to see overtime that open-ended choice was hard and she adjusted the approach because the culture here and the environment that they've grown up here for the last 40 years, it's too hard for them. I didn't realize it was so hard for them before . . . so, then I started giving them choices, narrow down the choices for them instead of just making it so wide and open. So then, "Okay, you can choose between," and I'll pick out three things and let them choose between those three things . . . instead of open-ended. So, then it made things easier, but it still held to my belief that I should give people the right to choose. . . . Because they can't think for themselves very well, and OBT really helps them think for themselves. That's part of what we do, teaching them critical thinking skills, but meeting them where they're at so that instead of just saying, "Okay. This is your problem. What should we do?" I'll say, "This is our problem. Here are a few ways we can solve our problem. What do you think?" So then giving them more narrow choices, but still giving them a choice. So, I think that's one of the most significant change that I've made.

A learning curve is expressed though this narrative of social remittance as certain values are being intentionally remitted through this discipleship program. The value of promoting critical thinking is part of the OBT curriculum. This is not in any way unique to this particular OBT program or Quyen. This intention was shared by many respondents.

The Transnational Việt Kiều lean towards the evangelism side along with discipleship classes to equip the new believers and other local leaders. Being transnational has a potential range of benefits and weaknesses as it pertains to discipleship ministry in the natal homeland. One of the benefits is that they have potentially less scrutiny than one that has fully relocated back to the natal homeland. For contemporary Vietnam, this means that the transnational Việt Kiều are able to do more crusade or conference event orientated ministries under the radar, that might carry a greater risk for those that live in country. As Van mentions, "if you come here as a tourist for a few months, everything is very easy for you. You want to stay here? Work here? Open a business here? Then at that time you will face the bureaucratic." For instance, Kiet has been returning every summer participating in evangelistic crusade events in rural villages with a local itinerant evangelist. He works with what are called the 'home churches' in the countryside. The logistics are organized by the local contact and his team, Kiet shows up for the evangelistic event and training discipleship classes for home church pastors and local leaders. Sometimes it is easier to engage in evangelistic events when you are not needing the residency permit as evangelism has its limits in Vietnam.

Evangelist rallies/crusade kind of events might be open to inflated numbers. Number inflation and "rice Christians" was a point that several returnees discussed in the context of what they have observed in other ministries and as a rational for their ministry philosophy. The usage of the term suggests people participating in ministry events primarily for the material gain rather than the spiritual benefit.[15] The term applies to both non-Christians and Christians. As such, "rice Christians" could be non-Christians participating in an evangelistic event, and potentially even saying a prayer confessing faith, primarily for the purpose of receiving the material benefit being distributed at the event. It could also be descriptive of Christians participating in activities such as a discipleship training program primarily for the financial benefits that the program offers (such as the trip to the city, hotel lodging, food, etc,). Interestingly, only the transnational Việt Kiều discussed salvation numbers as they told their stories. At the same time, transnational Việt Kiều did express awareness of the potential for "rice Christians" and spoke of the safeguards in place to help with this pitfall. Additionally, some of the transnational ministries utilize the wonders of modern technology to remain connected and conduct discipleship trainings while not physically in the homeland. This has been a more recent development and one that might have a significant impact moving forward.

Development Centric Ministries

A significant segment of the respondents engage in development centric ministries as an overarching cluster of ministry engagement. Participants with this ministry foci can be found in both registered NGO and unregistered work that seeks to contribute to individual and community flourishing. This would include work such as work with orphans, medical projects, and educational ventures usually aimed at the less advantaged in society among other ministries. These ministries are undertaken in direct response to the perception of need in the homeland. Additionally, it is often entered into in pragmatic responsiveness given the ministry context. Many respondents spoke of this ministry platform as the most direct and effective means to express Christian love and charity that blesses the largely non-Christian

---

15. "Rice Christians" was the term used by several respondents as they discussed their experiences and observations.

society. It is a tangible way to share the gospel in a context in which verbal gospel proclamation can be restricted.[16]

As Nhan says, "we learned that it's like you have to integrate social service into evangelism. You can't just share the gospel and expect people to believe. We saw it so effective in [a rural area] when [her medically trained husband] providing the healthcare. We were saying, he [her husband] can't heal you but we know God can. They were able to pray for the patients and directly testify to the working of God as you would see the patient for like three weeks or so. God healed them." Nhan went on to describe how this broke down the walls and opened up relationships with the locals who were very suspicious and had their guards up initially. The tangible expression of the love of Christ built relationships and tore down barriers. In time, the community came to see that "wow, these people are really genuinely." Their hearts begin to open as the love of Christ was shared in the context of this healthcare ministry. The healthcare they provide has been both a practical means to bless the people and an opening to conversations that move people closer to Christ.

Time and time again, returnees spoke to the reality that people respond to the love of Christ as it is tangibly demonstrated through these good deeds. When you are genuine and come with the intention to bless people because of the love of Christ, people respond and their hearts are open. Specific strategies vary but the intention is important. Anh Dung describes their approach and its long-term effectiveness in the following way:

> We're not just doing this so that we draw you into Christianity, but we love you because Christ loved you. We cannot share the gospel, but we do tell them that at the church we are Christian, and Jesus loves us, and so we want to share that love to you, and we show it genuinely. I think over time, people have realized that. There are many people now that, slowly, they're coming to the Lord, without us have to directly tell them about it. As they see us as Christian, how we live our lives and how we love them and share with them, God gives them the opportunity to hear the gospel through somebody else, and they accept the Lord. I think that's just, through our work, that they see . . . you probably heard it, this kind of phrase, that people don't care what you know until they know that you care.

---

16. Sometimes this has a pragmatic function as a necessary ministry platform that is necessary to open the doors to access a local population or even the best means available to legally be in the country.

They describe the ministry approach they have learned as "transformational, holistic transformation, or development. They learned this from years of experience. Relationships are formed, the love of God is tangibly demonstrated, and lives and communities are slowly transformed. It is a sometimes slow, but impactful movement as lives are shared over many encounters. Furthermore, their approach also comes from a place of humility as "we come to the people not because we think that our money, our resources are going to change them, but we come to them because God loves us and we have these resources to share them, plus we want them to be transformed." Intention is key for planting Christian influence amidst the limitations of the NGO visa.

When it comes to development centric work one key question quickly confront the returning Việt Kiều. To register or not register, that is the question.[17] My respondents were split on this question. Regardless, of where one came down on this question, it is true that one's approach has a profound impact on ministry experiences. The work of Anh Dung represents perhaps the most traditional community development approach. They are also firm on the opinion that one ought to register for long-term ministry effectiveness in Vietnam. They have been legally working in Vietnam for over twenty-years. They also have perhaps the closest relationship with Vietnamese diaspora churches represented among the returnees that I interviewed, having been commissioned and sent by the Vietnamese district of a national denomination as international workers. They entered the country legally with NGO visas.[18] This openness and legal status have

---

17. The question of registration is complicated and unavoidable for any returnee. In the current era, a returnee can hold a tourist or five-year multi-entry visa to enter Vietnam. This visa comes with potentially less initial oversight. However, these visas are issued with clear work restrictions and doing activities outside of the visa permission carries potential risk. Additionally, daily life function tasks such as renting a house or driving are more complicated with these visas. The Vietnamese State will issue NGO visas to returnees who return to work in this capacity. Living in the country openly and with legal standing comes with certain benefits and also potential drawbacks. The legal permission generally permits humanitarian activities such as clean water projects, medical projects, income generation projects, etc. However, this visa does not permit open communication of religions messages or what is termed religious work in union with the projects. Hence, some respondents choose not to register.

18. Their ministry role in the early years was driven partially by government imposed limitations rather than intentional choice. They were trained, sent and personally desired to engage in church-planting ministries. However, as their story tells, being Việt Kiều does not spare them from the complications of visas, restrictions on what can be done, and even the freedom that a legal visa and established relationship can provide. In the

provided them freedom to do what they say they are going to do and build long-term belonging in the community. The patient approach has paid off for them as they testify that over the years they go as "God, he just opened doors for us."

One of those doors is a more recent opportunity to openly engage in theological education. A few years back, Anh Dung was invited to start teaching at a recently legally sanctioned Bible College. The Hanoi government approved his religious worker visa to legally be in the country and teach theology. He credits the reputation that has been cultivated with the years of open work as key to this. However, interestingly enough, with the visa change status, he can no longer engage in NGO work. It is one or the other.

Some of the Việt Kiều respondents engaged in community development centric work have chosen to avoid registering. This allows a certain benefit of increased freedom (read ability to directly share the gospel/ directly integrate proclamation with the good deeds) while also putting certain other limitations upon the worker (read higher risk for the person and their ministry partners). Lan and her family reflect this position as they engage in foster care/adoption work. They are firm in their opinion stating, "we don't want to do an NGO once you start an NGO here, the government steps in and controls everything. We're not here to do humanitarian work per se. We're here to help people, but as a basis to present the gospel as our primary focus and so. When you open NGO, your hands are tied that just that doesn't happen. So we found that working through the local church and through local Christians, listening to them provide for their needs, financially we're able to be staying at arms-length and just facilitate what they would love to do, what they can do." They are able to do this work through a very close partnership with a local pastor's wife who is the primary worker who cares for the girls they are helping. This allows for a closer and faster

---

early years, the expectation of ministry life in Vietnam clashed with the reality of ministry life leading to times of frustration and learning, growth and fruitful work and the eventual opportunity for a change in ministry platforms. As described, "The disappointing thing for me and my wife was that we had this traditional mission mindset, and we were told that, no, you cannot do that, absolutely not. You cannot preach the gospel, you cannot share. Right now we are . . . we were told that we are only allowed to do relief and development. That's what got frustrating, for one thing. Another thing is that we had no skill. We were never trained in relief and development. It was a little bit disconcerting. . . . It wasn't fun. We just followed the flow, waiting for the opportunity. We could not do any real ministry that we thought that we had to do, like church planting, leader trainings, anything like that."

integration of Christian charity and discipleship. However, as they say, it also necessitates that this couple takes a largely behind the scenes off the radar role in the ministry. It also carries a higher degree of risk as they are working outside the boundaries of their visa.

Việt Kiều that return to the country need to be aware of the dynamics in the region they will work in and intentionally choose their approach and be prepared to navigate the terrain that comes with that choice. There are pros and cons for both the registered and the unregistered approach to Christian development work. Registered NGO work often might be slower for transformational change, but it might foster greater depth and stability. Returnees that go this route have the long game in mind. It might be slow and hard won, but it is deliberate and there has been good fruit from this approach among the project respondents. On the other hand, not registering allows for quicker access for directly sharing the gospel as you are more easily able to integrate verbal proclamation with Christian charity. However, it is often work done on a smaller scale and more hands off on the part of the returning Việt Kiều as seen by the example of Lan. Yet, in a much shorter time span, they have seen people holistically changed (both the immediate material need cared for and the Christian gospel directly presented). It is a good work, but it is relatively small in scope. Regardless, respondents from both camps, find commonality in acknowledging the vital role that this ministry platform can play in Vietnam. Community development centric ministries are a vital component of the modern returnees tool set as they missionally engage in their natal homeland.

BAM Centric Ministries

Thirdly, approximately a third of project respondents are engaged in BAM centric ministries as a primary ministry avenue. This is easily the most favorable in the eyes of the government and perhaps the most favorable in the wider societal context (at least the business component, the influence from the integration of ministry piece is not as appreciated). The perception of the ability to start and effectively run businesses that contribute to the economic growth in Vietnam is one of the primary motivators for the Hanoi government to reach out to the diaspora community and woo them back home. Indeed, fewer tensions and struggles were reported for returnees that went the BAM route. As Cau says, "So because if they think that you have money, look, the government wants you to come here cause they want you to spend money. Your relatives and other people think you have money so they can depend on you. So money speaks volumes here in Vietnam." Việt Kiều who have the skill-set to start and grow business are generally welcomed. The climate tilts towards favorable. On the other hand, business in and of itself has to be a calling and demands a certain skill-set and acumen. As respondents report, being Việt Kiều does not mean automatically ease and a golden ticket to start or successfully operate a business venture in Vietnam. The stories of business failures that are woven through the various narratives make this point. Like the other ministry avenues, it is a path that requires creativity and grit. By and large, respondents demonstrate these qualities as they faithfully seek to build flourishing businesses that bless their natal homeland. For those that are vocationally called and equipped for this work, their experience can be rewarding in many ways and contribute to gospel witness.

Cau reports three reasons for wanting to return to Vietnam. Two motivations were of a more personal nature and have been completed by his self-assessment. He has reunited with his natal family and learned the language and culture. The third motivation for return has experienced many ups and downs over the years in Vietnam and remains unfinished. This unfinished nature of the motivation has contributed to a lengthening of his initial timeframe for return to Vietnam. This experience is common among the respondents. Taken as a whole, returning Việt Kiều respondents have tended to stay longer than originally anticipated. Objectives are hard to obtain whether they be business venture, discipleship ministries, or the work of Christian compassion. As Cau reports, "in the beginning, I only planned to stay here about three years. You know, things change, I stay on with that business for ten years now." For Cau, his businesses have very intentional ministry dimensions and motivations. As he says of his rationale for return; the "third, is to do BAM and all of that was because what? From a Christian perspective, I felt like it was something that God was calling us to do; because, it doesn't make sense when you live in a very developed country and you have all the amenities that you would go back to a developing country." During his time in Vietnam he has helped to start three businesses. Each business has a specific DNA of Christian witnesses baked into the business model. However, by Cau's assessment his business experience in Vietnam has not been a smooth route as "nothing has taken." In one case, a business venture was doing well, but his business partner suddenly passed away throwing the business into chaos. In another case, Cau feels that the business was self-sustaining, but it wasn't to the degree that was needed at that time. As he says, "actually, I felt like I didn't make as much money as I could if I did something else. Let's say if I did teaching. Then there would probably be much more money. Because really it's just not about me, but I had to take care of my family, in Vietnam too. So, it was important to me that I had a career, at that time, to have the financials to support my family and my parents. It was self-sustaining, but it wasn't to the degree that I would have liked it to be." In this specific case, the returnee took what is a more lucrative position teaching at an international school. This narrative highlights competing tensions within BAM enterprises for the returnees that are most likely not present for non- Việt Kiều missionaries. Cau's passion is in BAM and specifically in entrepreneurship. However, people in Vietnam are depending upon him for financial support. The business must produce a certain profit level. For a season, the business had to be put on the back burner as financial considerations led him to accept work outside of his passion.

Despite the rhetoric, being Việt Kiều ought not to be confused with an easy path for business ventures. Dao, like others, has had his hand in multiple projects over his time back in Vietnam to variant degrees of business success. His resolute conviction that this is where he needs to be has sustained him. As he states he has run out of money several times and thought "all right, time to pack up. But I think I just felt like this is where God wants me to be and so it really helps to persevere through them. I think I learned that persistent and just having what God told you to do is really important. Keep that really tight and hold that really close, because I feel like I would have given up and came back to the US if I didn't realize this is where God wants me to be." This sense of calling to remain is crucial because, again, it is seen that being Việt Kiều and having formal business education is in no way a guarantee of success. Businesses run as BAM kingdom ventures might fail at times.

This issue of who to work with comes up here as well. The returnees cannot go it alone, they must partner with locals. Who you partner with is one of the most important decisions one can make. As Dao says, "I learned that partnering with the right people is really important, you need to know who to partner with. I learned that to help other people, you need to be able to make money and help yourself first be financially stable as a company. I guess that's very obvious but it wasn't obvious for me." Two things are spoken of in his reflection. First, the issue of national partners is of upmost importance. The returnee and the national partner(s) bring different and hopefully complementary things to the table. For this to work, you need to know yourself and be honest with what you can contribute and your own limitations.

Second, only a financially healthy business can truly be a blessing to the local context. You must have a real, viable business. It cannot just be a side project or a front for geographical access. Interviewees discussed how one needs to sacrificially invest time, talent, and resources into the venture. Out of this can come a flourishing fruitful venture. Being a blessing happens when the business is stable and you are fully engaged. You cannot do this half-way. In other words, if you are going to do BAM; do BAM. Do not have a business in name only while your primary passion engages in other ministry avenues. It demands your best to be a blessing.

Returnees are engaged in a plurality of business ventures reflecting the passions and giftings of the individuals. They also frequently find their way to a conviction that an educational venture is one of the most strategic avenues to make a lasting impact. It was striking how many of the Việt Kiều that participated in this project tend to eventually develop a ministry vision that includes an educational component. This was spoken of as a perceived need by respondents in all regions of Vietnam and even by transnational Vietnamese. A handful of the Việt Kiều are actively engaged in the educational sector as an avenue of ministry at the time of the interview. For most, it is a vision they have caught and are working to launch this sort of venture.

The educational vision spoken of addresses the apparent deficiency in critical or creative thinking that is rampant in Vietnam as per the assessment of the interview participants. It's a root problem and one that the Việt Kiều feel especially well equipped to address. This comes from frequently shared convictions that education in Vietnam is "just not really a good environment for international learning, or critical thinking and learning. I think a lot of learning that goes through the public school is more memorization, which I think if Vietnam is going to advance as a country, you have to teach more critical thinking, more of that skill set, problem solving, things like that" (Dao). It is also often linked with weakness in discipleship, general church health, and a hindrance to economic wellbeing as seen by the Việt Kiều. Christians lack maturity; the lack of a robust educational foundation is a key contributing factor to poor church spiritual health as well as economic poverty. Most are proposing an educational venture akin to a school operating with a Montessori educational model or American homeschool based programs for the general population. These would be educational ventures built upon a foundation of "good quality education at an affordable level" (Dao) and that integrates a Christian worldview foundation. That mix of quality and affordability is largely missing in contemporary Vietnam. International schools have quality but they are unaffordable to all but the wealthiest of society. The educational quality and value of English language schools is questionable. Their inherent value as a missional platform was also questioned by some. Coming from the West and with English language fluency, this is one unique strategic investment that the Việt Kiều perceive they can make. It is also a very direct means of social remittance that allows for the introduction of Western based educational values.

BAM is one of the common strategies utilized in the twenty-first century. Nearly 30 percent of my project respondents are engaged in BAM related works as a primary ministry vehicle as they return to their natal homeland. As a Việt Kiều, they are privileged with certain potential advantages in the ministry context. Several respondents noted that it is easier as a Việt Kiều to start a business in Vietnam than it would be in the States. Despite that, I heard narratives of many unsuccessful businesses. Simply put, far more businesses failed than are currently thriving among my respondents. For those that feel God's calling to go down this ministry road, they need to enter with eyes wide open to the many challenges that lay in front of them. Among other considerations, any business needs to earn profit to be flourishing, it needs to organically integrate Christian witness to be a BAM enterprise, the returnee needs to have passion for the business project itself, trustworthy competent local partner(s) need to be in the right key positions, it needs to walk on the good side of various bureaucratic stipulations, and it need to be suitably local to flourish in Vietnam. This is really hard to achieve. But when it is done well it can be a beautiful venture that blesses the local context on many dimensions (material and spiritual).

As the respondents shared, a BAM enterprise can have a societal and kingdom value. The social value is fairly straightforward when built into the ethos of the business. The kingdom value can be harder to quantify. As a Christian, the evidences of a life of godliness and faith, can permeate the business culture and God can use this to draw people to himself. One narrative really captures this potential. A returnee shared how one of his employees that had been working with the company for a while and was not a believer shared that "after meeting me and working with me, and seeing that I prayed and reading the Bible, he started to believe in God and wanting to get closer" (Dao). Something was demonstrated that this non-believer wanted. He saw this as he worked together with the returnee. It was organic, something that cannot be forced. It did not come from direct verbal proclamation. Simply being a Christian in a secular space spoke profoundly. This is one of the hopes for BAM and a way that Việt Kiều can contribute missionally to their natal homeland.

Their Perceptions of Their Ministry: Reflections from the Returnees

In this section of the chapter, the attention shifts to exploring how the Việt Kiều perceive their ministry. This will be seen through the lens of four key questions: 1. The effectiveness lens—Do they see themselves as effective? 2. The frustration lens—What frustrations have they experienced in ministry, with partners, with adjustment, etc? 3. The reception lens—How do they feel they have been received by the national Vietnamese? 4. The personal emotional lens—personal emotional issues (identity and culture shock). This will add a dimension of analysis to the ministry experiences detailed in the three primary ministry platforms that my respondents are engaging missionally in their natal homeland. Lastly, this section will briefly wrap up with a summary of social remittance analysis.

Do They See Themselves as Effective?

This question addresses the concerns of RQ 2, Sub RQ3: How do the Việt Kiều perceive the fruitfulness of their return ministry? One can tackle this question from many angles. Objectively speaking, there are several valid metrics that one could use to attempt to measure effectiveness. For the question at hand, the key here simply is how the respondents themselves discuss their ministry. Do respondents, directly or indirectly, communicate that they view their time back in Vietnam as effective? How do they discuss the fruitfulness of their return ministry? Self-assessment is key for this analysis. The straightforward answer to this question is that it depends. There is not a simple yes or no answer to this question. This section will explore the common themes that respondents discussed when talking in relationship to effectiveness.[19]

One potential gauge of effectiveness is the accomplishment of ministry objectives and measurable outcomes. None of my respondents were presumptive enough to declare that they see themselves as highly effective. Most respondents were very humble as they described their experiences. However, indirectly, several respondents in describing their experience, demonstrated ways that they perceive they are effective. Effectiveness can be measured by churches being planted, by leaders being trained, by communities increasing in financial security, by businesses growing, and by people coming to saving faith in Jesus Christ. All of these things are reported by the returning Việt Kiều. All these things are measurable outcomes that demonstrate markers of effectiveness. Respondent narratives told of these wins. These are good stories that tell of the Kingdom of God advancing as they faithful serve in Vietnam.

While there are many potential markers of effectiveness, by and large, the returnees tell narratives that highlight the nature of a missionary journey that has many ups and downs. Undoubtedly good things are happening. However, respondents were candid to paint a realistic picture that the so-called wins are included in a basket of many strikeouts. Sometimes this might happen in the reflection context of what has been learned. Statements were made such as we did something this way and it failed or we learned that this approach would not work in this context. Every respondent had narratives along these lines. It comes with the territory. Being Việt Kiều does not inoculate one from this experience.

This happened in Lan's case. For them, the initial objectives were fairly quickly set aside as it was readily apparent that this approach did not work in Vietnam. "The goal we had, we were thinking of finding foster parents

---

19. Some Việt Kiều take the route of holding up faithfulness as the litmus test of effectiveness arguing that the question itself is flawed. As Suong states her conviction that, "ministry wise I don't see about meeting goals and all that our focus. Because in the mission field you have so many challenges and there's so many thing that we have to face, we don't know what is right and wrong but all we know is submit to God whatever he allow us to do and the rest is his. It's not for us to say we are successful or we are failure. Personally, both of us we never think about being a failure or being success, we just focus because if we look into that it can cause a lot of discourage. Because we know that God is the one who works in and through us to reach the people group he want to reach. And the point is that are being obedient to be used by him whichever way he want it or not." In the big picture, this is a helpful perspective. Obedience needs to come first and always remain in focus.

to take care of needy children. Like if they lose a parents or father or one of the father or mother. That was our goal but it changed." Husband: There just wasn't an opening to that ministry. "I mean, we had some, but we" Husband: very little success. "Yeah, as somebody is not as successful without would be, but the Lord was really good. The Lord opened other doors." Their initial approach found very little traction. However, this is not the full story. God opened other doors and they have a ministry that while measurably small, is unquestionably making a kingdom impact (as self-reported) as they work in ways that are tangential to their initial objectives. Adjustments have to be made along the way. The Việt Kiều demonstrate this creativity as they are able to adjust course. Lan finds herself in familiar company regarding this journey of finding that one way is not working and moving forward through other open doors. There is a learning process that goes into returning home after many years. As my respondents demonstrated, this should be expected. Effectiveness is not equated with a perfect record of glowing narratives. Rather you keep going, moving forward along other pathways, when one way is not landing with the hoped-for outcomes.

Across many interviews a common theme emerged as the Việt Kiều overwhelmingly report a finding that the pace of ministry in Vietnam is slow, and they have needed to learn to adjust accordingly. Vietnam is a relational culture and time is a key ingredient needed to nurture those relationships. As Thuc has experienced, the nationals ask, "Is this a real relationship? Or is it once and done thing?" A premium is placed upon consistency as "once you establish relationship, the doors wide open." Being Việt Kiều might get you in the door, but one still needs to adjust and walk the pace of the location. You just have to keep showing up. You have to keep inviting people over, keep going to the ministry center, and keep finding organic ways to spend time with people. It is a culmination of relationships formed over the course of many events and many conversations. By and large, the picture that emerges is that ministry is often not an exciting event, but a slow gradual process that impacts lasting transformation on an individual and community level. Authentic depth of relationship that overcomes the barriers and leads to individual and community wide transformation is a slow process that takes time to grow deep roots.

Simply stated, ministry in Vietnam takes the investment in time. It is not a fast change. This held true in every region of the country and among respondents engaged in all three ministry platforms. As Kiet says, "you cannot rush it when it comes to work with the church in Vietnam. There are no short cuts." Likewise, Anh Dung says, "We have to walk real slowly, and just waiting for the right time. We cannot push it. A lot of times, we thought that we need to do this . . . but because of the restriction, we just could not do it. We had to do things slowly, learn to be more patient." For some, ministry goals are reported as being in the process of being accomplished but they are five or more years behind schedule as one has discovered just "how hard it was to work cross-culturally" (Quyen). Daily life takes longer than what most Việt Kiều were accustomed to after living in the global West. As Quyen describes, accomplishing goals is difficult when in "coming back here and getting half an item, not half of your task list, but if you had a line item on your task list, and if you were able to get half of one item done, you had a good day. That was very difficult for me. So, I think the disappointing thing is not getting things done as quickly as I hoped to." Effective or not, this question is filtered through the lens of recognition that change is a long slow process for many respondents.

The on the ground lived reality does not correspond with the picture spoken of within the diaspora missiology literature which suggests a picture of excitement and rapid movement. There is no moving target imagery here. The picture painted by respondents details a steady and consistent, slowly built, hard won ministry. The Việt Kiều are faithfully serving in ways that are arguably effective. However, the ministry pattern and experiences are much closer in alignment with the paradigm of traditional missions. You move to a community, learn the language and culture, persevere and commit to a long-term engagement, and adjust course along the way. Ministry for the returning Việt Kiều is slow and laborious. Those that are interested in deep rooted gospel transformation in Vietnam should be prepared to engage for the long haul.

What Frustrations Have They Experienced in Ministry, With Partners, and With Adjustment to Life Back in Vietnam?

This question explores some of the perspectives of the Việt Kiều as they discussed areas of frustration with their ministry experiences, national partners, and general adjustment issues that emerged as they sought to live back in their natal homeland. This section hones in on RQ 2 Sub RQ 1, with the emphasis placed on the realm of the challenges.

The Việt Kiều that have returned tend to work closely with local Christian ministry partners. This is done very intentionally for a variety of reasons. For one thing, respondents commonly reported a sense of knowing that they are not in Vietnam forever. They want to build something that will last beyond when they once again leave Vietnam. They, therefore, are very intentional about raising up local leaders who can carry on the work.

Second, there is a Protestant church in Vietnam. Protestant missionaries first landed on the tropical shores in Vietnam one hundred and ten years ago. The contemporary Việt Kiều diaspora missionaries are well aware of this foundation and demonstrated that they want to respect and build off the work that has already been done rather than reinvent the wheel. For a few respondents, these are friendship social networks established pre diaspora that have been reignited. In these relationships, the returnees have childhood friends that have grown into Christian ministry leadership positions that serendipitously opened ministry doors. Sometimes it is re-established connections with the church they attended as a child prior to their relocation to the West. For most, these are new networks. However, very few participants work directly with the ECVN South or ECVN North on an official basis. Most Việt Kiều are open to working with anyone who shares similar ministry ethos. They also tend to express motivation to go to where there is the perception of greatest need. This leads them to tend to work with collaborative missionary groups, home churches, the younger and smaller registered denominations, and intentional working with ethnic minority populations. These kinds of groups are repeatedly seen as being more receptive, having greater need (both spiritually and materially), and less access to training.

Working closely with local Christian ministry partners is a noble pursuit. By default, this approach means you are rubbing shoulders with leaders in the local context as a regular part of your ministry. This opens the door to the full range of relational interactions. As was mentioned in the effectiveness section, the returnees can point to many wins as well as times when things have gone off the rails for any number of reasons. Sometimes the relationships that are built are perceived by the returnee to be genuine and mutually healthy relationships. Other times they are transactional and leave the returnee feeling frustrated and used. This was a common theme that emerged from the data. Working cross-culturally can be a frustrating experience at times. This section will dive into how the Việt Kiều describe times of frustration in ministry with local partners specifically in the area of transactional relationships, the national church, and adjustment to life back in Vietnam in a holistic sense.

First, the returning Việt Kiều know that they are working cross-culturally when they return to Vietnam. There is no illusion that they are one happy unified people and that returning to the natal homeland will be smooth sailing. For all the potential advantages that being Việt Kiều brings to the ministry experience in Vietnam, there are layers of complexity and expectations that are unique to citizens of the diaspora. One of the reoccurring most significant area of frustration voiced by the project participants is the transactional nature of relationships. This finds its clearest expression in the issues of economic remittance—the expectations surrounding Việt Kiều and money.

Interviewees reveal that the Việt Kiều perceive that they are viewed as having money when they return to their natal homeland. At times they feel personally devalued, and their ministry contributions as being devalued, as people are looking at them as an ATM for their livelihoods and personal ministry projects rather than as co-laborers in God's harvest field. There seems to be a sense of pay to play going on at times. As Kiet describes, "the sad thing is that they, the city pastor, a good number of them are just looking for finances, so that's the disappointing part." He reports that pastors would leave the meetings after they heard the messaging that their group would provide no monetary benefit for the trainings. Likewise, Suong reports, "when we begin, we talk we meet maybe more than a hundred different leaders from different church, especially the house churches. We begin with them and then at the end some of them come with, well we cannot take your program because your program don't have any money involved. It's like slap on the face. So we say okay, from the beginning we told you and you said you want God's word and we only have God's word to help you help your people." Quyen articulated some of the underlying expectations that can cause tensions when they are not met. As she explains, "I didn't lack the students. What I lacked were students who were willing to financially be a part of it, meaning there were so many different programs coming to Vietnam where people would pay for everything. I mean, they even paid for what is called a sitting fee. They'd pay for the students' transportation, lodging, food for the whole week, and even money to take home. I didn't lack students who were interested in the program, but I lacked the students who were willing to financially take part in it." The theme was woven into nearly every conversation as respondents shared tales of economic expectations for the various discipleship and other ministry activities. Financial arrangements come with the territory and each missionary has to come to their own convictions as to how they will operate. One cannot separate missions and money. Dynamics surrounding money played out for the Việt Kiều in a myriad of social and ministry relationships and was frequently listed as one of the greatest areas of frustration.

Some of the project participants describe the dynamic in theological terms. For example, Lan used theological language stating that "money can be a stumbling block, For the Vietnamese people, Christian." Likewise, Van discussed the prevalence of bad theology that manifests itself in the hand-out mentality in which, "people will just keep asking, they will never be mature." He has observed that "If they cannot make money themselves serving those ministries, just waiting for money from outside to do ministry it's like they create trouble and then it's very easy to misuse to abuse that amount of money. And also, some organizations came here to help churches to develop, to have more conversions or something like that and then they will play with numbers they have false reports like saying last year we have five hundred new members and things like that but it's just lying number, it's like four members or so." Bing agrees stating that, "I think a lot of organizations came and then they just give cash, and they do a short training, and then they left. So, it creates this, the leader that's the mentality that we do the same. That's why it's really hard for the church, and they focus a lot of money than spiritually. Some of the Korean as well, they give cash and for the leader, and they do whatever they want." He goes on to explain that "in the Vietnam church for a very long time until now they belong to outside support a lot. Everything they go to outside the church, the most is money, funding. There's many churches right now they look at Korean missionary, or American, or other missionary, they can see that money attached to it." Like most of the respondents, they are working very intentionally with how they use money to try to change the culture.

Several other respondents disclosed personal raw narratives of frustration stemming from transactional relationship expectations. Suong describes this experiencing of discovering that the Vietnamese, her people, are hard to love. In the context of wanting to serve people and love people, she has experienced deep frustration of being used. As she says,

> the most unexpected is realizing how cunning the people are. When I was young, when I was little I didn't know people are so cunning like nowadays. They stab you on the back and thing like that. I'll be very much careful, everything that we tried to help people, we had to think twice and do a lot of evaluation and

seeking before we jump to helping anybody. Because there's too much scheme, there's too much cunning going on, we don't know if its real and majority are all Christian. Most of the time we got schemed on by the Christians not the non-Christians. Because the non-Christians we wear our guard but with the Christians we don't wear the guard, we want to help them and we go all the way to help them, whatever we can do for them and oh my goodness.

The sacrificial ministry to help her people have left her and her husband feeling as if they have been stabbed in the back at times.

To varying degrees, this experience finds common ground with a sizable number of my respondents. Working in a different region of the nation, Nhan tells a similar cautionary tale that goes to the heart of the issue for the Việt Kiều when it comes to this frustration. As Nhan has experienced, "there's an expectation with foreigners as far as finance and when you don't supply that, then things can turn. I think because we felt like we were really taken advantage of. Because they know foreigners are very generous people, and especially when they want to come and share the Gospel. So if we are not careful and we don't have good boundaries, you can really be easily taken advantage of." She told of one specific conversation with a university age student that made things crystal clear. As she narrates, "I asked her, why are Vietnamese people really nice to foreigners? Because Vietnamese people are really nice. She says, 'Well because foreigners have money.' It was like a reality that, okay, well it's not genuine." There's a reason why.... We've had plenty of stories, but that one was typical."[20] Like Suong and Bach, Nhan and her husband have felt taken advantage of and have learned the hard way the need to set clear boundaries.

Most of the interview participants desire to be generous as they are motivated to make a difference in the Christian charity space. They would gladly join with others to help meet genuine needs in the homeland. Rather, it is the expectation, scheming, and sense of a lack of integrity that goes into it, and the way the Việt Kiều perceive that they are being used for this purpose or that training events must come with material benefits. For many, this dynamic distracts from gospel witness while causing immense personal frustration. The Việt Kiều desire to work together with the national

---

20. I could point to many more stories from the interviews. One in particular highlights integrity challenges. One returnee discussed the issue of inflation of need and added a story in which she was approached by a local pastor suggesting an arrangement in which she would raise the money for their project and keep 10 percent of the funds raised for themselves.

church rather than feel as if they have to be on their guard so as to not be taken advantage of. Authentic relationships not based on ones perceived potential to remit money are desired by the Việt Kiều.

Second, working with the existing local church in some capacity is a priority for many that return. This can be a place of great joy and fruitful ministry. However, this has also proved to be a messy path, leading to a common source of frustration (especially for those engaging in discipleship centric ministries, this does not really apply for BAM workers). The Việt Kiều are returning to a context that has developed and exponentially multiplied in complexity over the years and especially in the Doi Moi era. There are now multiple registered denominations and home churches and their various networks, power dynamics, theological preferences, and the weight of traditions among other dynamics that feed into the ministry climate for the returnees. It is a complex landscape to navigate for the returnees.

One of the reasons the Việt Kiều missionaries are motivated to return and remain working in Vietnam is because they perceive that they can contribute to the growth of the church in Vietnam. It is clear from the many stories, that God is active and working though these dedicated servants. Furthermore, despite rhetoric that suggests a harmonious oneness, Vietnam is remarkably diverse on a myriad of levels. Nuancing is necessary. The specific context for one worker might be very different than the context for another. One cannot easily speak of the church universal in Vietnam as the respondents are involved in a variety of ministries in a diversity of contexts (i.e. urban cities in the North, Central, South; rural providences, work with different denominations and independent unregistered home churches, serve the kinh majority population, and ethnic minority populations, student ministries, etc.). The diversity of experiences and geographic locations of the project respondents help to fill in a picture of what is happening on the ground. Simply put, this means that one's ministry experience can be radically different depending upon where in the country one goes and who one is attempting to work with, among many other variables. Nevertheless, there were common themes that emerged when the Việt Kiều discussed their work with the church as it pertains to the discussion on frustrations.

The Việt Kiều in interviews when talking about the church often discussed two aspects: numbers and maturity. There is not a consensus concerning if the church in Vietnam is growing numerically among those interviewed. Some say it has plateaued. It is merely larger numerically due to natural population growth, but it is not a larger percentage of the population. Others say it is still growing, but that the rate of growth has slowed in recent years. The idea that growth of the church was more robust during the many years of stronger persecution was a common sentiment. Some workers differentiate between the ethnic groups and majority population and cite recent (research conducted in 2018) research by OMF to buttress their position. As Hung referenced, "OMF that did some research and statistics last year, I think amongst the ethnic groups they are growing, but among the Kinh people it's not." Still others are convinced the church is growing. Respondents sometimes point to direct stories from their personal experience to testify to an increase of churches in their area and/or numerically larger churches. As Mai states, "before there were like twenty, thirty people and now they are like three-hundred people after fifteen years." In her localized church circle, growth has been phenomenal.

While respondents lack consensus as it pertains to the numerical growth of the church in Vietnam, there is an overwhelming consensus on maturity. This perception that the church is weak in maturity or discipleship is shared by workers in every region of Vietnam and pertains to each and every denomination and the home churches. This is an area that the Việt Kiều frequently discuss and care deeply about. As Mai shares, "the church is growing, but people lack real care, discipleship." Their missionary team focuses on small group discipleship ministry and running a community center that seeks to address this perceived need. Tuan shares this opinion stating that "I think it's kind of one of the problems where I see that a lot of churches are growing in numbers, but there's definitely a lack in bringing those numbers up to maturity." Likewise, Quyen has experienced, "I don't see the spiritual growth in the Christians that I'm talking to. I see a lot of rules obeying. I see a lot of pharisaical stuff. Percentage-wise, I don't see a lot of people really maturing in their faith, and growing and living that transformed life to being salt and a light to those in their environment. I see a lot of programs, pretty tee shirts and big parties, and yes, they're drawing people in that way for a lot of humanitarian work. So, we see 'rice Christians', people coming for the rice, or the medical outreaches, for what they can get from Christianity. But as Christians, I don't see them growing in their transformed life." Others such as Bing tell of a church in maturity decline while simultaneously materially enriched. "The church building is higher, bigger, more land, more equipment, you can see modern the church. They have sound system. One hundred percent has sound system. Maybe TV, LED TV. Back and forth. Vietnamese church equipment, resource, they're well. They're okay, they will compare even with Hmong church you can see they're okay with that. Every year, the church they notify that through Christmas event, through many evangelism events, I think approximately about five thousand people accept Christ in public. But the attendance of the church is fewer, fewer, and fewer. Most of the churches you go is empty." This goes back to the economic remittance tensions. The visible structures of church, such as church buildings and modern equipment has grown via outside funding, yet the internal spiritual condition of the church has not kept pace with the new and expanded buildings.

The Việt Kiều care deeply about the spiritual maturity of the church. This was a key motivator for many to return and they want to invest their time and resources into this space. Yet, in attempting to work with the church in these spaces, comes a repeated discussion of frustration. The word "politics" often came up as the returnees discussed their experiences working with the churches in Vietnam. This was true of respondents working in each of the three regions of Vietnam and among denominations (both registered and unregistered home churches). There is also a repeated theme of political fighting among the churches and church leadership. Some of the returnees have been caught in the cross-fire. Working with one group will sometimes mean that other groups will not work with you and vice-a-versa. It can be tricky. As Liem describes, "we have problem because if not the textbook, not label, the CMA will be tough to do that, not label on the Baptist, not label on the Assembly of God or whatever, and then we had a problem." Furthermore, it seems to be that the more established the denomination is in Vietnam, the harder it is for returnees to break in. Quyen's discipleship experience is shared by many as they discussed their ministry experiences. As she says, "the CMA South is the one that has been the most resistant to it. They only allow their people to be trained by programs that they have approved, and so I unofficially taught people from the CMA South, and they would have to do it kind of undercover because they don't want their denominational leaders to know about it. But I have trained CMA South people, but not officially." By and large, the returnees express that they will work with anyone with a similar ministry ethos. They do not always find this to be reciprocal. Additionally, conditions are added that they simply do not want to submit to or would be impractical for various reasons. To work with an established denomination like the ECVN South in a recognized official capacity, you need to go through their vetting process. Most returnees that participated in this project did not, even as some of them were originally from ECVN churches before they joined the diaspora and/or have been members of Vietnamese CMA churches in the West.

Sometimes respondents have landed in the middle of a political minefield and been caught in the crossfire causing immense frustration. As transnational Việt Kiều Liem says,

> you can hear the fight between denomination, or they fight with you because they feel like money involved or something like that. And we know that the devil, kill, steal and destroy. Kill the relationship, destroy so on and so on there and then walk away from you, they bad mouth you about you're doing with somebody from your denomination or even pastor, when you tired, you disappointed, but you say, Hey, at least they're not nail you on the cross. The only thing church politics, it hurt me that, Hey, God put you in that area to share the gospel, not playing God, not playing power, not playing politics . . . they don't have foundation. When they don't have a foundation they get in, they become some leader to church, that cause problems. That's what we tried to push it into our foundation through the discipleship program.

The lack of spiritual maturity is the genesis of ministry vision and simultaneously a place that has caused frustration. Discipleship is seen as a tool that can build a healthy foundation and slowly turn the tide in this area of frustration.

Other project participants have also experienced the negative aspects of power dynamics at work as they have been caught in the crossfire. Hung's discipleship focused work has experienced several ministry highlights over the years of dedicated service. Churches have been planted and grown numerically, unbelievers have found faith in Christ and joined the church, and people have been discipled and mentored as ministry apprentices. However, this has been accompanied in the midst of many a frustration as he has attempted to work directly with the local registered church. In fact, multiple experiences have ended with friction and frustration. Like many of the returnees, he first started out by trying to gain the lay of the land with a time of working with the main city church in various capacities. This ministry season ended in separation and he left feeling like many of his suggestions were kept on the sidelines. After that he helped another guy with church planting and the church was blessed with rapid growth and they decided to plant another church. In his own description he had a lot of freedom to do most of the work and do it in his style. However, the relationship became strained. "I had a falling out with him. He thought I was trying to take over, I wasn't. So, in there we decided to part way, and the church that we planted, a third one, he said I could just take that and look after it and he'll just look after the two existing ones. . . . So, I'm still looking after that church." Around that same time, he had applied to work directly and in an official capacity with the denomination and was rejected during the vetting process. In his estimation this came from a process that was a bit muddy and rendered a judgment before he felt like he was really known to them. It left him with a bad taste. Despite that experience,

> even though I had falling out with the CMA churches, I think it's been great to see some of the ministries grow and see people grow, and some people have become Christian. Even when I was involved in [city name church], the Young Adults Ministry grew, and there was about seven small groups, and it grew to about ten when I left. I just wanted to do more church planting that's all, and seeing the church plant grow as well, to two and three congregation. Even now, that church is pretty good because it's got foreigners going there who are helping out and enriching people even though me and the pastors we are not on good terms, that's okay, the Gospel keeps going out, it's great. (Hung)

You have the gospel going forward, people coming to saving faith in Christ, joining community, people being discipled, and new leaders being trained all amidst the backdrop of some frustrations experienced in working in this ministry context. One cannot put the Vietnamese church up on a pedestal. It has conflicts and its own idiosyncrasy. One ought to enter with an awareness of what they are getting into.

Lastly, the very act of returning to one's natal homeland can be an exercise in frustration at times. Be prepared to experience disappointments and unexpected challenges to the return experience as it relates to living in Vietnam. Adjusting to living back in Vietnam does not always come easily or naturally. Most of the Việt Kiều experienced a range of disappointments as expectations and lived ministry experiences clashed with reasons for return and anticipated ministry outcomes. Some were very intentional in trying to lower expectations and/or expect everything to be different to mitigate disappointment. Even still, ministry is a road marked by lows and times of little visible success that come along with the fruit. This is particularly hard for Việt Kiều that sacrificially give up what is perceived as the dream life in the West to return to their natal homeland and face misunderstanding or worse. Transnational Việt Kiều Liem says this

> I came in over here in 1975, I making $130,000 a year until 2005, and I drop everything to surrender all. I had my MBA, and I'm working for almost 27 years, making good money, beautiful house, everything. But then when God calling me, that the huge and walk away from what we have walking into that ministry is not easy. But when you came back from Vietnam and sometime people misunderstanding, they feel like you go there trying to making money or trying to using them to come back to the US and raise the money. sometimes there're not even knowing that I put my life on the line, on the moped we go visit pastors all the way deep in the jungle, you know, sleep not even in the house we just sleep on the street keep going what for? For the gospel. And the reason I doing this because I almost lost my life.

The diaspora community in the West and the Vietnamese you return to serve will not always understand. Some returnees reported the perception that local Vietnamese are quicker and harsher to critique a Việt Kiều for their American ways and/or cultural knowledge gaps than an American who does not exercise cultural competencies. On the other hand, a returnee might have a robust comprehension of local cultural dynamics and clash because they do not easily fit back in the natal homeland. In other words, they express understanding cultural dynamics and the lived reality that it is hard to return to Vietnam precisely because one has changed during the long diaspora sojourn. At other times, the returnee might not always understand the local Vietnamese cultural dynamics (even with the shared heritage). Respondents acknowledged that at times they did not fully understand all the local cultural dynamics.

In any event, people sacrificially return and reality is often muddier than anticipated. People get sick. Roadblocks are discovered. As Anh Dung stated, "we started out pretty frustrated, because we couldn't do what we thought we were supposed to do." This sentiment is expressed by others. They have expectations of what ministry and life will look like back in the natal homeland. Reality can look much different.

Suong and Bach had already worked among Vietnamese migrant workers in a South-East Asian nation for five years prior to the move back to Vietnam. As such, it might be assumed that the adjustment to working in Vietnam might be easier once they packed up their bags and followed the migrant workers home. Interestingly, this is far from their experience.

Their initial season back in Vietnam was punctuated as a time that was a deep struggle as Suong describes.

> I pray and I ask God to say, Lord, the Vietnamese people, they are very hard to love. I had a hard time of loving them but if you send me here so use them. And I just do not have what it takes to love them. And if you want me to love them you have to give me some special, more power or something, or more love to able for me to love them to continue. And He did. At first, because it's my childhood memory I was based here? and with my parents, they always said the Vietnamese are very friendly, they are very kind and they are very genuine. But when I go to Vietnam, I didn't see any of those but I know of especially where I come from, the family members they have respect from the children, I didn't see any of that. And so I was asking, is all this true or not? But my point is like forty years ago, thirty years ago when I depart from Vietnam, it was still like that and according to my parents it was like that but thirty years later it's not. I don't know all that. And so I go to Vietnam and all I see just like opposite.

Suong found the Vietnamese, her own people, hard to love. Part of the challenge in loving the people came from this place of memory and expectation regarding who the people were. Perhaps Vietnam has simply changed for the worse over time. Or perhaps, memory had formed an idealizing of the homeland among her family in the diaspora. The good was remembered and kept alive in the family memory. Regardless, Suong's experience of finding the people hard to love was expressed by a range of the participants.

Returnees have found it can be hard to live in Vietnam. Hung had visited twice for extended holiday prior to his relocation. His initial impressions have not held up over the years. "Initially my impression was friendly, nice people, new to the Gospel. Over years, I think there is still a lot of very nice people, but I think it's a very selfish culture. Selfish in the sense that, the positive thing I guess is that it's family orientated, so yeah, they respect the elders and family, which is good, which is honorable. But, outside of that it's like who cares for anybody else? If they are not your family, they are not your friends." As a Việt Kiều, it was one thing to traverse the country for three months, it is an entirely different experience to set down roots. The negative experiences of being on the outside living in a place and experiencing this selfishness has been a source of frustration.

Project participants readily shared the ups and downs of their return journey. Whether it be the frustrations revolving around economic remittance issues and the perception that relationships are transactional, having to be politically astute when working with the local church, or frustrations that come from the reality of daily life in the contemporary Vietnam, it is undeniable that frustrations are a part of the return missionary journey. As a missionary, you are working with people on a cross-cultural playing field. As these narratives demonstrate, being Việt Kiều does not free one from the complexities and challenges that this entails. The Việt Kiều did not sugar coat their journey. A shared heritage does not equate with a serene homecoming experience. Nor does it pave the way for a frustration free, dynamic, perpetually joyful, return and ever flourishing ministry. This is a deep cross-cultural adjustment and all that that entails.

Personal Perceptions of Reception

Reception by the local non-migrant people seems to vary based on ministry objectives, existing social networks, age at the time of return, and even gender as described by the project participants. Among other variables, Vietnam is an honor/shame high group culture. Therefore, who you are factors into how you are received. Additionally, how the returnee intends to engage with social spaces in Vietnam contributes to the reception. There are some spaces that returnees will find easier to enter into than others. Most notably, those that attempt to work closer with official church structures deal with a range of reception issues that those primarily engaged in BAM related works do not face.

Taken as a whole, the Việt Kiều in this study report the perception that they are welcomed back to Vietnam by the national Vietnamese. On the surface all is well. However, when you look deeper, it is striking that the embrace while warm for some returnees, is somewhat neutral or reserved for others. Complex social dynamic plays out across many interactions and social relationships for those that return. Bing expresses this well as he reflected upon his reception. He was in a favorable social category when he returned and was able to leverage this for ministry purposes. As he describes, "in Vietnamese culture . . . the social ranking it plays very important role when you work, when you connect, when you deal with people. So that kind of thing we have an advantage. Our age also, we're not too young, we're not too old, so we can approach to the young people, also approach to the old people, elder. Yeah, welcomed back. Everybody welcomed us, very amazingly. God opened the door for us." Who they were in the group was ideal maximize the reception.[21] Furthermore, they had strong social capital that opened many doors and the gifting set to make the most of opportunities given to them. This worked out positively for some; for others it did not. The overwhelming majority of project participants, while sharing some bonds of being Việt Kiều and even comparable gifting sets, did not have comparably robust social capital and/or the advantageous social ranking. The lack in these areas is noteworthy for the experience of reception and experiential outcomes.

Only a handful of my respondents had strong social capital. They are seen as credible and are in a serendipitous position to make use of that credibility with a positive reception. Reception and opportunity tilted towards favorable based on the robust social network. This in turn has been a great asset in ministry effectiveness and the scope of ministry. It goes to follow that the people with the highest social capital have been arguably the most effective. They leveraged these good relationships and went back into places of status and ascribed respect. Ha was pointed in this evaluation. "Bing have a lot of friend." Bing unpacked this some stating that "we had to connect with the top leadership. Okay the president of CMA North and CMA South. We had a good relationship with them. With the pastor, regional pastor, with our leader of the churches. So that's why, because we have a lot, renting, we have a lot many project, we know that very well and many friend of ours. We don't have any problems with to go organize like that." They did not have to work hard to build these relationships. They had a lot of friends in strategic positions. The positive reception of these friends who had influence in key spaces opened doors and allowed them to not have problems.

Likewise, Van talks about, "I think that in the church circle because I had been worked with the theological school so actually I already had some kind of respect when I come back. And with the one who had been trained well, at a doctoral programs and I proved the quality of that degree and that comes with some favor from the church circle. And when we opened this program I received many people, I have many people come to visit here. The fact that I had been working with the American educational system got a high degree in the US and good schools also give me credit to work with them.... I was talking to a lady... they are not Christian and they just heard about me and what I'm doing. So it's like being trained in the US with a

---

21. Additionally, they had experienced a high degree of business success in the West and they had a respected ministry role at a large church prior to their return.

good equipping, well equipped, it gives me good credibility to work with the people." When it comes to church related ministries; social capital can prove extremely beneficial. A handful of the returnees had strong social capital networks that were utilized as valuable conduits for ministry engagement at the local church level. They would not be able to do what they have done without these established friendship networks that welcomed them back.

By the same token, a well-positioned local friend who vouches for you can make all the difference in accessing guarded worlds and smooth over many a difference. As Kiet explains, "in the back of my mind, I have always, that thing that's always bothering me, is that because I have a different accent, I'm not sure how they will receive me but because I didn't come in cold (but) along with another brother, a missionary (a local recognized evangelist), and so everywhere we goes he introduces me." The social capital of this local benefited the transnational respondent. He was welcomed in and trusted because of his friend. He was invited into the networks through this individual. It is not simply a matter of your training or the generalized bonds of a shared heritage. Who you know matters greatly for ministry effectiveness.

Social capital matters for reception. Additionally, money, or rather the perception that Việt Kiều have money, factors into how a returnee perceives their reception. At times, respondents report their perception that the warm welcome they have received can be partially or even mostly attributed back to money issues. More specifically, the perception that economic remittance might flow to the national Vietnamese was seen as a key variable in reception. As discussed, the national Vietnamese view foreigners and especially Việt Kiều through economic lenses at times. This has led to experiences where sometimes people have a mostly positive reception but for less-than-optimal reasons. As Cau has experienced "mostly I think it has been positive. Positive in a sense because I think people think that you have money. So, because if they think that you have money, look, the government wants you to come here because they want you to spend money. Your relatives and other people think you have money so they can depend on you. So, money speaks volumes here in Vietnam." The government welcomes the returnees back for their money. The local people think you have money. This perception is an important variable for reception.

Furthermore, gender matters for reception. Men doing business related ministries expressed a generally favorable reception. Women in educational or BAM related ministries expressed some reception challenges or even overt discrimination. Sometimes they perceived they were not considered "foreign" enough to play certain ministry or educational roles. Women also seemed to be given less grace when it comes to language and cultural knowledge (i.e. women should know how to perform certain life function tasks such as purchasing food at the market). Interestingly, Việt Kiều men did not discuss these cultural knowledge reception issues as challenges to their time in Vietnam.[22] Women also reported perceiving more societal judgment on their linguistic competency than men did.[23]

Across the interviews, men were more likely to report being received favorably than Việt Kiều women. Their descriptions of reception consistently leaned towards positive expressions. For instance, Dao reported a highly favorable reception. As he says, "well, I think it's been amazing. I think people here are so welcoming. That's probably one big reason why I stayed, because of the hospitality of the local people. Then just their understanding. I think also just the opportunity here, I honestly would not be able to start two companies in the US with the finance I had. Maybe start it and run it for a month, and then that's probably it. But just the opportunity here is really amazing. People have received me, even though I don't speak Vietnamese very well, they're very forgiving in that sense. They've been really, really amazing." He gushes about the hospitality and the lack judgment and favorable business climate even though he lacks high language proficiency. For some men, they report a first level reaction that points out the noticeable language accent and beginner fluency but quickly overcomes this barrier. For example, Thuc reports there are immediate questions such as, "why do you speak funny? Speak funny Vietnamese?" For Thuc, this is quickly overcome as people care more about the sincerity of the relationship and that he keeps coming back and investing. They seem to quickly accept his family's story as he has found that "generally the Christians and people are very accepting, and welcoming of you." The initial reaction of curiosity can be turned into acceptance as the language issue is not much of an issue once the sincerity of the relationship is established.[24] He has experienced a generally very favorable and accepting return reception.

22. This should not be equated with a complete absence of such challenges, it simply was not something any men spoke of in their interviews whereas almost all the women brought up these life function tasks.

23. Language competency at the point of returned varied among the returnees. The average interview participant self-reported a third-grade language fluency when they returned.

24. This returnee is working hard to learn the language, he is on the earlier end of the return experience and earlier into the language acquisition journey.

This generally favorable warm experience does not come through as an experience shared by women for the most part. Consistently, Việt Kiều women reported less warm receptions than men did in the data collection. Language used to describe them and the kinds of questions they received were consistently more pointed and harsher than the Việt Kiều men received. For example, Quyen was introduced by extended family as "my stupid niece or my crazy niece from the US." The idea of returning to live in Vietnam is very hard to accept for her extended family that never left. From their perspective, "We would give up our right hand, our right foot, or both, to go to the US, and here she is coming back to Vietnam to live. . . . So, it was a very difficult process for them because. . . . Also, they knew that my dad risked his life to take me to the US, and here I am coming back." Overtime, they have come to accept her even though they still do not understand. Elements of her family story of leaving for the "promised land" would be relatable to many of the interviewees (both men and women). Yet, none of the men mentioned similar language used by national Vietnamese to describe them as being crazy (some level of confusion was the strongest terminology used) for returning in light of the sacrifices to leave.

Additionally, project participants disclosed times when they perceived receiving discrimination for being Vietnamese-American. For instance, the Việt Kiều wife and her American husband have taught English as part of their return vocations. The wife needed to be CELTA certified. The husband needs no such certification. As a white American foreigner, he is offered the teaching roles no additional qualifications necessary. Most notably, Ping reports she has been rejected from jobs because she is Vietnamese-American. She reports, "finding out that people discriminate Vietnamese American here, like when you go find a job, they look for native speakers. It was a shock for me because I was so naive, and then in America their racism is more discrete. Here, it's very open. And then people think, "Oh, you would be more favored if you're Việt Kiều. But that's not the case." She goes on to share how her family in Vietnam "were afraid I was wasting my future because people would pay to move to America, The Promise Land. Why would I go back?" She was also told very bluntly that she must learn the language if she was to live in Vietnam long-term. The general picture presented between men and women showcases a harder reception for women. As such, not all is equal for the returnees. While there is room for further research, it is consistent across the interviews conducted for this project that Việt Kiều men can anticipate a more favorable reception than Việt Kiều women.

Moving beyond the specific analysis categories, as a whole group, the Việt Kiều used a variety of words to express their general reception. Commonly used words included surprised and curious. As in "I think they are surprised that I chose to live here instead of living in Germany and often they think, Ah, because it's cooler to live here. Because it's more fun right? And then they like the idea that I do speak English fluently and that I can teach them western mentality on one hand but I understand them as a Vietnamese somehow. I think they like that and of course people approach me and they want to study English first, but then the more they know me, the more they speak Vietnamese and they like deep conversations, they trust me" (Mai). Others use the term curious to talk about the reception. "I think they're very curious. Let's say the teachers at my school, they're Christians, they're Westernized. They're very curious as far as what my life is in the US. I think in a way, they're actually very nice to me" (Nhan). Anh Dung and others share this experience. The national Vietnamese are generally curious about what life was like in the West and why their overseas brethren elected to return after living as citizens of the diaspora. This is a very natural line of questions. People are curious. Curiosity can be something that is leveraged towards building deeper trusting relationships. It might characterize early encounters and be turned towards building future relationships.

A general curiosity or surprise is but one layer of the reception. Digging deeper, several layers of common experience emerged. When it comes to reception several respondents discussed a certain ambiguity about the whole thing. They report not neatly fitting into existing categories. As Nhan said, "They don't really know who I am." Yes, the Việt Kiều generally report that they feel welcomed in the return. The teachers at her school are generally curious and nice to her. Yet, at the same time, many respondents discussed frequent experiences that demonstrate that they are accepted at certain levels but in other interactions and relationships it is apparent to them that they are different than the local population. For example, daily life interactions can be a window into how one is perceived. For instance, as one respondent says, "they (sellers in the market) gave me the foreign price. They look at me in a different eye" (Nhan). Experiences of this nature plays out in all aspect of life and ministry/work in Vietam. Tai expresses this tension well. He reports, "Accepted is, yeah, I'm welcome and accepted. Yes. To answer that. But frankly it's God's given me a beautiful trait, is that

I'm a minority everywhere I go. And that shines because I'm different. Growing up in America, I was different. Coming back here, even though I looked like them, I'm different." While he feels that he is accepted, he also articulates the sense of divisions that make him a "minority" and different.

Several respondents elucidated on this understanding that they feel they are received as foreigners. They know they are not really the same as the local Vietnamese and they are generally not received as the same. They are received differently having lived as citizens of the global diaspora. Yet, at the same time, when it comes down to reception, they also do not fit neatly in the foreign category. The national Vietnamese are not always sure how to categorize their overseas brethren. As Quyen discusses, "the Vietnamese people's attitude towards you, and it's we're in a breed of our own. We're never going to be completely American, and we're never going to be completely Vietnamese, and I know some of my friends struggle with that because they want to be in one or the other, and I knew that I never fit in either way." Indeed, respondents report this as a struggle as "it's like, 'Oh, she's Vietnamese but really not a Vietnamese person.' So I saw that I wasn't accepted" (Nhan). To be in this ambiguous place relationally can be a challenge to navigate. Anh Dung revealed, sometimes national Vietnamese come to him as a foreigner thinking that perhaps as someone living there as an outsider, he can do something for their situation. Yet, at the same time he is not always received as foreign enough at times. He does not neatly fit into the foreign category. This comes with a linguistic and trust advantage, but also weaknesses. As he says, "I think as a Việt Kiều, with my language, I do have more of an advantage, because I can understand a lot of the nuances and things like that when I talk to the students. That's a plus for me to be there, but as a foreigner, the Vietnamese, they just love foreigners. They just want to flock to foreigners, so there's a positive thing. I'm being looked at as only a Vietnamese overseas" (Anh Dung). The fact that returnees are Việt Kiều places them into a category that has points of convergence with both the national Vietnamese and foreigners. This can be ambiguous and complicated at times. This reveals that people in the Việt Kiều category are typically viewed differently and can be held to different standards than both national Vietnamese and foreigners.

There is the personal and communal levels of reception and then there is the bureaucratic dimensions of reception. Official government propaganda welcomes back the Việt Kiều with open arms as heroes in the nation building project. Reality is more nuanced. While the government wants the Việt Kiều return; that does not mean that it is an easy or natural relationship once one is back in their natal homeland. Only a few respondents directly discussed bureaucratic spaces.[25] This is a highly sensitive area so it was danced around or mostly alluded to in discussions. One place this came out in was in discussion of visas. Visas to remain in the country is a thing of uncertainty for most of my respondents. Even those with the five-year multi-entry visa, say that it does not mean much. One always has to be cautious in this area as a Việt Kiều. As Anh Dung says, "We couldn't tell them the real story, just tell them that we're here to help the people. For the government, they were very watchful. Even now, you kept living in fear that you do something wrong and you get kicked out. We had only three months multiple entry visa, so every three months we had to renew it. A lot of tense situations where we just tried to do our best to show them that, yeah, we're there to help the people. We could not do anything else." He went onto mention, "You may meet with an official who may seem to be very friendly, but they're watching you. Just be careful with that." As one respondent mentioned when "there's people who live in Vietnam as a Vietnamese, they will face many difficulties. If you come here as a tourist for a few months, everything is very easy for you. You want to stay here? Work here? Open a business here? Then at that time you will face the bureaucratic (things). My wife, usually she, recently when she goes back to the U.S, when we landed to the airport she said "Oh, it's like the air freedom." Here you are constantly under a feeling of you are not free. You are watched" (Van). At times, one needs to strategically lay low to see another day. As Hung says, "I'm going to still kind of be quiet a little bit because I've got a church, the authorities know, but I don't want to jeopardize that. So, I want to help out but just be careful. I don't want to get kicked out and no one's going to look after our church." Things can be made hard for people. Sometimes the legal ground to be in Vietnam can be unsteady even for Việt Kiều. The Việt Kiều are officially welcomed back, yet that welcome back has conditions attached to it that make the return a little less of a sure thing. There is a sense of we are here now and committed now, but who knows how long we will really be permitted to be here. Things are held a little loose.

Lastly, it is worth noting that reception issues can change or fade over time. In other words, the longer one has lived in Vietnam the more certain

---

25. This is one dimension that the transnational Việt Kiều have a distinct advantage. They can more easily slip under the radar and as such do more risky ministry events or more directly secure government approval as they have less to lose if their request is denied.

issues might dissipate as one gains an advanced language fluency and deepens an integration into the natal homeland. When you can look mostly local and can speak like a local, you can start to gain agency in terms of how you present yourself. Over time, some of the distinctives of diaspora can become less apparent as the person increasingly adapts to life in Vietnam. Some of my respondents that have been in Vietnam the longest discuss this. As Suong said, "well usually I don't identify myself Việt Kiều, I always present myself as the Vietnamese. I don't let them know I'm Việt Kiều, they pick out that I am abnormal Vietnamese that's all. It's the way I speak and my Vietnamese is not so great so they say I have some accent that I don't look like a local Vietnamese, that's all." Likewise, Hung mentioned that "I don't think they know I'm foreigner, I just look Vietnamese, and I speak. My language skills was originally about 10 percent, I understood about 10 percent. I didn't know how to read or write, so I had to learn that. So, I learnt that over the years, now I don't think they know the difference. They just think I'm a Vietnamese person." This can be a strategic advantage at times to play a local.

Personal Emotional Issues: Identity and Culture Shock

This section of the chapter will examine personal emotional issues that emerged from the interviews. In the act of migration, a sojourner can return home. However, the home they return to is not the same home they have kept alive in memory as they live in the diaspora. The homeland evolves over time. Nor are the sojourners the same as prior to departure. The diaspora journey changes people. Therefore, personal emotional issues are points of discussion that emerged in each and every interview. The Việt Kiều respondents frequently engaged with topics of identity, culture shock and other emotions as they discussed their experiences in returning to their natal homeland.

First, identity. Identity is complex for the returnees. Conversations entered into the territory of personal identity during every interview. This is a topic on everyone's mind. Even as they take the act of returning to Vietnam, the Việt Kiều returnees articulate the understanding that Vietnam is not their permanent home. Nor are they the same as their brethren that never left. One of the ways that this is expressed in their self-description language. Some of the interview participants bristled at the label Việt Kiều. It is considered a term imposed by the Hanoi government. They are clear to make a distinction between Vietnamese people that have gone abroad, but do not have a foreign citizenship, such as a Vietnamese overseas worker in Malaysia, and themselves. In self-description my respondents used terminology that emphasized their biculturalism and foreign citizenship (i.e., Vietnamese-American) rather than Hanoi government promoted descriptive terminology, Việt Kiều. Bing passionately explained this identity framing, "we call exactly Vietnamese-American. You get American citizenship. We hold American passport, but original with Vietnamese. So, they call it Vietnamese-American. And Việt Kiều people, Vietnamese live overseas, but they do not have citizenship in the country." Consistently, interview participants self-described themselves as Vietnamese-American or Vietnamese-German etc. Việt Kiều would not be their preferred label. It is important to note that you can come home again. However, you are not the same as the non-migrants that never left, or Vietnamese that temporarily went abroad to work or for study. There might be shared roots, but the tree has branched out and has new growth.

The returnees are bicultural folk as evidenced from their repeated use of bicultural self-identifying terminology. As Mai says, "I'm still a Vietnamese, somehow. Half of me." As Nhan says "I realized that I am Vietnamese-American." However, this is not a simple painless discovery. This discovery was crystalized when she visited her extended family for the first time. It was not the smooth joyful meeting that she had envisioned. Rather, "I think they were just trying to figure out who I am. I'm trying to figure out who they are. So, it's not like an automatic where in my mind, my imagination was to come back and I look like them. Yeah, we're like now one happy family, but it just wasn't like that. They see me as an American-Vietnamese, not a total Vietnamese person." This came as a surprise and a hard letdown for this returnee. As "because I envisioned when I was in the US that my identity will be solved. I go back there and they said, You're Vietnamese? I said, Yes, I am Vietnamese. We're all kumbaya. I came back and they're like, no, you're not (Nhan). This was a struggle as "if I'm not Vietnamese, if I'm not American, who on earth am I?" This is an experience that is relatable on various levels to many of the returnees as they shared tales from the return. One can return to Vietnam, but you return as an American-Vietnamese, not a total Vietnamese person.

Indeed, the act of return to one's natal homeland can force an identity crisis. It is not easy to resolve. As Ping remarks that, "I just dealt a lot with identity issue that I didn't deal with in America. Like, where do I fit in? Vietnamese American, but they don't see me as a Vietnamese local. But I'm not an expat in a way. I didn't come here for a job, or to have a better life, more income and more to save. It just I couldn't fit in. Questions such as what does it mean to be Vietnamese but not really accepted as 100 percent Vietnamese in Vietnam or American but not 100 percent American and the same as the majority culture are interwoven into the return journey for many of my respondents. Several reported not really being at home in the States and also not really being at home in Vietnam. They are overseas Vietnamese that have returned. In other words, Vietnamese-American or Vietnamese-Australian, etc. The overseas sojourn makes the returnees culturally different from the local Vietnamese even with the shared heritage. At the same time, the layers of shared heritage and same face give the Việt Kiều degrees of difference from the foreign expats that also live in Vietnam. This can be confusing to navigate. In coming home, they know they are in their own category.

For some, the degree of foreignness became evident over a period of years, even while similarities of shared Vietnamese identity and linguistic exposure provide the Việt Kiều with certain ministry advantages. As Quyen describes, "advantage is you have a little bit of the language. You have a little bit of the culture. The disadvantage is you have no grace whatsoever because they have a certain expectation of you. But definitely, it's very helpful to have some of the language and to have some of the culture. Sometimes being Việt Kiều means that you face a situation of expectations placed upon you that you are not able to achieve. You are not given the grace foreigners receive (no one expects the visible foreigner to speak the language and be culturally proficient), yet you lack the cultural tool set to sufficiently live up to expectations of locals. You are a breed of your own. As you live in Vietnam, you feel these tensions as your personal identity is introspectively considered by the environment in which you are not accepted as completely Western nor as completely Vietnamese.

Returning "home" forces an identity reckoning and process that moves the returnee to eventual acceptance if they are going to remain and flourish in life and ministry back in their natal homeland. For some, this might mean coming to accept the places of cultural dissonance. Tuan makes a profoundly self-aware observation as he has developed a growing awareness of his foreignness over the years of living back in Vietnam. As he articulates, when I first wanted to come to Vietnam, I thought, 'Oh yeah, I'll be super involved in ministry and I'll be able to build this thing up myself.' But then I realized that by paperwork, I'm Vietnamese, and there's I'm a third culture person. I'm very Vietnamese in some ways, but I'm very foreign in others, and that foreignness means that I will never be fully Vietnamese, and I'll never be able to fully integrate, you could say. And then because my wife is Việt Kiều, and she grew up completely overseas and just came here as an adult, it's even more difficult for her to integrate. So, there's kind of a realization that I can perform a supporting role, but probably I'll never have a superstar role, because I won't be. . . . I'm too foreign.

One can hold to parts of both identities. However, as Tuan so clearly articulated, this means that as returning diaspora they will never be able to fully integrate. The foreignness will always situate them as semi-outsiders. Project participants that had been back the longest perhaps realize this the clearest.

The personal identity questions that surface for the returnees upon returning are perhaps exacerbated by the reactions of their fellow diaspora members. Most returnees report that they did not enjoy widespread support among their family and friends in the Vietnamese diaspora community. It is one thing to visit for a short holiday. Vietnamese living in the West are curious about the natal homeland and look to it with nostalgia and vivid memories (both good and bad). It is an entirely different thing to return to the nation that your family worked so hard and risked their lives to get out of and reestablish belonging. Respondents reported that for the most part, family and friends do not understand or support the decision to return. They have concerns. Many remain distrustful of the current government and express worry about what will happen to the loved one that returns. Thuc describes a fairly typically response, "so, my family, my parents, they didn't want us to go, because they left in the 70s, and that's their memories. Of how Vietnam was, even though they've been back, there was a reason why they left. And so that was kind of a lot of questioning on why." Likewise, Cau says, "they thought I was little crazy. They thought, they didn't know why I would come back." The word crazy or stupid was used by several. After all the sacrifices, how could you throw it all away to return to Vietnam? Returnees reported receiving a lot of questions, especially for those that returned to engage in discipleship or community development ministries. Granted, some Christian Việt Kiều communicated that think it is noble for the returnee to take up their mission, yet still hard to comprehend. Returning to start a business (and engage in BAM) was a little easier to understand. Visible economic success can smooth over confusion. Money speaks loudly. However, for most, the journey to return is confusing to their fellow sojourners in the diaspora.

Identity is but one layer of personal emotional issues that arise in the return journey. Culture shock is a feature of the return journey. Being Việt Kiều does not spare one from the ups and downs of living in a different culture. Returning to live in Vietnam is cross-cultural. The respondents are in unison on this perspective. This manifests itself in so many ways in the daily life and grind of ministry in a different culture.

How respondents mentally prepared for cultural shock varied. Some came with awareness that culture shock would happen and tried to mitigate some of the culture shock lows by intentionally lowering expectations. However, it was more common to be surprised by the experience of culture shock. For some respondents, they thought that because they were working with Vietnamese communities in the West, it would be a natural or minimal adjustment. As Nhan reports "so we would say that we would take cross-cultural class, but the thing is because in the US, we've worked with the Vietnamese church, but it's very different. Very different. This Vietnamese-American. This is Vietnamese-Vietnamese. The culture is so different. You can't take this experience and say, okay, it's going to work here. Nothing works." In other words, she reflected that she wishes they could have had some cross-cultural training, but they did not realize the need because they were already working with Vietnamese people.[26] Likewise, Hung was surprised by the cross-cultural learning curve. As he says, "I think I would say I was adequate at the time. But I know how inadequate it was, now that I'm here. Because my original thinking was, yeah, I'm Vietnamese, I'm doing cross-culture ministry in Sydney anyway. So, those basic stuff in cross-culture ministry, and knowing that it's going to be different I understood, but the experience, I guess is a bit different to what you may know. . . . So, I evaluate what I do, and I'm still learning. I've made a lot of mistakes culturally." Returnees readily acknowledged times where they made cultural blunders, misunderstood or misread the situation, or had incorrect assumptions.

---

26. Some Việt Kiều that I had been in contact with for interviews, ended up being out of the country at the time receiving cross-cultural training.

This demonstrates that returning to Vietnam is truly a cross-cultural experience for the diaspora citizens, even though people came from multicultural situations as Vietnamese diaspora living in the global West. As Quyen reflected, "I wasn't really prepared for cross-cultural work, even though I grew up cross-culturally." She discovered just "how hard it was to work cross-culturally." There is a need for cross-cultural training even with the shared heritage. All of this adds up to the general pattern in which most respondents report the desire that they could have had more cultural training so that they can be better equipped to navigate the tidal waves, the lows, the highs, and the various experiences that come from living in a different culture. Returnees ought not to be caught unprepared once the euphoria of return evaporates. Return was harder than expected for many. Culture shock is a taxing, unavoidable companion of the cross-cultural return journey. As people return, they come face to face with the reality that there is Vietnamese-American and Vietnamese-American cultural spaces in the West and then there is Vietnamese-Vietnamese. While there is natural overlap, there are deep differences. Navigating these differences is unavoidable in the return journey and will look different for Việt Kiều than it does for Western foreigners that move to Vietnam.

Respondents spoke of a wide variety of cultural issues that have contributed to challenges in the return journey. One of the most consequential cultural issues discussed was communication styles. The high level of indirect communication was spoken of by many as being especially tricky to navigate. As Nhan has learned, the "relationship is different. Just the fact that you're talking with somebody. You talk and they talk. You listen and you both listen. But what is said to somebody else is something different." Or Anh Dung says, "Culturally, they can smile at you, but they may hate you, those kinds of things." Listening for what is really being communicated is a learned art form. Being Việt Kiều can give an insight that these communication dynamics are happening as elements of these communication patterns are alive in the diaspora. Even still, this cultural form of indirect communication is hard for many returnees. There is Vietnamese-American and then there is Vietnamese-Vietnamese indirect communication.

Proficiency in the language can provide a window into what is really being communicated at times. Quyen relayed an interesting experience that touches deep cultural values and group expectations that shape the communication exchange.

> One of the advantages that I had, especially when I had short-term teams come, and the Vietnamese, they will talk in front of me as if I'm an American, forgetting that I understand everything they said. With the way that the Vietnamese work, in front of the Caucasian, everything will be great and wonderful. 'Yes, great. Love your program. We love you,' blah, blah, blah. They'll turn around, they'll speak Vietnamese to each other, and they'll say, 'Oh, that was awful. I don't know why we're doing this.' Or, 'this is such a waste of money.' Or, 'this is' . . . whatever it is that they want to say that is in the negative, that they wouldn't have said to the foreigner because they want to save the foreigner's face, so honor/shame culture and all that. So, then here I am, standing there. They're forgetting that I understand Vietnamese, and that they'll say all this in front of me, or they will have the attitude of, okay, she might understand, but she's not going to tell them, because she's on your side, because she's Vietnamese. So, then that has helped me understand things, because they wouldn't have said those things otherwise, or I wouldn't have understood it otherwise.

This narrative is highly informative. It is not that people are lying as a Westerner might say. Rather, the value is placed on saving the face of the honored guest. Shifting though this to hear what is truly being said or felt by local Vietnamese is not an easy process. As this demonstrates, there are times in which Vietnamese on the receiving end of trainings, projects, etc., are sending strikingly different messages depending upon the audience. The cross-cultural worker needs to take on the learner's posture and be open to hearing all the feedback and seek understanding for what the feedback truly means, what is being indirectly communicated and how honor/shame categories can be employed to elicit understanding.

Cultural shock issues extend beyond communication styles to include aspects that touch on most points of life and ministry in Vietnam. Respondents discussed a wide range of issues including but not limited to: humor (my Vietnamese friends will laugh and I do not understand why something is funny and vis-a-versa), cleanliness expectations, order of the traffic, time expectations, cultural faux pas made in daily life tasks such as shopping at the market and in ministry events, age (how you relate in society is largely determined by ones age), the order of queuing up or rather lack thereof, just to name a few that were spoken of by respondents.

Social Remittance

This final section of the findings chapter will employ the concept of social remittance as a tool to analyze the data. As has been established, there is Vietnamese-American and then there is Vietnamese-Vietnamese. Returning to Vietnam is a cross-cultural ministry experience for the Việt Kiều returnees. Having lived in the global West for a formative and lengthy time they naturally have been shaped by their diaspora experiences. It is well documented that the Việt Kiều are conduits of economic remittance.[27] However, it is not simply money that flows back to the homeland. The Việt Kiều that have returned tend to be conduits of social remittance. They do things differently and introduce new ideas back into their natal homeland. Who they have become is brought back to the homeland as they interact and engage in a variety of capacities in Vietnam.

Taken as a whole, the transnational links being built between the returning Việt Kiều, churches in Vietnam and Vietnamese churches in the West are relatively weak at best as seen in this project. For the most part, the returnees do not have strong transnational connections with Vietnamese churches in the West. If they have a sending church, it tended to be an American or multi-ethnic church. A majority of respondents that went through a mission organization went through a non-denominational faith-based organization. A significant percentage went independently. Only one Việt Kiều couple is an exception to this pattern. They are sent as global personnel (missionaries) by their Vietnamese district. They hold a unique place. On a whole, the transnational Việt Kiều hold stronger ties in both communities and better bridge the two worlds. One Việt Kiều is involved with a drug rehab center run by a local Vietnamese church that is heavily supported by Vietnamese-American churches. This is an example of durable link between the two groups. Some of these drug rehab centers are brilliant models of partnership between Vietnamese churches in the West and local Vietnamese churches. The transnational Việt Kiều have built stronger ties between diaspora communities and churches in Vietnam. Two of these respondents are pastors of Vietnamese-American churches and have included their extended family living in the West in the ministry back in Vietnam.

The transnational links are relatively weak at this point in time among these project participants. By and large, they are not multidirectional

---

27. See for example, Bui, *Returns of War*, 186.

bridges to the larger diaspora community. However, the social remittance of the returnees is substantial on a personal dimension. Social remittance flows through each of the primary modes of ministry of the Việt Kiều. For example, ministry convictions introduce new ideas into Vietnam such as foster adoption. As the returnees testify, this is a foreign concept in Vietnam. Some that are involved in BAM operationalize ideas that draw from their time in the West or Western way of being the boss. Việt Kiều are involved in trying to introduce organic or other new farming methods. Some things are incorporated into the ministry philosophy in organic moments that introduce opportunities for social remittance. As an example, one respondent talked about the intentional effort put into helping local leaders make decisions rather than relying on the missionary facilitating the training session to make all decisions on small things such as what the group will eat for dinner. Although small, this is an intentional way to foster non-local forms of leadership. However, it was in the educational spaces (both secular and religious) that social remittance was discussed with the most depth. General education (specifically the intentional introducing of the value of education that builds a foundation of creative thinking) and the various discipleship/theological training programs that are flowing into Vietnam are commonly spoken of by project participants.

First, the discipleship/theological education is a core concern of many of the returnees. Many of the returnees and national partners spoke of the sizable amount of content that is flowing into Vietnam. Several of the Việt Kiều that participated in this project are directly involved in this knowledge flow to a certain extent. By and large, the content that is being delivered draws heavily from Western sources. For some, their ministry includes translating Western Christian literature for distribution to local churches. They use their bilingualism to accurately translate. However, they are not necessarily producing or promoting indigenous theology (a few exceptions could be made from my respondents). Rather, by and large, they are translating, producing, and teaching from Western Christian source material. For some, this is a replica of discipleship programs from their home church translated and dropped into the Vietnamese space. Sometimes the content comes from multinational non-denominational discipleship programs. The extent that the content is contextualized for the local audience in Vietnam is unclear. Other times the Việt Kiều write their own training material in Vietnamese from their own knowledge basins and preferred theologians. However, by self-description, these teachings draw heavy influence from theologians that they view as having good theology and teach it to their networks. Commentaries from theologians such as Don Carson, John Stott, C. S. Lewis, and Matthew Henry were mentioned by one transnational Việt Kiều as the basis for the Biblical course material he has developed and teaches to his network in Vietnam. It was telling that the list only included American and English theologians. The general pattern clearly emerges that Việt Kiều are remitting these packages of discipleship trainings that are heavily influenced by source material they were exposed to as they lived in the global West.

Educationally, respondents report wanting to cultivate values that are seen as Western educational values. I will briefly mention two examples here. First, there is a growing 'home school' movement in Vietnam that teaches US public school curriculum. The Việt Kiều are involved in these ventures as a ministry and social remittance platform, and their participation lends credibility to the home school. It was eye-opening how many respondents already have or desire to open a school as part of their five-year ministry vision, which has a philosophical value of creative thinking as its foundation. This vision addresses a perceived deficit that exists in the current learning environment. Second, Ping, a trained academic counselor working at an international school, is reflective and says bluntly in her assessment, "my ways are American." She labors to help as a counselor applying American values of social emotional well-being and child protection policies for the Vietnamese families attending an international school. It is truly a foreign concept that she is employing in her daily work with Vietnamese families in an educational space.

Withholding any value judgment, it is seen from these respondents that they bring a social remittance back to their natal homeland with them as the live and serve in Vietnam. You can come home again, but you are not the same person as when you left. Living in the diaspora changes you. These values are being remitted back to the homeland.

CHAPTER 5
On the Receiving End

Non-Migrant Protestant Christian Vietnamese Experiences of the Phenomenon of Return

Chapter Introduction

WHEN WALKING THE STREETS of a contemporary city in Vietnam, one is confronted with the sights and sounds of globalization on busy street intersections. One might drink coffee at a Starbucks, eat KFC chicken, drive a Honda motorbike, listen to K-pop, shop at a Lotte Mart, watch a Hollywood or Korean movie,[1] and eat from a variety of late-night Vietnamese street food delicacies after the film. Tour groups from mainland China, Korea, European nations and the United States rub shoulders with local inhabitants in the narrow corridors of the historic city centers and popular resort towns. The economy is buzzing in the big cities as life in contemporary Doi Moi Vietnam has experienced rapid growth over the past two decades.[2] A global reintegration and rapid economic development anchored in the legacies of the past and protected by the self-described benevolent ruling class,

---

1. "Hallyu, the Korean wave, has had a strong influence in Vietnam. Researchers and the media stated that the three-phase coverage strategy of the Korean wave was successful. The first stage is the coverage of dramas, the second phase is connecting music (K-pop) with the actors and the final stage is bringing products from Korea to conquer Vietnamese consumers. The Vietnamese Z generation warmly welcomes Korean values. Phuoc, "Marketing in Vietnam," 96.

2. The World Bank details that GDP per capita increased between 1986 and 2018 from US$ 231.45 to US$ 2566.59. GDP growth rate has remained between 5–8 percent per year since 1990 (Thuy, "Road to Doi Moi," 38). Between 2002 and 2018, Vietnam has achieved a remarkable transformation in which "more than 45 million people were lifted out of poverty. Poverty rates declined sharply from over 70 percent to below 6 percent (US$3.2/day PPP). The vast majority of Vietnam's remaining poor—86 percent—are ethnic minorities." The World Bank, "World Bank in Viet Nam," para. 1.

guide and guard the future. In the midst of this upheaval, the Vietnamese diaspora is returning to their natal homeland in large numbers.

There is strong consensus within sociological literature on Vietnam that there are seismic changes occurring in Vietnam. Vietnam has undergone a profound change as the nation has pivoted towards reintegration with the wider world in recent years. The discussions with the non-migrant local Vietnamese speak to these changes. Much is happening and converging in intriguing ways that are reshaping public spaces for all societal actors. The Protestant Christian Church is living out and navigating their ongoing mission in the midst of this new social reality being constructed by these rapid changes. The returning Việt Kiều are one stream that fits into a bigger picture of a society that is undergoing rapid change. Within this larger framework of global connections formed (or perhaps rekindled in some cases) as Vietnam pivots towards increasing global reintegration, the Việt Kiều have returned to their natal homeland. This return has not gone unnoticed by local non-migrant Protestant Christians. They are well aware that many are returning. They see the direct impact on their ministries and personal lives as they have been directly and indirectly impacted by this large-scale return. They see long missed friends and church members return to pay a visit and perhaps ascertain if there might be work for them to do in the natal homeland. They see the children of those that once fled as refugees returning. They see the impacts of economic and cultural investments from the diaspora reshaping their world. Indeed, the Việt Kiều return to a specific context, to people and places. They interact with various actors in the homeland that have their own agency, opinions, vision, and tried and true ways to navigate their context. The story of return is not to be written by the returnees alone.

This chapter dives into RQ3. Namely, how have the non-migrants (local Vietnamese) experienced the phenomenon of return? Space is devoted to how the non-migrant Protestant Christians perceive the motivations and missionary impact of the Việt Kiều, the experience of power dynamics in ministry, and to what extent Vietnamese Christians accept the returnees with solidarity among other topics that surfaced during the interview conversation and visits.

I interviewed non-migrant Vietnamese Protestant Christians directly working with returning overseas Vietnamese in the North, Central, and South of Vietnam to gain an understanding of how they are experiencing the phenomenon of return. Hearing the voice of the local non-migrants provides remarkable insight into the unfolding phenomenon. We are able to see the other side of the coin. The returnees and transnational Việt Kiều do not move in isolation. They return to serve in established social spaces in their natal homeland. The voices of the non-migrant national partners adds extraordinarily rich texture to the narrative of this unfolding phenomenon. They are irreplaceable actors in this drama.

The non-migrant interview participants have worked with the full spectrum of the returning Việt Kiều. Some of the respondents have worked closely with ministries that welcome many STM teams and individuals. Others serve directly with long term returnees. Still others, work with returnees directly on a smaller scale. They are friends, employees, mentees, and ministry partners with returnees. Local respondents are members of home churches, parachurch ministries, and registered denominational churches in the North, Central, and the South. Each come from the Kinh majority ethnic group. They serve in a variety of ministries and have interacted with returnees in multiple spaces to inform the findings discussed in this chapter. The stories of the returnees would be incomplete without locating their narratives within the context of where they are going and the people they are returning to. Their lives and their stories intersect with the stories of the people and ministries they are returning to and intertwine to form a new chapter in the story of the Protestant Christian Church in Vietnam. This story is over one hundred and ten years old, but it is far from complete.

How Do the Non-Migrant National Partners Perceive the Motivation of the Returnees?

Chapter 4 included a discussion on the stated motivations of the returnees. Clear and compelling motivations pull them back to reestablish belonging in their natal homeland. But what do the local Protestant Christians have to say about this? Is the essence of what the returnees communicated in terms of their motivation for return and ministry goal perceived by the people they are returning to? This chapter will explore what non-migrant national Vietnamese project participants have to say from their vantage point. This first section will unpack the question of motivation. To what extent are the stated motivations for return perceived and appreciated by local Christian communities?

When it comes to observable motivation, local Vietnamese identify a mixture of motivations pulling the Việt Kiều back to Vietnam. However, the answers given in conversations pointed to just a few common themes of motivation. Moreover, it is significant that the principal motivations for return that the Việt Kiều expressed are perceived by their non-migrant national partners (albeit with slightly different terminology). Namely, the observed motivations for return include the desire to do something good (especially for the poor or children) via some kind of Christian humanitarian compassion work, the salvation motivations, and the personal longings to explore and experience one's natal homeland and perhaps have some personal healing from returning "home." These observed motivations align closely with motivations that the returnees stated.

On the whole, observed motivations can be characterized as falling under positive descriptors. The local Christians consistently use favorable language to express their understanding of why the Christian diaspora is returning. The general picture is that local Christians see that returnees are coming back from a place of beneficial and appropriate motivations.

First, it is seen that returnees return with good intentions. Within interview discussions this understanding found life in a variety of specific expressions. Importantly, the overall interpretation expressed is largely comprised of positive language and imagery. It is perceived that the Việt Kiều are seen to "have a heart for Vietnam" (Hieu). A worker in a different region of the country says an almost identical statement, saying, "some Việt Kiều they have the heart, for the Vietnam people" (Thang). He adds the limiting language of 'some' to the statement of having a heart for Vietnam. Nevertheless, the concept is similar. Having a heart for the land and the people is bringing the diaspora community home. There is good will here for the returnees. The perception expressed is that people are motivated to return and invest in the homeland out of this character quality of having a heart for Vietnam.

Moreover, strictly speaking, for some national partners, it seems very natural for the national partners that the overseas Vietnamese would return now that the pathway to return has been cleared. The heart is there; now the legal way has been cleared. As Quy says, "I do not know in other country other cities. But in the big cities like Hanoi, Ho Chi Minh City, fifteen years ago its more closed. Less churches. But now there are more churches, more home churches. And then I see that Việt Kiều can come back easier and can involve more with more activities, religious activities." Her assessment of when the diaspora community started returning aligns with political changes implemented by the Hanoi government. The government allowed people to return and they started returning. She also observes that the number returning is increasing each year. The overseas brethren are painted in a positive light as having a good heart for Vietnam and being involved in many forms of activity in the homeland. The heart for Vietnam has been unbroken over years of diaspora sojourn and they having started return now that it is easier and legally permitted to do so.

Having a heart for the nation and the people goes hand in hand with this general perception that returnees want to do something good. The scope of this motivational concept of wanting to do something good is rather broad. As one person stated, "I kinda know they try to do something good to the country. Of a great variety" (Toan). Various activities are tied together under the common thread of this idea that the returnees are motivated to return out of a desire to do good. Sometimes it might be tied to specific Christian salvation experiences. For example, "some of the people return after extensive recovery experience of Christianity and they want to do something for the same people with the same background like gangsters and drug addicts" (Toan). These Christian drug rehab centers that have sprung up are an important mode of ministry and space of transnational ministry. The Việt Kiều might be motivated to return from their own recovery experience and good intentions to help their brethren in their natal homeland struggling with similar problems. This specific ministry is always spoken of with only the highest respect. Still others noted how some Việt Kiều are medically trained and specifically want to use their skill set to help the poor.

There is a spectrum spoken of in the discussion, but generally, the understanding is that returnees return from a motivational space of wanting to do something good and use their experiences and/or skill set to be a blessing in the homeland in a variety of ways. Many respondents speak to this concept. As Toan unpacked,

> some of them come here just to help. Say, for example, teach English or just figure out what people are into. They also want to teach psychology, counseling, Bible. They want to teach farming. They want to do business, entrepreneurship. They want to help people with orphanages. They also want to build community, rescue orphans and street children. Yeah. There are varieties of things. They want to work with the local people, and they want to make sure that there is collaboration between the locals and the donors in the US or in Germany or Australia and somehow create more like a trade.

This list is by no means exhaustive. The length and variety listed showcases the framework of understanding the phenomenon. Namely, those in the homeland see a plurality of good activities that the returnees are invested in a generally favorable light. These are the activities that motivate the overseas community to missionally return. The common thread is the perceived desire to do something good or the good heart for Vietnam and the people. The perception is communicated that the Việt Kiều generally want to do something good via a plurality of expressions as unique as each individual Việt Kiều. The doing of something good correlates with the motivations the returnees express as they spoke of the perception of need in the homeland. The Việt Kiều see need in the homeland; the locals see that returnees have a heart to do some kind of good.

The motivation of wanting to do good is not restricted to humanitarian concerns (although those are important), this concept of having a heart for Vietnam, is also seen as having a specifically religious proclamation and faith calling element to their motivation for return. This speaks to the salvation motivation expressed by the returnees. The national partners discern that the returnees they work with care not merely for humanitarian kind of works, but for the religious salvation motivation as well. Those that come back are "those who really love the Lord . . . and (share) resource to invest to extend the kingdom of God in Vietnam" (Quy). The motivation is specifically missional in nature. It goes beyond a desire to merely materially help an under-resourced community flourish. Lots of people send money for a variety of projects. This motivation is different in that the kingdom of God being extended is prized as well.

Later in the conversation Quy unpacked some of the rationale for why the returnees are motivated to return and specifically invest in extending the kingdom. As she stated,

> I think the most important things is that God touched their hearts and . . . even they live in the U.S. but Vietnam is still their home country so they still want to serve their home country especially children for the home country to know about Christ and receive Christ because to compare with the U.S. and Vietnam. Vietnam still considered like I do not tell about the other people groups but for example Kinh we have around more than 100 people group. For Kinh the percentage of people who receive Christ is 1.5 percent only. So still considered unreached people group and I see that their heart is they want their home country to receive Christ and know about Christ and still considered unreached people group.

This overview highlights the understanding that the overseas Vietnamese might be separated by distance, but Vietnam is their home country and the Vietnamese are their people. There are important bonds here that carry motivational weight as seen by those in the homeland. There is also the framing of relative salvation need. As a local Christian leader, she is well aware of the percentage of people that are Christians and is familiar with the terminology of unreached people group. From Quy's experience she knows that the Protestant Christian overseas community are familiar with the statistics as well, and this motivates them to return to Vietnam and invest their time, talents, and financial resources into their natal homeland. Seeing people in their own natal homeland labeled in the category of an unreached people group is an impetus for missional action. For Quy, the fact that her people are an unreached people makes it easy to understand why the overseas brethren would be returning to serve in Vietnam. She has worked with many returnees over the years that return for STM to teach Bible courses and conduct evangelism in response to the salvation need in the homeland.

Thang speaks to this motivation as well, with the added nuance of his regional context. For Thang, returnees experience some limitations to direct religious work, but they are able to find other outlets by supporting specifically Christian religious activities. As he describes, "some people ready support for Vietnam church. But they can't work direct, but they have support about money for the who share the gospel, for the building church and servant who serve the God, addicted drugs. Give a lot and help the church. Support a lot of the church." He has seen firsthand that some returning Việt Kiều want to sacrificially invest in religious activities to help reach people in their natal homeland. Returnees are motivated to and ready to help the church to the best that they can. There is a perception that the overseas community is motivated to return from the core value of this salvation motivation.

Relatedly, the notion that Việt Kiều sacrificially return out of their personal Christian faith convictions was expressed by many. Many Việt Kiều return to Vietnam for a variety of purposes, but there is a specific Christian faith dimension to why these specific Việt Kiều are returning. It is seen that their faith is motivating action. It is personal. One respondent in particular shared a narrative that encapsulates the best of the motivations and demonstrates how returning in and of itself can create a legacy in the natal homeland. She has worked closely with a specific Việt Kiều couple and is impressed by the deep sense of personal calling and faith that this couple expressed in their story when thinking about motivation for return and the specific place within Vietnam to return to. She shared the story of an early meeting with them and how they articulated the calling that the returnees expressed. The returning couple shared that, "they prayed and they asked God to show them which (region/city) to go back to Vietnam to serve and they didn't know where the city they will be and they go to many providence in Vietnam and observe and they pray and pray and God gives the picture and the word, the letter *H* and they tried to come the providence with letter *H* like Hanoi and Hai Phong and Ho Chi Minh and they observe what God is doing here and the more the prayed the more clear God guiding them to go back to [current *H* ministry city] not [other *H* cities]" The way this couple describes their calling has made an impact on this person. The deep faith that they live by is inspiring. They went to a region of the nation they are not from and to an unknown city, in response to the calling they prayerfully received. She is herself is now on a path working for a parachurch missions organization as a national missionary.

It is worth making mention of the direct extended family motivation. Simply put, this is not a motivation that the national partners observe. They see the concern for their homeland in a generalized sense as it pertains to doing good humanitarian work to make a positive impact in the natal homeland, specifically Christian religious motivations, and/or perhaps an interest in exploring their roots (especially for the 2nd or even 3rd generation returnees). However, connection with extended family is largely an insignificant variable to this equation of return. As Quy mentioned when directly asked if the returnees she has worked with have family social networks they are returning to visit. Her answer aligns with the stories of the majority of the returnees. As she stated, "most of them do not have relatives here anymore. Some of them have relatives in the South. And [northern city] we do not have many Việt Kiều most of Việt Kiều s they are from the South. So they just come here for mission." Time has moved forward and many in the diaspora community already have their entire family out of Vietnam, as the interviewees with the returnees attested to, or the bonds with those that remain is inconsequential as a motivation for return with the passage of time. Indeed, the absence of mentioning family as a motivation for return or as ministry bridges for the returnees is consequential. None of the local Vietnamese discussed extended family as a significant motivation for the Việt Kiều to return. It has simply been too long. Local Vietnamese, see that by and large, returnees are not restricted to the spheres of extended family or ancestral home villages as they return and explore and invest in their natal homeland. There is a perception of motivation born from a curiosity to explore the ancestral homeland in a generalized sense to see one's roots. However, this is mostly happening outside the connection of direct family lineage. This is broader than direct family.

Experiences Working Together

In this section, the attention shifts to exploring how the local Protestant Christians who participated in this project describe their experiences working with the Việt Kiều. What are their observations? What phrases and words are used to describe the reputation of the returnees? What are their observations concerning ministries the returnees are participating in and care most about as they return to Vietnam? What impressions have been formed and forged over the years of welcoming back their overseas brethren? This section drills down to explore specific questions and perceptions of the Việt Kiều in ministry in the natal homeland.

Taken as a whole, local Protestant Christians who participated in this project expressed a generally favorable impression of the phenomenon of return. This impression has been formed through many interactions over the years with a variety of returnees in a wide variety of social spaces. Furthermore, the three core ministry foci that characterize the returnee's missional engagement (discipleship-centric ministries, community development-centric ministries, and BAM-centric ministries) were all spoken of by the local project participants. It is illuminating that the ministries that are spoken of as being the primary avenues of ministry engagement by the returnees are seen in such a way by the local Christians. In other words, they observe what the returnees are focused on, and how they actually spend their time, and they articulate similar conclusions. There is a congruency here. What returnees say they are doing and care most about doing is in fact observed by the local community.

Local Christians themselves are active in some of these ministry spaces. Some, such as Quy served vocationally in a coordinator hosting role that allowed her opportunities for countless interaction with returnees. She served with a ministry that operates one of the Christian drug rehab centers. This ministry hosts many STM teams, including but not exclusively, teams of Việt Kiều. These Christian drug rehab centers were commonly mentioned in interviews as shining examples of Christian witness that have contributed to the growth of the church in Vietnam. This particular center, along with others, is also a positive example of ministry collaboration between national partners and Christian Việt Kiều in the West working together to support an impactful ministry in the natal homeland. This particular center is heavily supported by a particular association of Vietnamese churches in America. They raise funds to pay the fees of the brothers that live at the center.³ They have also paid the fees for qualified and called brothers and graduates of the program to come to the States and lead evangelistic outreach services and fundraisers with their churches in their home communities. They also, among others, come on regular STM trips. As Quy describes,

> When I worked for [name of center], [name of center] is a Christian rehab center to help the Vietnamese drug addicts to get out of drugs, and then to not only get out of drugs but being transformed to be a receive [sic] be a Christian and also get out of drugs. So in that center I have opportunity to meet many Việt Kiều who are mostly from the US and also some of them from Australia. And they are those who really love the Lord and they use their leaves and they have two weeks leave they use that leave to come back here and do missions like to come and teach the Bible for our brothers in [name of center] mostly most of the people are brothers, so teaching our brothers about the Bible, specific courses and also conduct outreach together with our pastor our church to conduct outreach and there are some outreach we already conduct in Vietnamese government rehab center, in that outreach we share gospel and also give some Bible.

It is noteworthy that her impression is highly favorable as it has been formed over the years of working closely with teams of returnees. From her perspective, she sees the STM members as mature believers, positively contributing to the ministry, and as working well with and under the direction of the pastor and other local leaders of the center. Indeed, she is very thankful for the many that have sacrificially returned and invested in this ministry.

Quy has interacted with many returnees on short-term basis. Some have returned several times; others she has only worked with once. They

---

3. "Brothers" is the term used for the residents living at the center going through the eighteen-month program. Only men live at this center. The church operates a separate home for women that the author did not visit.

come for a short time, but the impact is substantial and has born much fruit out this healthy transnational partnership. Several of the non-migrant local Vietnamese speak from the personal experiences of relationships with Việt Kiều that have relocated and established a residency in Vietnam in addition to STM visitors (many have relationships with both groups). The nature of the relationships varies. For some, at providential times, their lives intersected and they directly benefited through their relationship formed with the returnees as the returnees engage in various forms of ministry. For example, Hue was studying for the ILETS exam when she was introduced to a Việt Kiều returning couple that had taken up residency in her city.[4] This couple helped her prepare for the important exam and she helped them with some translation of medical information. The relationship was mutually beneficial. She was given the best of tutoring as it came from people with native speaker fluency. For the couple, the help with this project was important as she was able to aid in a core ministry initiative as this couple is invested in teaching English to medical students. It was mutually beneficial for specific season, but has not been a deep ongoing relationship.

This same Việt Kiều couple has played a significant ongoing mentor relationship for Thi. One of the means of impact has been in via their translation work. Like many returnees, this couple spends their time in many projects, including work in the area of the translation of Christian resources from English into Vietnamese. One such resource that they translated was a spiritual formation/discipleship motivational book. They started distributing and teaching this book that to anyone who would participate in their region. Thi has received this teaching and testifies that the introduction of the ideas in this book have changed her mindset. Changing her mindset has helped her grow in Christian maturity and helped her along her pathway to vocationally serving as a faith based missionary worker within Vietnam. She spoke in glowing terms about the experience saying, "I don't know much about how they the way they do they know. It's the book *Experiencing God* and they translate that book from English to Vietnamese and they open the class in the main church in [city name] and they invite those who want to study that book because it important the way that you want to share God and do ministry and that is the way that they can share their

---

4. The International English Language Testing System (IELTS) can be considered the gold standard for demonstrating English proficiency. ILETS is designed to help you work, study or migrate to a country where English is the native language. This includes countries such as Australia, Canada, New Zealand, the UK and USA (https://www.ielts.org/).

opinion and what they learn from that book and change peoples mindset also me to." As members of the diaspora, these returnees have access to Christian literature that is not available in Vietnam. As Thi articulated, they have access to learning opportunities/discipleship training that Christians in Vietnam might not have access to. The diaspora sharing these resources is seen in a very positive light in this case for Thi.

For Thi, being on the receiving end of a translated resource was personal and highly formative. Most of the others did not share such personal stories. Rather, the idea that Việt Kiều are uniquely positioned to help with translation and dissemination of Christian resources was spoken of by most all the local respondents. The national partners see that some of the returning Việt Kiều have high fluency in both Vietnamese and English. It is seen simply as a factual reality that this is one ministry that Việt Kiều tend to do, and also that this is generally a good role to play. Those that have the linguistic competency can contribute in this way by adding to the availability of Christian literature resources in Vietnam by translating these Western Christian works. Locals gave the impression that this is a good ministry avenue.

At least two of the respondents have personally been on the receiving end of economic remittance. For both, they testify that this has been a predominately positive experience. Hieu, who has an official vocational position in a registered denomination, connected with a returnee some eight years prior to the interview. He was able to play the role of informed national host and help connect the individual Việt Kiều to local ministry opportunities. He has ended up meeting with this diaspora individual on an annual basis when she returned for STM purposes. In this relationship, he also ended up receiving a certain amount of economic support during years of formal theological study from this Việt Kiều. As he tells his story,

> I know a lady when I was in [hometown], the lady Việt Kiều, and she come back to [hometown] she met me because before she left Vietnam to come to US she a member of [hometown] registered church my father's church so when she come back she want to help and she didn't know what to help and she asked me what to do sometimes she send me money so I and her go to some poor churches to help people, young people or children even some pastor not have enough money to . . . yeah so I think I have a good experience of her for a few years, she faithful give money (laugh) for me to do that she trust me just we meet in [hometown] and she come to visit the church and 'oh Hieu, she said, I am so happy

because you come back to Vietnam that church need I was in the US and not stay in US but come back to Vietnam and sometime she might give me money to she give me $500 for a few years until I got back to [current city] yeah, so very very successful I mean she encouraged me.

This story illustrates positive ministry synergy that can happen between a returnee and the local church. This Việt Kiều has been able to join with ministries and support the outreach work of the local church. In this case, the Việt Kiều started by going first to the church that she had attended as a child before her relocation. She was very intentional about working under the authority of the local church. She also was very helpful and encouraging to this particular person at a liminal season in his life. It is worth noting that this particular worker is now ordained through a registered denomination, and now that he is working vocationally, he no longer receives any direct economic remittance. He received some support during a time period of study and preparation for vocational ministry. At a key time, she played the role of encourager to him. She also has made other connections over the years and no longer works directly with this person when she returns. This is a positive experience of relationship with someone who has become a transnational Việt Kiều. It was also not an indefinite relationship that planted the seeds of dependency. The relationship had a time and place. As illustrated, both the returnee and the local project respondent have moved forward in healthy ways. From Hieu's perspective, in this situation, the ability of the Việt Kiều to support ministry in her natal homeland church and him personally has been a good experience.

Expanding the view out beyond Hieu's personal narrative, it is evident that there is a generalized articulation widely shared that the Việt Kiều can and do support financially the various Christian ministries and workers. Sometimes this comes with the acknowledgment of certain limitations that Việt Kiều might encounter. As Hieu has observed, "some Việt Kiều come back and they can help the church by money. For example, they buy something facility for the church the Việt Kiều help a lot too, buy material Việt Kiều donate money for the church. They cannot work but they can fund it for the church Vietnam." Likewise, as Thang and Hoa shared, "some Việt Kiều they have the heart, for the Vietnam people. Some people ready support for Vietnam church. But they, they can't work direct, they can't direct (inaudible) foreign but they have support about money for the who share the gospel. They ready for support with money." They have observed that money tends to go "for the building church and servant who, who serve the God." These are two unconnected workers laboring in different regions of Vietnam. The observations are very similar. Within this statement, Thang acknowledges a reality of the situation from his perspective. The Việt Kiều can return and they do want to do good, yet they might and do experience certain limitations in regards to religious work. Indeed, as a worker with a faith-based mission, he himself can and does receive some small ongoing sponsorship from overseas Vietnamese. In this way, some Việt Kiều can play an indirect role and contribute economically to workers engaged in ways that are closed for the Việt Kiều at times. Reasons why Việt Kiều cannot directly engage in the religious work vary. Nevertheless, it is known and accepted pattern that some Việt Kiều will not be able to directly engage in ministry work, but can contribute with economic remittance to fund ministries and play more of a behind the scene supporting role.

The question of economic remittance fits into the worldview for how local non-migrants perceive the Việt Kiều. Quy makes a revealing statement when she says, "for the government Việt Kiều is already foreigner. But for Vietnamese people we still consider Việt Kiều is Vietnamese but they live in other countries so we consider that they have more resources than the local people." Economic remittance does flow back to the natal homeland to Christian religious work as my respondents attest both by personal experience and generalized observation. More than that, there are expectation regarding this. As Quy attests, it is simply assumed that the diaspora community has more resources. Being considered one of us, and having more resources, perhaps places expectations on the relationship. The wording in this statement is intriguing as it reveals worldview. In her thinking, the government considers the Việt Kiều "foreign." This despite the very intentional wooing of the overseas community to return that utilizes insider terminology. The 'we', the Vietnamese people, is distinct from the government in how they view the Việt Kiều. But at the same time, in the same sentence, a distinction is made between the 'we' and the Việt Kiều. They are the same, but in ways they are not. In this case, it has to do with economics. The Việt Kiều are not included in the 'we' of this sentence in the same way the local Vietnamese are, even while they are considered as Vietnamese. They live in other countries; they have more resources. Expectations are baked into the ministry equation. They are considered to be better resourced. Yet money issues cut deeper and will be explored further in this chapter. More will be said on this later.

A balanced picture of how the national partners experience working with the returnees comes from several conversations. It is wise to recognize that some local Vietnamese have not always had unblemished encounters working with returnees. For instance, Thi considers her Việt Kiều mentor couple in contrast to others that have less impactful ministry in her perspective. As she explains, "for me I have met and worked with the some people American Vietnamese-American in the South and they some of them just go back and do the short-term ministry like short trip like outreach or mission trip like short and didn't follow-up like for the next step for the future that I feel like doesn't impact more for the Christian Vietnamese Christian but the couple I work with and I feel like is benefit for Christian Vietnamese-American can go back and can share their lives their faith different culture because they cross the culture a lot they know that their experience God how God did the ministry with this country and this country and they have real big picture that God doing in the world and this is also helpful." I do not know what the STM people said about their trip. However, as the national partner working with teams, Thi determined these trips to be largely low impact. The reason given is that these trips lacked real collaboration and follow-up. On the other hand, the Việt Kiều couple that have relocated to her city are able to avoid these weakness as they are share.

Additionally, respondents report times of seeing Việt Kiều run ministries and BAM initiatives fail. Sometimes while they are on the team. They have gone down with the ship. It is a harsh place to land. Even with the best of intentions, the Việt Kiều run businesses and various ministry initiatives are not guaranteed to be fruitful. Sometimes businesses fold, ministries run out of money, and progress in establishing transformational ministries can be painstakingly slow. The local Christians do not avoid mentioning these examples to complete the narrative. The tales told are realistic to the reality on the ground. Nevertheless, the general impression is positive and non-migrant local Christians welcome the diaspora returnees with certain admonitions as will be discussed later in this chapter. Respondents report an overall favorable perception of the phenomenon. As Hieu states, "I would love to see more and more Việt Kiều come back."

Local Perceptions of the Việt Kiều in Ministry

The non-migrant local Christians testify to holding a generally favorable impression of the motivations for return. They are able to articulate positive stories of relationships built with returnees. As the data demonstrates, the Việt Kiều are seen as contributors to the kingdom of God in Vietnam from the perspective of local Christians. There is goodwill for the returnees. But that is not the full story. The picture that emerges from the conversations is more complex. It is clear from the respondents that having a good heart and wanting to do good, only carries you so far in the cross-cultural missional task. Indeed, this section will dive in to explore the wide range of crucial issues that surfaced in the course of conversations.

Do Local Protestant Christian Vietnamese See the Returning Việt Kiều as Effective?

This question address sub RQ1: How do the non-migrants perceive the missionary impact of the Việt Kiều? It is one thing to say that people are motivated to do good deeds and that they are following through on that desire. It is a different question to probe about relative effectiveness, and strengths and weakness to approaches. As a caveat, this is a hard question to properly gauge for at least two reasons from a qualitative study. First, impact and effectiveness are relative markers that are often measured in relationship to goals. A person might not have full access to all the relevant information to answer this sufficiently from their vantage point. They might see some tangible measurable outcomes, but not know all the goals or internal operations of various ministries. For example, a returnee might be working in a BAM ministry. National partners might not have full disclosure to completely assess how successful or not the business is in terms of helping the local people, being a viable business in the community, and being a positive Christian witness in a community. Perspective can be limited, but that does not mean that locals have not formed opinions as they have observed the lives and works of returnees. As Toan says, "I'm not sure how successful they are. And its really had to assess the success, the rate and ration of what they're doing, and whether or not they're doing something else on the side. It's hard to assess, but we kind of know what kind of business they're trying and to help the local people." Specifics might not be known. However, a general impression is formed and local leaders are not unaware of what is happening or naïve to the community perceptions as it pertains to the returnees and the various works they are doing.

Second, impact and effectiveness can be profound, yet hardly visible at a certain point in time. By this I mean that, ministry can be effective without creating many flashy or immediately visible outcomes. The most impactful ministry in Vietnam is often not flashy, so gauging missionary impact a somewhat imperfect observation. For example, a returnee might have built a life and ministry back in Vietnam that impact scores of people, yet this impact is quiet and harder to see from some vantage points. Also, ministry dividends might be seen in the future. It takes a long time for the plant to grow and produce the abundant harvest. Lastly, perhaps very little visible fruit might be produced, yet this does not mean the returnee was ineffective if the returnee was faithful to God's calling. Vietnam can be a hard place to serve, and life transformation is hard to quantify. As one respondent said, "am I saying that what I'm doing is fruitful because I can count on my fingers or just the fact that I am faithful in doing the things that I believe God is giving me to do. Just trust that I cannot see the fruit now, but just pray over the things that you're doing and feel that's the thing that you want to give, you want to do." With these caveats, local Christians did express opinions on the matter of perceived missionary impact by the returnees. This was commonly discussed by pointing to specific examples that show a picture of perceived effectiveness in the receiving communities. Additionally, two key variables consistently came to the surface that enter the equation for considering missionary impact and effectiveness.

As has already been illuminated, Thi has a favorable view of the Việt Kiều couple that she works with. This is not merely a matter of her personally enriching mentoring relationship she has with this couple. This opinion has been formed by the observations of their ministry approach and community response that have characterized their time in Vietnam. She points to their ministry of teaching English to medical students and the community that has been formed as an illustration of success. Thi points to the hospitality and wisdom that this couple freely shares and the church community that has increased in size over a three-year time period to frame her answer. As she has observed,

> All his student and church member attend every Sunday morning in his church and I have known three or four student(s) become Christian and rest of them is non-Christian but they come and want to learn because his church worship service is bilingual like

> worship or preaching is by Vietnam and English and have translate to Vietnamese. I'm so impressed when I look back three years, the first year I meet them just two three people but now twenty student(s). Like twenty student attend his church and also they I think so important because both of them husband and wife because they have life experience that they can do counselor with the student like they did not just teach them English but they do counselor for the student because not like most student but some people they go to work already and got married already but a lot of problem in their family and they do counselor and some the student in university they give some advice stay healthy work and good way for study.

The number is relatively small. Yet there is a visible increase both in the size of the church community and the number of students that have come to saving faith. Likewise, Hue, who does not worship with this community, praises God that a least a few people have become Christians through this ministry. Living in the same city, she is aware that some have come to faith. The growth of this young community is plainly evident to see. People have come to saving faith in Christ. The worshiping community has increased in numbers. Students are being counseled. Numerical increase is a one metric of missionary impact. Two unconnected local leaders offer a similar testimony about this ministry.

Furthermore, as mentioned earlier, this couple helped Hue to reach her immediate goal of passing the ILETS exam and continue forward vocationally. On a small individual scale, you can say this is a measure of effectiveness and impact. When the interviewer met Hue, she was attending a training program intended to help students missionally engage as English language teachers in their own homeland. This is one life that has been directly and positively impacted by intersecting with a returnee. Improving in her foundational language competency has helped this local leader on her vocational pathway. Teaching English is one tangible means that returnees can bless people in their natal homeland. Hue is one of many potential examples of this ministry in action. She has not had a long-term ongoing deep relationship with the returnees in this case. Even still, a life has been blessed by the relationship.

On the other hand, it was shared that the ability of this couple to work directly with the university as instructors has been blocked. They are not permitted to teach legally in the university as they intended when they moved to the city. They faced, and continue to encounter, bureaucratic restrictions. This variable has had the result of narrowing the potential scope of their missionary impact. As such, local leaders relay that this couple has pivoted in strategy so that they are still engaging the same population. The access point has changed. Ministry perhaps looks different than the couple envisioned to a certain extent. The local Christian leaders see this playing out.

Additionally, this ministry approach of working outside of the main registered church in the city has also resulted in a certain level of disappointment for Hue. From the perspective of Hue, the registered church and this couple do not know each other well. As a member of a registered church, she bemoans the lack of a strong relationship between her church and the couple as they mostly do separate things (their primary ministry space is the work with students attending the local medical university and shepherding the home church) and she would like to see more help as there are many students in her church that would like to learn English. She expresses the desire for the couple to have started with her church because they also have great needs.[5] Hue sees signs of ministry impact from the specific couple and has heard the reputation; she also is a little ambivalent as direct relationship is weak as it intersects with her direct ministry spaces.

The approach of highlighting both positive and negative examples of perceived missionary impact and effectiveness was common in conversations. Visible outcomes can be one measuring stick to gauge missionary impact on a case-by-case basis. The ministry work of the returnees lands in communities and makes a discernible impact. Results on the ground are seen by locals. Taken as a whole, stories of the returnees reveal that the results can be mixed as discerned by local non-migrant Christians. For instance, Hieu pointed to the example of the Việt Kiều woman that has been returning every year as a positive example of impactful work. He can recount all the tangible things that have occurred over the years of returning and investing in the homeland. This is a true measurement of impact. Lives have been improved through the work she has engaged in. This transnational returnee has formed bonds, helped reduce poverty, aided in equipping lay leaders, and prayed. There is a clear correlation of cause and effect and positive impact in a community and in individual lives in the homeland. Many similar positive stories of individuals who return

---

5. Hue acknowledges that she does not know all the details for how one pathway was chosen or what factors contributed to the returnee's ministry decisions. I.e., she does not know if her lead pastor invited them into ministry partnership.

on STM basis to places such as the drug rehab centers or have relocated back to Vietnam were relayed.

Toan pointed to an example of a certain couple that have returned and built a very successful business. Admittedly, this has come at a certain cost. They have carried on with a long-term vision but have needed to be "cutthroat" to survive. Success and how this success has been achieved is community collective knowledge. This can potentially harm the mission dynamic of their work. Their reputation, both the good and the not so good aspects, are known. However, on the other end of the spectrum, Toan pointed to a specific experience he had working with a Việt Kiều BAM work in which the "ship sunk." Meaning the whole BAM business venture failed and folded, even under what ought to have been good advantages. As he unpacked, "remember the worst-case scenario, the business that went sour, more sour than sourdough. That particular experience came from more than a decade of being in Vietnam, and it still failed like anything else before that. What does it teach us though? It teaches us that failure is part of the journey." Not every ministry is going to be successful. Being Việt Kiều does not make you immune from this potential outcome. Local partners are well aware of this reality. It is worth mentioning that the end result is not to be taken as a verdict on comprehensive missionary impact. In other words, the end result and stresses of living through this experience did not negate all potential positive community impact. Nevertheless, it was the ultimate outcome in this case and a very real scenario for any returnee. The returnees themselves attested to the unescapable reality that not every venture will flourish. It is significant that the non-migrant Vietnamese that participated in this project collaborated that understanding. They did not paint a one-dimensional rosy picture of the work of the returnees. By this, locals acknowledge that they see good, the bad, and the ugly. It is both ends of the spectrum, and everything in between. Simply stated, being Việt Kiều does not automatically equate with missionary impact effectiveness for the national partners. Failure can be a part of the journey even for the Việt Kiều.

The microscope can be zoomed out to see a larger picture of perceived missionary impact and effectiveness that goes beyond looking at specific Việt Kiều returnees on a case-by-case basis. Two key variables come into consideration here that fit into a pattern of a bigger consideration regarding perceived missionary impact. First, Việt Kiều missions is a team sport that is truly only done in collaboration with locals rather than an individual sport. The non-migrant local Christians each spoke to this dynamic. As Quy said, "but they need to work with the local people, they cannot do it alone." Quy is speaking from her lens of experience working with the many STM that come to the drug rehab center and to support other ministries of the local churches in her city. These teams have a reputation of strong collaboration. From her vantage point, any impact is contingent upon robust collaboration with the local peoples. Apart from that, there is no impact. Simply put, they would never have access without collaboration. A close working relationship with local Christians is the difference between being a tourist and having the opportunity to be effective as the overseas community is invited into these restricted spaces. Furthermore, the returnees play a supporting role taking their cues from the local leaders who are largely responsible for setting the agenda. It is impactful and important, but ultimately it is supportive in this ministry relationship.

Likewise, in a different region of the country, Thang and Hoa make a similar observation as they note that the Việt Kiều need to collaborate with the local people. As Thang conveyed, "I think missionary, foreigner missionary, they work with the, the same Vietnamese, but they need to cooperate." He was sure to communicate that from his perspective, the foreign missionaries, including the Việt Kiều, must cooperate and collaborate with the local workers. As a local ministry leader, he knows from experience that the returning Việt Kiều need to cooperate with local peoples. They see examples of this happening and the better range of potential outcomes that come through ministry collaboration, as well as, other times that lack robust collaboration.

While collaboration as a core ministry principle is key, it is not simply an issue of collaboration, or lack of collaboration, with local people. It is a more nuanced and consequential range of social choices that confronts the returning Việt Kiều. The returning Việt Kiều have choices to make that directly impact their sphere of influence and hence their missionary impact. How is the returnee going to interact as a social being in their natal homeland? How are they going to relate and work with the various ministry networks? Returnees spoke to the challenges of this aspect of return. Likewise, the non-migrant national partners speak to this choice that must be made. This touches on some core decisions that will impact the ministry in profound ways. This also has legal implications (i.e., is the person going to try to go the route of a registered non-profit or business). This has various ministry implications that directly impact the range of potential outcomes the missionary Việt Kiều will have. In this context, registered non-profits can openly do certain tasks while perhaps having their hands tied more tightly in other meaningful ways. Namely, direct Christian teaching and gospel presentation might be curtailed.

The issue of collaboration while relevant in each ministry avenue is perhaps the most relevant to missionary work done via discipleship centric ministries that directly engage with the local church. Potential national partners are well aware of their context. The twin narratives of Hue and Thi illuminates the relational complexities of this dynamic. The choice that the Việt Kiều couple made to work primarily with a home church and focus outreach on medical university students meant that the relationship was weak with the registered main church in this city. This led to a level of disappointment for Hue. It is not necessarily a broken or bad relationship; it is simply a matter of not knowing each other in this case. For Thi, it is a thriving relationship. This clearly illustrates from the perspective of local leaders that in the same city, to work and make an impact in one area, also means that other potential ministry spaces are given less attention and people in that camp might be a little disappointed or unsure why one pathway was chosen. Indeed, who you choose to collaborate with is not simply a matter of working with one group, but can be a choice that closes the door to other ministry spaces. Pointedly, do you seek to work with and under the authority of a registered denomination or do you pursue a more independent route and work primarily with home churches and/or parachurch ministries?[6] As potential national partners, there might not be a complete understanding when one pathway is elevated over others as they see returnees at work. The national partners have their own networks and ministry spaces. As Việt Kiều, you are entering their home turf. You crash into a unique story that has continued forward in the time that the Việt

---

6. In fairness, it is necessary to note that this is not a choice simply to be made unilaterally by the returning Việt Kiều. This is a complex social choice. The national partners also choose to work with the Việt Kiều and the government might not grant the recognition. The interviewer has been told that the government and a certain denomination in a part of Vietnam has only opened up two classes for students who studied abroad to come back to Vietnam (this could be international students that study MDiv or other theological programs outside of Vietnam, not necessarily limited to Việt Kiều as this study is exploring) to study and recognize the credentials in Vietnam. Only two classes. The first class is said to have only thirty students. The second one only ten. This is a small number relative to the potential number of people that might be qualified for such a program. Some returnees and study abroad students might not even have the option to work in a recognized way with their denomination.

Kiều lived abroad. As the outsider, you are joining with them and have access to certain groups based on who you are collaborating with. Project respondents hold their own opinions on these matters.

Hieu spoke of collaboration in these terms:

> I would tell them the church overseas when you want to help the Vietnamese church you have to come through the denomination leader here ask them what do what help available for them submit you need to be humble, not only you have knowledge and can tell people what to do you come to the church here leader here ask them what you can help them. So if the overseas want to help the Tin Lanh church they have to go tell them what the need.

This really applies to any denomination, "if they belong to the other denomination their home church they can do it there. But I think they also work don't see the results much but I think they work good thing come out also even though no recognition." For Hieu, the operational principle here is submission to work with and under the authority of the denomination of which you belong. An emphasis is placed on the need to humbly learn from the local leaders and follow their leading. This statement also reveals a common frustration. As Hieu alluded, some return with knowledge and perhaps in their zeal to help or share that knowledge they are perceived as telling people what to do. This is the opposite of the spirit of collaboration that Hieu and others call for. Local leaders that participated in this research project are in unison in the opinion that the overseas Vietnamese can help. However, they articulated the profile of a returnee that can be most helpful. They are looking to serve alongside returnees that return with humility and a learner's attitude. Namely, the exhortation was shared that local leaders request those that do not go thinking too highly of oneself and one's status as an overseas Vietnamese. This is the core character quality that opens a door for collaboration with local leaders.

Hieu went on to describe two kinds of Việt Kiều and the ministry pathways available to each group. A small percentage go under the authority of the local church denomination while the majority do not take this path. By his estimation only one or two out of every ten that come back belong to the denomination. Going independently, "they can work for the intervarsity or CCC or outreach student or translation books or some other things but not in the large scale. Just small things they can do it." By this Hieu, is stating the lay of the land from his perspective. Returning Việt Kiều might only do "small things" when they are outside the spaces of denominational structure and minister without the official recognition that comes from the title of pastor.[7]

Working from within the denominational approved structure gives a specified freedom and clear range to ministry in Vietnam. However, this freedom is accompanied by certain other restrictive parameters. Hieu describes his own situation to explain this.

> I can travel because I belong to my denomination, and I understand authority. I submit, I agree. Even though part of me don't want it. The other people from study of Việt Kiều come back here and they can do many things normal society or they can work with the different organization but they don't have title like me, pastor. I am under the line of my father, and my denomination. Easy for me. Any church in Vietnam I can come I preach officially the government recognize my credential.

So why would returnees not elect to work within official structures of their respective denominations? From Hieu's perspective returning Việt Kiều might not want to go under this authority because "some they come back to Vietnam and they want to be freedom. They don't want to become pastor and then have to come to that church. They said oh no you cannot get to, you have to submit. They want to be freedom to work anywhere. Home church or Tin Lanh church. They work anywhere. A lot just come back and don't want to belong to any denomination." The majority of returnees are seen as desiring to be unshackled or not limited by various local structures or authorities. In this context, denominational belonging comes with a price of giving up certain freedoms.

---

7. One example of this comes from the discussion with Thi and Hue. Both local Vietnamese know a returning Việt Kiều that has chosen to work primarily outside of the space of the registered denominational structure. The reasons for this decision are not fully clear to either respondent. What is clear is that this couple has started an independent "home church" and seem to work largely independently of the established denominations in their ministry area and the denomination that they belong to in their Western homeland. As such, they have a level of freedom to minister in the way that they see is the most meaningful as independent workers without official recognition (either from a denomination or the government). For Quy, the returning Việt Kiều that she has worked with over the years are stellar examples of submission to work under local leadership. However, she is predominantly working with STM teams that are coming specifically to serve in Vietnam at the particular ministry site. It is a different dynamic for a short-term visitor. I am not aware of any Việt Kiều relocating to Vietnam to work under this network. In this case, the local leadership are the gatekeepers into this ministry space and Quy has seen many working under this structure during their visits.

How one chooses to engage with the various homeland ecclesial structures is a crucial and consequential choice for returning Việt Kiều. Local leaders attest that how a returnee answers this key question directly impacts the potential scope of missionary impact. It is not an easy question to answer as there are many variables at play that factor into this important decision. Regardless, how one engages with the church speaks into conversation concerning relative missionary impact. Potential parameters of impact are set by who or what groups one associates with and how they associate with these groups. Local partners know this well as they have learned to navigate this ministry context. Moreover, they know that the Việt Kiều are not able to escape from this social context as they reenter the social terrain of Vietnam. Returnees enter into the thick of it. Indeed, this lived reality was discussed frequently in the Việt Kiều returnee discussions. Many described how they wrestled through these issues and how they came to their current working relationships with various ministry organizations. Some might not perceive a calling to belong to the denomination in their natal homeland. It might be the right choice to join a home church or home church networks. It might be the right ministry choice to serve with CRU or other parachurch ministries. Regardless, it is complex choice with complex layers of relationship and ramifications that might not always be apparent at the time of the choice. When Việt Kiều do not work under official registered entities, they have certain benefits and certain limiting factors. There might be good work being done, but it might be on a smaller scale, more behind the scenes ministry. This might be the prudent path. Regardless, who you work with or associate with and your official position/status in society will factor into the range of your impact. This is simply the way it is in Vietnam. Local leaders know this well from their own experiences.

On the other hand, returnees may give up too easily on joining the existing church structures. Other times they convey an attitude that is inclined towards critiquing and undervaluing local leaders who might not have had the same learning opportunities. Indeed, among the local leaders interviewed, there is some perception of judgment at times and looking down on what exists in the homeland or a prideful attitude that might lead the overseas community to resist submitting to local leadership. For instance, Toan articulates returnees might "speak about faith very boldly, insensitively to the things that people have been taught." This might even come from a good desire on the part of the returnee. They are passionate about their faith and have returned to share it. They tend to be passionate about areas that are of deep concern to them. For example, a returnee newsletter discussed the lack of pre-marriage counseling that he has observed among the churches in Vietnam. To remedy a perceived weakness, he has been doing pre-marriage counseling with several couples this year and teaching about the sensitive topic of divorce and remarriage in sermons as it comes up in the Biblical text. Attempting to meet this need might come across to local leaders as critical and condescending due to the wording choices used in the newsletter. Language used to emphasize the importance and impact of this teaching is framed in a tone that could be seen as being depreciatory of the local church. While well-intentioned, if this is perceived by locals as a case of a returnee acting in ministry in a manner that "disregards the importance of respecting the cultural setting at the time," tensions will enter into the relationships. The national partners do not want to be on the receiving end when returnees attempt to serve in ways that are insensitive to the local context.

Secondly, some respondents speak of the phenomenon from the vantage point that seeks to take the complete picture into account. While Việt Kiều missionaries can be effective, it is perceived that certain expectations are brought into the relationship by the Việt Kiều that are harmful. Beyond the questions of collaboration, missionary impact needs to be filtered through the lens of a realistic mindset. By this local Christians mean that there is a perception challenge here. Respondents shared that the Việt Kiều can want things to happen faster than what the ecosystem can produce and sustain. The pace can be slow to build relationships and grow ministries. Relationships can be built with non-Christian Vietnamese that eventually lead to a friend becoming a Christian. But this can take some five years of intentional friendship. Some returnees do have success in building transformational ministries, but it is hard-earned and takes time to come to fruition. Sometimes it can be hard to work with Việt Kiều as they sometimes expect too much too quickly. As Toan unpacks,

> for some other people, they struggled quite a bit. Say, for example, their farming and Bible teaching region, they struggled to find support. They barely had any support at all, and it's very hard for them to come to terms with it that it might suck for a while before they can get on their feet and get it going in a system. Because it is, the nature of ministry is hard. It's hard to keep giving, giving, giving, giving and investing until finally it can come to fruition. A lot of people feel discouraged at first. Yeah. Working with returnees is good, but there is also for locals, it's sometimes a challenge.

> Or they don't realize that it takes a decade or more to invest in something like a country. It would take a lot longer for someone to say that okay, I'm committed to be in Vietnam, and it's going to be two or three decades before I can even start being influential.

Toan's statement finds congruency with the experiential reality shared by many of the returnees. Real transformational impact demands a long-term time investment. The non-migrant local Christians know this reality well and caution returnees in this regard. It tends to be slow to build relationships. It is slow to start ministries. It is slow to disciple. It is slow to work in Vietnam and have impact. It can be hard for locals to work with returnees at times as they do not approach the work with this long-term view or perhaps face bouts of discouragement when reality hits. Indeed, non-migrants encouraged potential returnees to count the cost because it is an investment to return and seek to serve in the natal homeland. Flashy events or economic remittance for a building project might produce numbers for a newsletter but that is not the most meaningful way to build a lasting missionary impact.

Additionally, local Christian interviewees indicated that at times one can have their hand in too many jars. In other words, Việt Kiều can have too many ministries going on at once. Ministry attention and energy can be scattered. This pitfall surfaced in interviews with returnees. This speaks to the fact that overextending oneself is a natural temptation in ministry. Việt Kiều missionaries are cautioned to keep their eye on the guiding vision that brought them back to Vietnam. One can do many good things that only amount to an impact that is an inch deep. You simply cannot do everything. A more focused approach can lead to a deeper long-term impact. As Toan said in his cleaver wording, "A mixture of too many things into the mission spoils the soup. Either make Pho or Bun Thit Ngnon. You can't make Bun Thit Nong and Pho. You cannot blend too many things into business and ministry and this and that. You burn out before you even know it. If you come into the country to explore, sure, you'll really explore. But then what do you want to do?" In this case, consistency, commitment, and depth win the long-term holistic transformation and make that rich Pho broth.

Finally, it is noteworthy that while discussing perceived missionary impact, the larger context was spoken of. The returning Việt Kiều are but one movement impacting contemporary Vietnam. Quy, when speaking of the growth of the church in the North over the past decade speaks that while there is an increase each year in the Việt Kiều returning they are but one variable to the growth. Each of these has come into existence as globalization has become entrenched in Vietnam. She speaks of three movements; international students that find Christ while studying abroad, migrant workers in Malaysia and Korea that find Christ while working abroad and return and plant churches, and finally former drug addicts that enter the ministry. Within this, the "Việt Kiều pastors or Việt Kiều visitors they also play some part of the activities. I also see that they send many Việt Kiều to Malaysia. In the past many Việt Kiều migrant workers so receive Christ from there." These three movements speak to contemporary ministry in the globalized world. Yes, the returning Việt Kiều play a role. Yet, they are far from the only movement. When we think of the question of impact, it is important not to overlook the fact that non-migrant see that there are many things converging and contributing to the growth of the Kingdom. This picture points to the need for humility among the Việt Kiều. They can join in fruitful ministry and can effectively collaborate with local ministry partners. At the same time, God is active and this phenomenon is but one globalization trend that is coming together to impact the natal homeland. Ultimately, a wise word of counsel is offered for the returnees that hints at a perception of returnees. "Maybe they're all going to benefit more if they follow what the Lord is telling them to do and just be happy with that, just that. That the Lord asked them to follow on the journey and they report just that, that journey. Leave the fruits and the growth for the Lord. We just water, and we just sow the seeds" (Toan).

How do Local Christians Describe Frustration Fault Lines that Emerge in Working with Returning Missional Việt Kiều?

This section will highlight two issues surfaced in the conversations with the non-migrant local Christians. The exploration of frustrations falls into two main concerns that will be addressed in this section: economic remittance and power dynamics.

First, as already discussed, economic remittance is happening in Christian ministry spaces. The fact is well established and supremely relevant as various aspects of economic remittance were discussed in every conversation (both with returnees and local Christians). As the stories from respondents such as Hieu illustrated, this can be a positive encouraging experience on a personal level. At the same time, as chapter four demonstrated, dynamics of economic remittance are a major point of frustration.

Returnees are not alone in this frustration. Economic remittance can also be a source of frustration for local Christians, albeit for different reasons. The non-migrant local Christians have wisdom to share from their perspective on this topic.

In the relationship, economic remittance dynamics are experienced differently by all actors. The themes that emerge from the local Christian respondents highlight transparency in giving that best empowers all local stakeholders. One theme of frustration that emerges in this realm is that giving is not the space to make power plays or overly onerous stipulations to the gift. There is sometimes a frustration with returnees who at times are seen as attempting to leverage money for influence and control over its destination. There can be unhealthy actions surrounding money that take place at times. Namely, "some people have money and they want to do in their own way they [sic] way you have to do this I give money otherwise, but it not the right thing to do even though you think that's good. The local people they know more than you" (Hieu). In other words, give in humility with an open hand and a listening posture. From the perspective of my respondents, sometimes the Việt Kiều might want to do things their own way as they have the resources. They might want to control the resource distribution and destination. However, this is not necessarily the most helpful way to operate from the perspective of the local people. Operating in this way can create internal and external problems for the local church that the overseas community might not even be aware of.

Hieu describes a situation that is fairly common. Việt Kiều have some connection back in their natal homeland. Perhaps this is the church they attended as a child before they migrated to the West, or they still have some extended family or childhood friend in Vietnam that tells them of a need of a certain church or among a community. The Việt Kiều contribute as they see fit. They believe they are helping to meet a need or they desire to fund a project that is of particular importance to them for personal reasons. From Hieu's vantage point

> I think its helpful to do the way they want to do but they should make connection with the pastor local church than do whatever you want because the local church leader they know what to do so you have to connect with the people local to help so because they know the need otherwise you go and do something and then you go back home the government can say you can create conflict in the church for example or something like that but after you leave. After you left you can create some conflict or make problem for

> the church you helped because you didn't do it the right way or government issue so be careful how you help so when you have the money I believe that the pastor and the leader of the church have to know what to do, connect to them and tell them, the what the need of the church. Rely on local church. And you have to respect the leader otherwise difficult for you how to help. Do openly not only pastor but deacon they have to together also important together can know. Because sometime pastor just believe that they get money and do this that and don't tell the deacon, it create a problem at the church any decision has be pastor and deacon otherwise cause conflict a lot of people.

Enhanced transparency is the key variable here. Even an act done with good intention can cause problems that the overseas Việt Kiều do not anticipate when they do not fully understand all the relationship dynamics within the local church ecosystem and its relationships in society (especially with government officials). Economic remittance, while a potential blessing, can be a double edge sword that unleashes difficulties internally and externally for the local church at times. So, how do you help in the right way? For Hieu, this internal conflict can be mitigated by openness in giving and humility. Therefore, the Việt Kiều are advised to connect with more than just their extended family that remain locally or a contact they have at a church they attended as a child. Connect with multiple stakeholders, listen to them, and humbly respect them. Make it open so the community, or at least the larger leadership team, are in on the happenings so that the potential for conflict can be minimized. The Việt Kiều might have the economic resource in their personal bank account. However, it is not something to be held as leverage over individuals or groups to accomplish what they want. The whole community can be brought in as stakeholders to maximize the positive contribution of the remittance and lower the potential for money to cause conflict (either internal or external).

Both Việt Kiều returnees and local Vietnamese are well aware of the large amount of money flowing into Vietnam. These personal, on the ground stories that were woven into the interviewee ministry narratives confirm the repeated theme of economic remittance that tends to be a prominent feature of Vietnamese diaspora studies. When it comes to economic remittance the topic of accountability came up in several of the conversations with returnees. Returnees shared many stories that raised red flags in their perception of the events surrounding money and ministry (some of these are shared in chapter four).⁸ Non-migrant local Christian leaders did not tend to address the topic of accountability with the details of bad examples or red flags in a similar manner. Their concerns are more about best use of remittance and transparency for both the giver and the receiving community as in Hieu's advice. Regardless, as this section demonstrates, the giving of economic remittance is happening, and it can be helpful. However, it is an act that has many potential pitfalls. Both the Việt Kiều and the local church need to proceed carefully to lower the potential of the exchange leading to frustration or worse for all involved.

A second theme of concern related to economic remittance is the themes of destination and dependency. This is a concern on the forefront of the minds of most of my Việt Kiều respondents. It is significant that the non-migrant local Christians also articulate concern of a similar nature. For example, Thang and Hoa, articulated the concern that while money is flowing to local churches for various building projects, they are more concerned about Vietnamese non-believers. As they articulated, "I want to help the Vietnamese know the Jesus in their life. If the Việt Kiều can invest money in, for the, for, about the not believe to help them know the Jesus. I think this the important thing." This concerns the destination or primary purposes of economic remittance. Both local leader and returnees are in

---

8. The interviewer had one conversation exchange with a local partner that raised red flags akin to those commonly spoken of by returnees. In this case, it was not what was said directly in an interview, but the email correspondences with a local ministry partner that raised red flags. In summary, a transnational Việt Kiều shared the email contact of his primary in-country ministry partner. This person was described as being very helpful. This person is the primary contact for ministry operations back in the homeland and has extensive oversight over the financial resources of this ministry as the in-country leader. In any case, the transnational Việt Kiều was sure that this person would be happy to meet and talk. Indeed, initially, this person was quick to respond to emails and eagerly started setting up times to visit ministry sites and offering to help with logistics, such as lodging in the city. That is until the meeting dates were nearer and the purpose of the visit was emphasized. Suddenly, it would be difficult to meet because of rain and the interviewer was given the runaround. No one needs to participate in the research project. Anyone can say no at any time. What was striking was the sudden and dramatic tone shift and sudden unavailability of all people connected to this ministry once this national partner clearly understood that the interviewer did not simply desire to visit an orphanage and give support or see the in-country work, but rather wanted to have a conversation with the contact and some of the other pastors regarding their experiences working with returnees. Once this person clearly understood that I wanted to ask questions, the shift in the tone of the conversation and excuses given was immediate. While I cannot claim to know for certain why the conversation took such a sharp turn, it certainly raised red flags.

unison in the opinion that a significant amount of economic remittance flows into Vietnam. The physical landscape changes as building projects are funded by outside dollars. However, not all are comfortable with this arrangement. They, like other respondents, pray that money will go towards means that expands the horizons of the church rather than more building projects. Do you give primarily to fund in-house projects, the various edifices of Christianity in Vietnam, or do you give in a way that makes a deeper legacy and more directly expand the boundaries of Christianity? This is the concern of Thang.

Further research would need to be undertaken to clearly demonstrate how much money is flowing back for in-house building projects versus how much is going towards externally focused outreach related works. However, I can say that this concern certainly echoes the concern expressed by some of my Việt Kiều respondents who cautioned that the many building projects are not producing a more mature church. For example, Bing in his heartfelt sorrow states,

> The church building is higher, bigger, more land, more equipment, you can see modern the church. They have sound system. One hundred percent has sound system. Maybe TV, LED TV. Back and forth. Vietnamese church equipment, resource, they're well. They're okay, they will compare even with Hmong church you can see they're okay with that. Every year, the church they notify that through Christmas event, through many evangelism events, I think approximately about five thousand people accept Christ in public. But the attendance of the church is fewer, fewer, and fewer. Most of the churches you go is empty. Where people that know the Lord, where do they go? We can see that, if you look outside, you can see, now church grow, look at the building equipment they have. But if you look into the service, look into their personal lives, you can see the church decline, the church decline.

Economic remittance is building modern looking church buildings, but is it growing the church spiritually and is it expanding the Kingdom?

These concerns were spoken of by others as well. For example, Quy shared similar sentiments while adding a concern was spoken of by most all returnees. She states that

> For my view point I see that the Việt Kiều pastor if they can more realize more people should work to reach the unreached people groups because I see that for Kinhs people group there are many resources pay attention but in Vietnam there are many other

> people group in Vietnam they receive less resources or they don't have any resources and also we are thinking of how the Việt Kiều can help the local churches to bless them in their own feet because I see that if we receive finance support from foreign countries the Việt Kiều often bring the resources in but now I see that if we can stand on our own it will be much better. . . . I think that Việt Kiều has very good heart they just would like to bring back the resources here but I think that how can they help the local churches to stand on their own feet and share their even small resources to other people groups or other countries.

She sees that the church often receives resources, but are resources being used to the best of their potential? Over the years, she expresses that she has grown increasingly uncomfortable with so much one-sided receiving.

Moreover, the issue of dependency is not just a matter of economic remittance. It goes to the heart of the identity of the Vietnamese church. In conversations, the desire that local believers ought to be equipped as co-laborers and missional agents was shared. For potential returnees, there is a call to look beyond the national borders of the natal homeland and to engage in the task of equipping local Christians to do likewise when they do return. The Church in Vietnam, while numerically small relative to the percentage of the total population, has a multi-generational history. This creates calls for not just receiving missionaries, but for those Việt Kiều missionaries to help the church develop her own missionary vocation. Vietnam has been receiving Protestant missionaries since 1910. As Quy implored, "from my perspective I am thinking that Việt Kiều can help the local churches to transform to shift their mind that no more just receive even receive missionary but to think how about be a blessing to other people groups in our country. In other country we will start to send missionary to other people groups to other country because even we Vietnamese Christian here is still small but if we do not do it maybe we will not grow up." The mindset of the missional returnee can be one that helps to encourage the local Christians to take ownership as co-laborers in the worldwide missionary task, not simply receive money or expertise from the outside (diaspora or others). It speaks to a shift in the relationship dynamics that money is a part of, but not the full story. Money flows in and is part of the ministry equation, yet even for those on the receiving end there is a certain degree of uncomfortableness with the status quo at this point in time. Christian leaders on the ground can see that the money does not always go to the greatest need at times. They can see it can create a culture of expectation that can perpetuate immaturity. Even when it goes to legitimate needs, it might not be the best use of the resources as it pertains to equipping a spiritually mature missionally minded local church as the local Vietnamese attest. Dependency is a concern here and it echoes the concern that several of the returnees discussed.

Second, the conversations with the non-migrant Vietnamese regarding collaboration between the returning the Việt Kiều and non-migrant local Christians often touched upon the sometimes frustrating and often complex issue of power dynamics. This addresses Sub RQ 3: How do non-migrant church leaders experience power dynamics in relationship to the ministry of the Việt Kiều?

Sometimes, the narrative is rather glowing as in the context of Quy's personal narrative of her years working with the many STM teams that return and come alongside the ministry of the drug rehab center. In her experience, the teams bring their giftings and life experiences to freely share and are good partners with the local ministry. As she tells it,

> in our [ministry center] we work with many Việt Kiều from the U.S. and from Australia and they really respect our local leaders. There are two different groups. For the groups if they have already the purpose, for example they bring the medical team here, so their purpose is to serve the poor people, serve the people then after that share the gospel, they already have purpose. For those that are pastors, who are church deacons, who already have Bible background, they ask us what Bible courses we want to conduct and they will find the people who are suitable to send. They just look for like we have the need so we request and then if it fit with their purpose they will send for example. If we would like to conduct an outreach and it costs about 2000 and it fits with their church goal something like that they can send the money and also some of them go to conduct together with us. We need to conduct a Bible course so they send respond their church people can do so they send the church people. For example, they know that they cannot do things alone so they always do with the local churches here. That is the thing that I really respect them and they are the one that bring the resources but they do not act as they own the resources.

In this example, the healthy pattern is demonstrated in which the Việt Kiều work well with their national partners at the ministry center(s). They demonstrate humility, generosity, and allow the local leaders to lead. They are seen as contributing rather than seeking to be controlling. In this way, the Việt Kiều are actively contributing to this dynamic ministry in Vietnam.

At the same time, the brothers at the center offered a consequential caution from their perspectives as it pertains to the transnational teaching ministry that occurs at the center. It was disclosed that the brothers expressed a certain confusion about the carrousel of visiting teachers that pass through the center, each with their own styles and messages and sometimes obviously competing theologies or as Tai says, "wrong teachings and different doctrines." By this he means that the brothers at the center are exposed to a wide variety of teachings through the teams of Việt Kiều (and other foreigners) that come to the center who often have formal training and a higher status as a returnee. There is an unbalanced power dynamic. As a brother in the center, it appears as if the Việt Kiều have a degree of freedom to teach as they see best with little oversight. By and large the brothers have a lower level of education in general and little to no theological training (most are not Christian when they enter the center). As Tai expresses, "not a lot of the brothers here understand, or they have the chance to do a lot of research on their own. But there's a lot of teachings, there's a lot of pastors who come here and give seminars and stuff, and I have to be very careful, from who or what I learn." (Interviewer: So do different pastors have different theologies, different messages when they come?) "Absolutely. Absolutely. It is confusing." It is worth lingering on this point. The national partner sees a positive synergy at work at the drug rehab ministry. Quy's description of the many teachings from overseas pastors sounds very positive. She used phrases such as "they ask us what Bible courses we want to conduct and they will find the people who are suitable to send." The brothers sit under the teachings of the many different people that come to the center, yet their lived experience as receivers of the teaching is not clearly in alignment with Quy's perspective. Rather, the experience can be one of confusion and a basic level of not understanding as the brothers are exposed to the many seminars and sermons coming from many different pastors who teach from their own theological convictions, perspectives, and concerns. The brothers in the center receiving the teachings do not have the foundational training and framework to make sense of these various messages and are left with times of confusion. How teachings are received is an important perspective for the Việt Kiều to hear. Likewise, it is even good for the national partners involved in organizing trainings to hear as people in the center might not be receiving the learning that they think they are receiving from the many STM teachers that come. This is one specific example from one specific ministry site. However, it is a reasonable assumption to make that the brothers at this center are not alone in this perspective given the many different people that visit and teach Bible courses, seminars, and training events in Vietnam. Further research could be done among various local faith communities and ministry sites to test this messaging.

Now, beyond the specific location of the drug rehab center, instances of misunderstanding or points of tension surfaced in nearly every interview as it relates to the web of power dynamic issues. For instance, one respondent admitted to having seen many misunderstandings or points of tension between the local churches and returnees. One specific story was mentioned when the interview asked if he had personally witnessed any points of tension or misunderstanding when the local churches and Việt Kiều attempt to work together. The straightforward answer is informative. He said, "Quite a lot, actually" (Toan). This came from a place of the returnees speaking "about faith very boldly, insensitively to the things that people have been taught." It is not necessarily that the message is theologically right or wrong. The issue cited was insensitivity. It is in the communication delivery punctuated by the lack of humility. The returning Việt Kiều have an ascribed high status that often gives them a certain platform to teach or share their perspective when they visit. They have traveled thousands of miles. They are ascribed the social status to publicly share. However, how or what they share might clash with the teachings or culture of the local people. It is seen that "a lot of people" share this trait. Power is out of balance and the local people experience the effects of ministry and teachings from Việt Kiều that do not respect the cultural setting or demonstrate sufficient humility in their eagerness to share the faith and correct areas they perceive as lacking in the homeland church.

Likewise, there is commonality with the story that another respondent told. She mentioned that a certain Việt Kiều couple "go back and observe many churches in [ministry city] and also from the North because they belong, they live in the South more than in the North and they observe understand the culture in the North and the South both of them and they can observe like what the churches in Vietnam kind they do and sometimes they feel its different with their ways and some things that they didn't agree that like the churches in Vietnam do." She provided a specific example centering on forms and expressions of worship that this Việt Kiều couple do not agree with.

> For example, in the way the worship like when we worship we proclaim that God is healer, God is wisdom, God is but for them because they experience we do not like proclaim God is healer God is but we have to experience his name like healer God is healer and if we experience that God heals like something part our lives and proclaim we have experience then we proclaim its not just proclaim like follow the saying or the saying or some didn't agree I will share that they feel like the way people show up here and some of the focus is I do I do forgot God is the important thing, God is work, and His work is not the people work. (Thi)

This calls attention to one specific church practice that a specific Việt Kiều couple have found that they do not agree with. This highlights the understanding between the two groups that there are differences in ecclesial praxis. It is not the place of this study to make any attempt at a theological judgment that sides with one group or another in these matters. It is simply to bring the observation to the forefront that the local church is not unaware that observations of this nature are made by returning Việt Kiều. Is the stated assessment fair to the local church practice and beliefs? Is the assessment biblical? Is their assessment formed from the lens of their own church practices and experiences living as diaspora citizens? In theory, the idea of traveling around and observing the culture sounds like implementation of good missionary practice. Indeed, several of the returnees spoke of a season of visiting many different churches as a component of their early phases of ministry back in Vietnam. For these participants, these travels and visits were most commonly presented as taking on the posture of a learner. It was presented as a method to be a good missionary. However, in this conversation the practice is more closely linked with critical critique as a feeling that returnees find fault with "different with their ways and some things that they didn't agree with" (Thi). They are included in the same train of thought. In this linkage the observation finds common ground with other interview conversations. The traveling and observation is most commonly linked with judgment of what the returnees find lacking in the local church context. The returnee is seen as observing, judging, and attempting to correct what they see as lacking in the home church context.

The frustration at the perceived judgment is articulated in Hieu's plea that the Việt Kiều need "to help understand the church culture in Vietnam different than the American or US or European culture so they don't have to do their own thing in Vietnam." The perceived action of doing their own thing most likely comes from a place of good intentions on the part of the returnee. They are passionate about their faith and have returned to share it. They tend to be particularly passionate about areas that are of deep concern to them. One returnee newsletter highlighted his ministry initiative offering pre-marital counseling. He wrote of starting this ministry in part due to the lack of pre-marriage counseling that he has observed among the churches in Vietnam he visited. To meet this perceived need, he has led several couples through pre-marital counseling sessions since the inception of the ministry and intentionally teaches about the sensitive topic of divorce and remarriage in sermons as it comes up in the Biblical text. In his newsletters his ministry practice is upheld as good and in contrast to local Vietnamese pastors who might not broach the subject. He made the observation that local pastors might avoid sensitive topics such as this, as they do not want to offend people. Criticism of this nature is heard by local ministry partners. As Hieu lamented,

> because some people criticize the denomination after they come back from America oh the church I have to do this or that but they don't understand we live in Vietnamese communist country different than the way and I feel like some church leader and even some pastor of the US Việt Kiều come back and conflict because of that so I would tell them the church overseas when you want to help the Vietnamese church you have to come through the denomination leader here ask them what do what help available for them submit you need to be humble, not only you have knowledge and can tell people what to do you come to the church here leader here ask them what you can help them.

This statement is global in nature rather than specific as the narratives of Thi or Toan which pointed to specific instances when returning Việt Kiều took actions or promoted positions that demonstrate a critical vantage point while not truly understanding and appreciating the context of the local church.

Each of these narratives come from three different regions of Vietnam and different church ministry contexts. Yet, they speak to a similar theme. The knowledge that the Việt Kiều remit back can be helpful to the church. Appreciation by local Christian leaders has been stated for the ability of the Việt Kiều to help with valuable ministry activities such as translation. However, points of tension or misunderstanding can surface with the Việt Kiều when they express verbally or non-verbally, an attitude of higher status and do not demonstrate humble respect of local church leaders and/

or social context. Returnees can be seen as being people that are critical of the church in their natal homeland. This is not to say that the local church is perfect. It is simply an acknowledgment that the returning Việt Kiều are semi-outsiders and when they return the local leaders do not always feel that the returnees fully understand and appreciate the local church cultural setting or try to teach something they believe is important without really appreciating the audience. Perhaps returnees do not fully take the time to deeply understand what the local church has gone through. As an overseas visitor, the returning Việt Kiều have a certain ascribed status, especially when they are pastors or have had access to theological training in the West. The implementing of this power has sometimes created tensions in church settings as these respondents illuminated.

Personal Emotional Issues: Reception, Identity, and Belonging in the Natal Homeland

This final section will discuss the complex issues of reception, identity, and belonging from the vantage point of the local Vietnamese. The returnees had quite a lot to say on this topic. Likewise, the local population holds their own perspectives on this topic.

As official numbers demonstrate, Vietnam receives many foreigners through ports of entry each year. Việt Kiều are included among many expats that are finding their way to contemporary Vietnam as there has been a "surge in work opportunities" in Vietnam in highly skilled professions as the "Socialist Republic of Vietnam sought to attract global companies and talented workers to bridge economic ties between the United States and the Asia Pacific Region."[9] The influx of Protestant Christian Việt Kiều is situated within this larger story of a rapidly changing society. That to say that how the local Vietnamese receive the returning diaspora is a story situated within a society undergoing rapid change as people are increasingly becoming global citizens.[10] Globalization has been unleashed in the

---

9. Nguyen-Akbar, "Finding the American Dream Abroad?," 96–97.

10. Foreign direct investment has brought scores of new factories, office buildings and resorts in the rapid development project and workers reshaping Vietnam. This is particularly true in the major urban areas where the lives of many different nationalities intersect on a regular basis. Koreans rise to the tops as the most ubiquitous of expats residing in and visiting contemporary Vietnam. Indeed, sections of Vietnam have Korean billboards, business signs, and sell a wide range of Korean products marketed to both the Korea tourists and the Korean business community that has set up shop in Vietnam.

homeland. While the larger context informs opinions, these finds are kept tightly to the research topic. Namely, this section seeks to examine how local Christian leaders that participated in this research project are receiving the returning Việt Kiều in the context of Christian ministry in Vietnam.

First, and most significantly, it is meaningful that the non-migrant national Vietnamese that participated in this research articulated a generally positive experience of the phenomenon of return. As Toan summarized, "I would say that overall the experience is good." Each respondent was able to tell positive stories of returning Việt Kiều. They personally attest to good things happening through the waves of returnees. This comes from the cumulative impressions formed over the course of time observing and working directly with returnees. This affirmation is not given naively. After all, as this chapter demonstrates, there are times when ministry experiences and relationships have missed the mark or gone sour. Rather, as well-informed participants, the impression and bent towards reception is favorable considering all variables. The invitation to return is extended (sometimes directly in the conversations) and the locals that participated in this project are favorable to the continued collaboration with returnees.

The generally positive stance comes through in the tone of conversations and specific language used to characterize the return. Phrases used in interviews frequently exhibited positive terminology. This includes respondents such as Quy. She was sure to express her appreciation for the returnees saying, "I would like to thank the Lord for them for the Việt Kiều who have the heart to come back and expand the kingdom of God here in Vietnam. Thang uses similar language as Quy saying, "some Việt Kiều they have the heart, for the Vietnam people. Some people ready support for Vietnam church." Thang works for a parachurch ministry and counts Việt Kiều among his direct supporters and has welcomed them to join with him in various activities. He also knows that they support ministries such as the drug rehab centers. This specific activity is seen as especially meaningful. This concept of having a heart for Vietnam demonstrates that local leaders can see the good intentions that returnees have. While the degree of good feelings varied some, the overall impression expressed by my respondents was favorable.

Korea is but one nation to invest heavily in Vietnam. Other groundbreaking research explores some of the economic dimensions of this context. This project is focused specifically on those that return with a specific missional intention among other reasons.

Moreover, the returnees that have already been back to Vietnam have made a generally favorable impression as seen in the hope expressed that more will return. An invitation to the overseas community is extended from some of the local church leaders. Hieu expressed his positive affirmations of the phenomenon stating, "I can say that I love to see more and more Việt Kiều come back." Like the others, Hieu has close personal experience with returnees on a personal level as well as the vocational level in his current ministry role. He looked forward to the future, hoping more and more would return. This in and of itself speaks volumes into the perspective of the phenomenon.

It is significant that while the national partners are very supportive of the Việt Kiều returning and engaging in ministry in the natal homeland, the sense of distinction and boundaries remain in place. Toan articulates this clearly. He says that "but after all the identity of the Việt Kiều, they're still Việt Kiều. After a while in Vietnam, their rescue is wherever home is for them." He went onto use an incarnational theological metaphor as an analogy.

> When we say that Jesus became human to become exactly like us, to walk our walk and to cry our cry and to eat the food that we eat, that's very true. But when the disciples was detached from him, they're like, 'Where has he gone? Where has he gone?' When Jesus say, 'Well, I'm going to go to father to prepare a place. There are many places in my father's house.' That in some ways, the locals, they're not going to have a promise like that from the Việt Kiều. I'm going to go back to the US and I'm going to prepare a place for you. It's not like that, see. I'm just saying when they decide to return home to take care of their parents, it's going to be for good.[11] They're not going to be here to continue to visit the faith, to encourage the faith, whatever they did. It's going to be for good. There is that reality, that inevitable deadline. They will return.

In this sense, the Việt Kiều share similarities with any of the foreigners who come to Vietnam. They have a home outside of Vietnam. They will inevitably, for one reason or another, return to that home. They are unable to take their local friends with them anymore than any other foreigner can. Yes, there are bonds of shared history and points of connection. Yes, they

---

11. This observation has held true in the two years since the field research was completed. One of the returnees that participated in this project has recently left Vietnam (in January 2022) after a decade in Vietnam and returned to their diaspora homeland. The primary reason given was the desire/need to care for an aging parent.

can break bread and build relationships with local faith communities. Yet, when it comes down to it, they simply are not the same as the local people that have not left and joined the Vietnamese diaspora community. They are back in the historic homeland, yet it is not their home any longer. There is an expiration date to how long they will be in Vietnam. They are not the same as the local people, after all "they're still Việt Kiều." This identity and belong boundary is not lost on the non-migrant local Christians. They are Vietnamese-American or Vietnamese-Australian, Vietnamese-German, etc.

It was common for local Christian respondents to use language that showed a worldview understanding of the foreignness of the returnees while simultaneously having some shared points of belonging. As Toan warns, "You're going to encounter everyone on this earth the same way you encounter your own people because they grew apart from you fifty years ago." On one hand, people in Vietnam are "your own people." On the other hand, they really are not. Distance has replaced belonging and you will encounter people in Vietnam cross-culturally as you would "encounter everyone on this earth." This paradox of similarity and distance is expressed in many conversations in different linguistic forms.

The category terminology used by locals for the returnees is illuminating. Returnees are welcomed back. However, that stance, while generally favorable, is not the end of the discussion. For instance, Quy in her conversation of the STM teams that come to serve with the center used the word "foreigner" in her natural speaking. The term is used in the context of all the teams that come from overseas, including Việt Kiều and Westerners (mostly American and Australian of other ethnic heritage). She clarifies within the conversation as she says, "for Vietnamese people we still consider Việt Kiều is Vietnamese but they live in other countries" this contrast to her perspective that the "for the government Việt Kiều is already foreigner." However, the good relationship that her local pastor has with government officials allows her pastor to take teams of foreigners (both Việt Kiều and other ethnic heritage foreigners) into various government drug rehab centers. The Việt Kiều might still be Vietnamese for Quy, but they are associated in the foreigner category even while they are not the same as other foreigners. There are connection points that help Quy to see the overseas diaspora as Vietnamese, but the Việt Kiều are not the same as the local Vietnamese that have not migrated.

The word foreigner was used in a similar manner in Thang and Hoa's conversation. Within their ministry they have had various STM teams and long-term workers helping. Thang made a distinction that STM teams with foreigners might be able to help with the conversational English club, but not share the gospel. Whereas STM that have Việt Kiều, the Việt Kiều foreigners might be able to share the gospel. The condition is that they must speak the same language. Because they are Việt Kiều, they might speak the local language well enough. Bilingualism opens more ministry than the monolingual foreigners in this context. Hence, it might be appropriate to share the gospel in addition to helping with the English club conversation time. It is worth noting that for this couple, it was not assumed that Việt Kiều automatically possess the language competency. Furthermore, the face is spoken of as an important factor for determining the appropriateness of sharing the gospel in these gatherings. Overseas Vietnamese share the same face as the local Vietnamese. Outwardly, "we" (the local and the Việt Kiều) look similar. The shared ethnic heritage is significant for the appropriateness of sharing the gospel in this context. In Thang and Hoa's worldview, Việt Kiều are foreigners, but not the same as the interviewer (White American). The interviewer has a visibly different face. Because of this it might be appropriate for a Việt Kiều to share the gospel in addition to helping with the English conversation. Nevertheless, the Việt Kiều are not the same as the local people. The distinction is between Việt Kiều foreigners and non Việt Kiều foreigners in Thang's conversation. The groups are distinct, but they both have the foreign group association.

Furthermore, the historical events that launched the phenomenon of the largest diaspora wave is certainly not unknown to the local people. Thi's story is a clear articulation of some of this surfacing. The break in shared history does impact the way the Việt Kiều are perceived. This is especially true before they are known in the community. A lot of this can be overcome through the building of authentic relationships. Nevertheless, as an example, Thi made it clear that the local people wondered what the Việt Kiều couple were doing in their city as, "we ask them why you choose [Northern ministry city] to come back and even though both of them is from the South not the North and the pastor husband does was born in the North but his family moved to South for a long time when Americans and Vietnamese fight and her his family take refugee to go from the South to America and the wife she follow her family went to America" The fact that they are not from that Northern city or providence, is an automatic identity distinction. It raised questions. The local Christians knew this about the returning couple and were curious. This is neither automatically good nor bad. Perhaps it simply is. Kinship bonds are traced to regions, villages, and family clans. The Việt Kiều have been gone for a period of up to forty years. Still, this history is relevant. It can be a barrier or it can be an inspirational teaching point. After all, Thi is greatly impressed with this Việt Kiều couple's demonstration of faith. The fact that they moved to a Northern city in which they had no familial connection only serves to enhance that testimony. It was also telling that when she described some of the STM teams that she has experience working with the term she used to describe the team members was Vietnamese-American. She did not refer to the group as Vietnamese or even with the term Việt Kiều. Rather she used the bicultural identity terminology.

Some local leaders provided warnings regarding the nature of return to Vietnam for those that might embark on the return journey. Yes, you can return, but there is a message that ought to give pause to returnees. As Toan expands on his warning,

> I would say return to Matthew, the end of Matthew. Go to the whole world, not just your own country. You're going to encounter everyone on this earth the same way you encounter your own people because they grew apart from you fifty years ago. They speak an entirely new language. They speak the same words you understand but a different meaning and a different context. That is a completely new world for you. You have the advantage of understanding what I mean, but it's not the same kind of assumption you can build. There are things you find offensive that they don't. There are things you don't find offensive, but they do. Even though are the same people, they're going to take it that you have the same approach.

Several variables are mentioned here that showcase how the Vietnamese and Vietnamese-Americans have grown apart. The language has changed drastically. Words have new meanings; others are simply entirely new words that the diaspora do not know. Non-verbal communication patterns are new. Ways to offend the other are plentiful. Local leaders know that it is a cross-cultural communication exchange with returnees. This reality is not lost on the returnees who describe this discovery in chapter four.

In fact, Toan made an observation that given these differences, at times local leaders can interact with returnees with a patronizing attitude. Being one of us, but not really the same can lead to an interesting phenomenon as Toan articulated. "There is that patronizing attitude, oh yeah, you're not really one of us, so you might not understand. So let us slow things down for you for a little bit or give you this excuse or that excuse and also the special treatment. Or explaining you, that is not how things work around here, which I think is just patronizing. . . . Just because they have a different upbringing or a different cultural experience doesn't mean that you can disqualify the way they feel or their contribution." Locals can be patronizing to returnees or disqualify them sometimes simply because the returnees are not really one of us. They will not deeply understand.

Lastly, it is an interesting and relevant observation that Toan also made the distinction that sometime the Việt Kiều are not foreign enough for the local job market. In other words, Việt Kiều while having certain advantages, might also face disadvantages in situations in which they are foreign but not foreign enough. By this he means the visible image of the stereotypical blue-eyed brown-haired foreigner has certain advantages when it comes to playing roles as a foreigner in contemporary Vietnam. He describes a teacher who has a US passport but he is "considered native." That is to say, this foreign teacher is not

> preferred by the teachers or by the parents when it comes to learning English. The parents prefer the full white Caucasian. As he says, 'it's funny, but we work with what the market wants, right.' That is one of the things that is unpredictable. (Interviewer: When you say teacher, do you mean English teacher or do you also mean theological teacher?) Not just that. Not just that. Mathematics, art, literature. Because we're not talking about just pronunciation. We're talking also about the image as well. The schools here would rather have a foreign teacher that looks foreign.

This is a reality that is certainty not unknown to my Việt Kiều respondents. After all, a Việt Kiều respondent and her Caucasian-American husband were invited to teach English at a language school. One needed credentials, the other did not. As he says, "we got busy into teaching English. Nhan, his Việt Kiều wife, is CELTA certified for teaching English. I am Caucasian. That's my certification. Unfortunately, that's all I have in my training for teaching English. But she (school owner) wanted to use us to bring in business." His training or lack thereof is a non-issue. He is a valuable marketing draw as a visible foreigner. He does not have an educational background nor any training. On the other hand, his wife who has a background and training in education, needed to complete a formal CELTA certification program to teach in Vietnam. During my interviews, this dynamic surfaced most often as project participants discussed experiences in the education sector in Vietnam. To what extent it applies to other sectors society is a question that could be explore in more detail in future research.

Returning to Vietnam will be a cross-cultural experience. Time has moved the homeland and people forward. There will be a steep learning curve for any that return. Interviews with local leaders establish that the returnees are welcomed back and can contribute in many ways in their natal homeland. This is meaningful. However, the welcoming posture needs to be understood for what it is and what it is not. To say that the returnees are welcome back is placed within the framework of understanding that it will be a cross-cultural work for returnees and one that drudges up identity issues as the two groups have grown apart over time. The Vietnamese and their diaspora, Vietnamese-Americans, Vietnamese-Germans, Vietnamese-Australians, etc., are distinct groups that share points of connection and disconnection. The posture of a welcoming back stance does ignore these considerable differences.

Looking at all the variables, it becomes clear that this is a complex social setting to navigate for all involved in the relationship. Overseas Vietnamese returning to Vietnam and reestablishing belonging in the natal homeland is a relatively new phenomenon. There is identity and belonging ambiguity on both sides. On one hand, the Việt Kiều are associated with the foreign category. However, they are not like all the other foreigners. They have closer ties with the local people than foreigners of other ethnicities. On the other hand, in some settings, the Việt Kiều might not be the ideal foreigner. They are foreign, but not like other foreigners. They share similarities with local Vietnamese but are clearly not the same as the local Vietnamese. Locals know that their time back in Vietnam will expire at one point or another. They know returnees maintain a belonging outside of Vietnam that cannot be shared with their local friends. When they go on holiday to visit their parents or children, they are going to their diaspora homeland. Their identity and belonging is situated in this third category as seen from the vantage point of local Vietnamese. After all, they are still Việt Kiều. Undoubtedly, this observation fits the lived experiences shared by the Việt Kiều respondents. It is not an easy riddle to solve. This is an area that invites further research.

CHAPTER 6

Summary, Missiological Implications, and Recommendations

Summary

THIS PROJECT HAS INVESTIGATED the experiences of the returning Protestant Christian Vietnamese diaspora community who have returned and reestablished belonging in Vietnam with a missional purpose and the perspective of non-migrant local Protestant Christian leaders. The paper is organized around the discussion of motivations and experiences both those of the returnees and how the local community is experiencing the phenomenon.

It is well documented that the Vietnamese diaspora is returning to the natal homeland in large numbers as the homeland policies have changed in the evolving Doi Moi era. The various layers of transnational ties to the homeland people and places have remained durable over the years of diaspora sojourn, even as the diaspora have settled and established belonging in their adopted homelands. Common motivations discussed in the academy emphasize personal relational reasons for return such as visiting family and friends that remained behind and in response to the emerging economic opportunities in the natal homeland (a preferred pathway of the Hanoi government).

One of the significant findings of this project is that the dimension of religion is seen to be a salient variable for some returnees. Specifically, members of the Vietnamese diaspora community are returning to carry the Christian gospel back to their natal homeland. Some returnees are transnational religious actors having established a regular pattern of returning and ministering in Vietnam while maintaining belonging in the adopted homelands. Others have returned to live once again in their natal homeland. The majority of participants in this study are in the latter category, having returned and reestablished belonging in Vietnam with a missional purpose among other reasons for return.

Moreover, the act of returning with a religious motivation is seen as being part of a larger journey that leads the diaspora to return and reestablish belonging in the natal homeland. In other words, individuals did not necessarily start with a missional vision of life back in Vietnam. The majority of returnees articulated a sense of unfolding movement back towards Vietnam as multiple short trips were taken before they decided to return and reestablish belonging. These trips were discussed as being influential towards the formation and actualization of their eventual return and missional activity, regardless of one's initial stance towards the concept of return. Indeed, many returnees voiced strong stances toward the concept of returning to Vietnam at the start of their journey. The relationship with the historic homeland is complicated, as many of the returnees fled as involuntary migrants. They are refugees or children of the refugees returning 'home'. Three overarching categories describe the returnees' stance toward return: those who always wanted to return, those who never wanted to return, and those who returned from a neutral starting point.

Furthermore, returnees articulated three crucial motivations for coming back. These key attributable motivations are the philanthropist motivation to bestow charitable goodwill, the explicit religious motivation, and how bonds of kinship contributed to the return experience. These three salient motivations served as core impetuses towards return for project respondents. Additionally, these motivations are not mutually exclusive. Most respondents described a combination of all three working to pull them back to return and reestablish belonging in Vietnam. Moreover, it is significant that the non-migrants also perceive these core motivations among the returnees. Furthermore, by and large, they see the motivations to return in a positive light. Language used to describe the motivations pulling the overseas Vietnamese back home is painted in positive terminology. Returnees engaging in religious work in the natal homeland are seen as those with good hearts.

The second research question explores the lived experiences of the diaspora returning to their natal homeland and engaging in Christian ministry. Not only are the salvation and charitable motivations salient motivations for return but they are also powerful determiners of one's mode of

SUMMARY, MISSIOLOGICAL IMPLICATIONS, AND RECOMMENDATIONS

ministry engagement in the homeland. The shape of one's missional action often displays congruency with stated motivations for return. For example, returnees care about spiritual maturity so they eventually land in a discipleship ministry. Others that desire to generate community flourishing, gravitate towards launching a BAM enterprise or undertake a community development project. The ministries of the Protestant Christian Việt Kiều are characterized by three primary ministry clusters or common avenues of ministry engagement. At the same time, it is important to note that ministry foci are not mutually exclusive or fixed. The scope of ministry is fluid and flexible with many variables that contribute to experience. Often one person is involved in many different ministries at different points in time as they have creatively engaged in the homeland. Sometimes primary ministries overlap; sometimes they might be contained to different seasons over the course of their missionary career. The ministry foci are discipleship-centric ministries, community development-centric ministries, and BAM-centric ministries.

While success can be a difficult metric to pin down, it is clear from the narratives of the returnees, and the local leaders, that in their eyes returnees are contributing to the growth of Christianity in Vietnam in many intriguing and tangible ways. People are being discipled, new leaders are being trained, the gospel is being winsomely presented to those that have previously not heard the good news, people are coming to saving faith, drug addicts are receiving treatment, individuals and communities are experiencing the positive impacts of Christian development work, and kingdom-minded business are generating a societal value. There are many inspiring stories of labor bearing fruit. With that stated, it is seen that life and ministry in Vietnam rarely align neatly with expectations and anticipated ministry pathways. Ministry can be messy. Roadblocks are discovered along the way. The pace of ministry flourishing is often portrayed as being painstakingly slow. The conviction that one is called to be back in Vietnam was frequently mentioned as critical to riding out the hard times and disappointments that come with the terrain. Life and ministry do not work the way it did in the West. One might be Vietnamese, but that is not to be equated with ease in returning to live and serve in Vietnam. On the contrary, for many, it adds new layers of complexity to the missionary encounter that will be discussed in the implications. Returning "home" is a cross-cultural experience; one that surfaces many deep and difficult questions. A wide skill set is often drawn upon and honed over time as returnees navigate the cross-culture encounter. Even for those who always wanted to return and thought they knew what they were getting into and returning with clearly articulated ministry goals, the actual experience on the ground has rarely neatly aligned with expectations. Methods often shift along the way as returnees find dissidence as they labor to implement the vision.

As the data demonstrated, the Protestant Christian Vietnamese diaspora community is returning and reestablishing belonging in Vietnam. Evidence is seen for ministry through the diaspora and by and beyond the diaspora as delineated by Wan.[1] The Việt Kiều respondents are ministering to their kinsmen (through the diaspora) and beyond ethnic boundaries as they return to Vietnam (by and beyond the diaspora). Indeed, the majority of respondents actively engage in ministry to ethnic minority populations in Vietnam, while others have this as a core component of their ministry vision. Ministry to Vietnam's ethnic minority populations is prioritized for the majority of the respondents. Not a single respondent in this study narrows their ministry to only serve their fellow kinsmen. Rather, as the data demonstrates, there is an openness to minister to anyone and everyone that God brings into their sphere of influence. In this regard, this is an example of missions by and beyond the diaspora.

Furthermore, individuals and couples returning to Vietnam are amalgamating with existing religious institutions in the homeland when they return. This is a guiding ministry principle for many. They are well aware that the Protestant Church has a long history in Vietnam, and they use language of desiring to complement and join with this movement rather than launch new independent or competing ventures. However, who to work with in the homeland is a zone of many complications and pitfalls. It is noteworthy that the work with religious institutions in the homeland is predominantly outside the space of the legally registered Protestant denominations. Most returnees expressed that they were willing to work with individuals and networks that share their ministry ethos and seem receptive to them. However, they do not always perceive that this ministry value is shared by certain established homeland networks. In practice, the ministry philosophy of returnees tends to gravitate towards casting a wide net. Many returnees do not want the scope of ministry to be limited to one denomination and/or one church, or geographically to one village/city. Furthermore, they are motivated to invest where they observe the greatest need. Functionally, this leads most into the space of unregistered home church networks and

---

1. Wan, *Diaspora Missiology*, 5.

various parachurch ministries laboring to provide theological education and discipleship programs and the like (especially among Vietnam's ethnic minority populations). Most perceive that more established denominations, such as the ECVN South or ECVN North, while it has needs, are not the places of greatest need. This potentially has a significant impact on the further development of the Christian movement in Vietnam. Regardless, working with local faith communities is a priority, but it comes with many complications for returnees as the Protestant Church in Vietnam has its own unique history, idiosyncrasies, power dynamics, and internal debates.

The third research question was addressed in chapter 5. This brought the voice of the local Vietnamese into the conversation as they discussed the phenomenon of return from their perspective. The tides of globalization have washed ashore in Vietnam and local leaders must navigate these choppy uncharted waters as they press on in service. North, Central, South, urban or rural, no space is untouched by global trends. This is their ministry context. The return of their overseas brethren to the rapidly globalizing homeland has not gone unnoticed or without impact. As such, it is significant that they are generally positive toward the phenomenon. By and large, they express stances that welcome back returnees and appreciation for the hearts of the returnees and their contributions. They affirm that the returnees are engaging in many tasks which largely correlate with the primary ministry foci expressed by the returnees.

Constructive wisdom was shared from their vantage point that could potentially enhance the relationship. The themes of ministerial character qualities that the locals desire for the returnees to embody were remarkably consistent among different regions and ministry contexts. Locals know that returnees have gained valuable competencies, and they voiced appreciation for this. These varied skills are needed. However, the overall perception expressed by respondents is that as a group whole, character does not always match the competency of the returnee. They desire to work with returnees for whom competencies are congruent with character. Specifically, the wisdom shared rests upon the stance of relating to the local church and local communities. Namely, locals want to work with returnees who value collaboration, are slow to critique (especially the Church), operate with a philosophy and actions that empower locals, do not insist upon or claim a diaspora status that holds power over a local individual or community, desire to be a blessing, listen and learn from the local context regarding how to best be a blessing, recognize that there will be frustrations along the way and that not all projects will flourish, and know that they are not the same as those that have not embarked on a diaspora sojourn.

A posture of cultural sensitivity is called for in the exchange. Whether one is ministering through the diaspora to fellow Vietnamese in Vietnam, or by and beyond the diaspora to other ethnic groups in Vietnam, it is a cross-cultural task that the returnees are engaging in. Abundant evidence of this was woven throughout the conversations. Experiences that revealed cultural tensions, dynamics of misunderstanding, and language differences between returnees and locals were ubiquitous in the discussions with returnees and local Christians.

Dynamics of cross-cultural tensions are seen in spaces where one might expect to see some complications, such as the thorny practices of economic remittance or money and missions. However, tension points are also seen in seemingly innocuous practices such as returnees traveling, visiting, and observing various local faith communities before they launch their ministry. It is seen that different meanings are attached to the practice. At times, returnees are perceived as holding a posture tilted towards critique of the church in their natal homeland. This is not to say that the local church is perfect. It is simply an acknowledgment that the returning Việt Kiều are semi-outsiders when they return. In working together, local leaders have developed the impression that returnees do not fully understand and appreciate the sociocultural setting. Teaching ministries are one such space that sees this attitude bubble to the surface. Respondents pointed to experiences of returnees teaching in which the timing, content, and pedagogy betray a weak understanding of how to best communicate with the intended audience. Perhaps returnees do not fully take the time to understand what the local church has gone through. As an overseas visitor, the returning Việt Kiều have a certain ascribed status, especially when they are pastors or have had access to theological training in the West. The implementation of this power has sometimes created tensions in church settings as illustrated in the findings.

Nevertheless, the local leaders who participated in this project expressed a desire that more and more returnees would come back and serve in Vietnam. One can do many good things back in Vietnam. The locals who participated in this project affirmed this. There is space for returnees to be woven into the tapestry of ministry in contemporary Vietnam. They have a role to play in God's redemptive mission. This role can be performed in partnership with the local church and in step with other trends fueling the growth of the Vietnamese church.

Missiological Implications

In this section, I will address some of the implications that have surfaced from this project. These implications speak to the practice of Christian missions in the twenty-first century and specifically engage with the construct of diaspora missiology as discussed and promoted by its leading proponents.

First, the diaspora missiology conversation can benefit from a more nuanced and robust understanding of the actual ministry motivations and lived experiences of people in migration. The diaspora missiology conversation is punctuated with passionate excitement as we are living in an era characterized as containing a new and consequential "karios opportunity,"[2] one which is waiting to be seized. Literature leans heavily on inspirational messaging. The Great Commission could be fulfilled if only Christians could see what is occurring and capture a vision to participate. As such, much of the literature takes on a motivational tone. Moreover, diaspora missiology literature tends to myopically highlight ministry to various diaspora communities in the global North and possibly how these diaspora communities need to be mobilized towards missionary engagement. The agency of the diaspora people is underappreciated as diaspora people need our help. Hence, the discourse highlights imagery such as hitting a moving target, borderless ministry/no boundary to worry about, and a ministry focus characterized by a strong integration of evangelism with Christian charity.[3] Ministry is borderless and holistic because people are displaced and we in the West can reach them outside of their traditional homelands, or we can engage in the task of mobilizing migrant workers that are already part of the global workforce to go with a missional vision as in the case of the Filipino overseas workers.[4]

Diaspora missiology aspects might be descriptive of missional praxis for first engagement for Westerners ministering to a diaspora group in the

---

2. Tira, "Diaspora Missiology and the Lausanne Movement," 217.
3. Wan and Tira, "Mission Practice," 48–49.
4. The Global Diaspora Institute has a twofold vision. 1. To equip, connect, resource, and mobilize missional leaders in diaspora communities. 2. To help the North American church to engage with diasporas and the global church (https://wheatonbillygraham.com/institutes/global-diaspora/global-diaspora-institute/).

West (ministry to the diaspora), but as this study demonstrates, this is not representative of ministry by or beyond the diaspora as in the case of the Protestant Christian Việt Kiều that are returning to Vietnam with a missional purpose. It is not representative of the fullness of the multidirectional migration and missions or the complexity and challenges of missionary engagement. In light of this research, this study raises the question of how far diaspora as an overarching framework can take us. The Vietnamese diaspora is one story of migration and missions in the "age of migration."[5] Yet, their lived migratory and missional experiences do not fit with the descriptive paradigm. This suggests a limitation to the framework. Diaspora as an overarching construct might not be the optimal framework for the twenty-first-century phenomenon. The picture that emerges from examining the missionary movement of the Vietnamese diaspora suggests a far more nuanced picture of ministry by and beyond the diaspora than the leading proponents of diaspora missiology imagine. This study would agree with Krabill and Norton's conclusion, "the way diaspora missiology is often described and strategically presented represents a narrow understanding of the significance of migration and missiological reflection and praxis."[6]

On the surface, the diaspora missiology framework fits as the data demonstrates that this is a contemporary story of a diaspora community engaging in missions through and by the diaspora. However, under closer scrutiny, as a diaspora community currently engaged in missionary work, the Việt Kiều, do not neatly fit the diaspora missiology paradigm. The lived ministry experiences, perspectives, conceptualizations, opportunities and challenges, focus, and missional orientation do not neatly fit the descriptive paradigm of the returning Việt Kiều. Moreover, contrary to the working definition, existing networks of friendship and kinship are not significant to the ministry strategy for most of these respondents as they live out missions through the diaspora. Ninety-three percent of returnees did not return to their hometown. The diaspora returns and engages in ministry, yet kinship ties are weak. Moreover, any kinship ties that remain presently durable, can be expected to wane as we move beyond ministry by the first generation. Therefore, as a framework for understanding the returning Vietnamese and their contribution to global missions, diaspora missiology is not the optimal descriptor as the diaspora group under consideration is not operating in ways consistent with the diaspora missiology paradigm.

5. Castles and Miller, *Age of Migration*, 2.
6. Krabill and Norton, "New Wine," 452.

Wan focuses on four aspects of diaspora missiology as a new paradigm to supplement traditional missiology. Wan describes the new paradigm of diaspora missiology using numerous minimally defined terms including, "holistic," "deterritorialization," "glocal," "hybridity," "mutuality & reciprocity," "no boundary to worry about," and "moving targets."[7] By this yardstick, my respondents do not fit the picture. This paradigm is not descriptive of their modus operandi. As noted, most "diaspora missiology" literature is highly idealized at a strategic level of conceptualization. This empirical study of the real experiences on the ground of missions by and beyond the diaspora, while encouraging in many regards, tempers the enthusiasm of the paradigm. It demonstrates a far more complex and messy real-world picture.

While the Việt Kiều are engaging in ministry by and beyond the diaspora, characterizations of the diaspora missiology paradigm are not salient to their lived missional experiences. Data demonstrates that Việt Kiều ministry focus, conceptualization, perspective and orientation are reflective of the paradigm of "traditional missiology" rather than the characterizations associated with the paradigm of "diaspora missiology."[8] For instance, "deterritorialization" is defined simply as "the loss of social and cultural boundaries."[9] As seen in this project, the social and cultural boundaries are most certainly present and highly relevant for the ministry experience of this diaspora community. Evidence was commonly shared that pointed to the dichotomized thinking in the focus and conceptualization of missions, the experiential reality that the concept of nation-state and geo-political boundaries, and that personal cultural identifications remain salient to the encounter. Furthermore, specialization remains high, even as individuals demonstrate engagement in different ministry platforms over the course of their missionary careers. The flow is conceptualized primarily as going in one direction from the West back to Vietnam. Conceptually, Vietnam is the place of mission. Individuals who are going to Vietnam are doing missionary work, especially when they engage in activities traditionally considered missionary work, such as teaching the Bible or evangelistic conversations. Moreover, concepts Wan labels under "traditional missiology"[10] were specifically cited by returnees as motivations for return and as a part of

---

7. Wan, *Diaspora Missiology*, 99.
8. Wan, *Diaspora Missiology*, 98–99.
9. Wan, *Diaspora Missiology*, 99.
10. Wan, *Diaspora Missiology*, 98.

their missionary strategy. For instance, the concept of "unreached people groups"[11] was cited as a salient motivation for many to return to Vietnam and engage in missionary work among the most unreached.

All this suggests, that in this case, this diaspora community engaged in missions through and by and beyond the diaspora, is not operating with the aspects of the different paradigm proposed to supplement "traditional missiology"[12] in the twenty-first century. Admittedly, the peculiarities of living and attempting to serve with the restrictions imposed in contemporary Vietnam factor into this equation. While the door is open for the overseas community to return, homeland policies are designed to weaken religious work and mute any narrative that does not originate from the Party State. Indeed, the lived reality highlights that despite rapid globalization and widespread migration among Vietnamese, national borders and politics are very much alive and well for missionary work amongst this population. For instance, the law of the land discourages integration and holistic work. As returnees in chapter four articulated, a returnee working with a legally recognized Christian charity does not have the freedom to integrate church planting or evangelism into the work. Nevertheless, many respondents regardless of government restrictions, expressed an outlook more closely aligned with the traditional missiology paradigm in this key ministerial perspective. Ministry is often siloed in practice with little evidence of substantial holistic ministry or integrative crossover for most respondents. Some respondents spoke of learning that they need to integrate Christian charity into their evangelism work, but it was spoken of in the context of a hard lesson learned on the ground. Namely, they realized they had to broaden beyond a focus on "saving souls" to see fruit in "saving souls," their core objective. For these workers aspects of Christian charity have become integrated into their practice of evangelism to an extent, but the practice does not have the same integrative weight as in the diaspora missiology paradigm. Most ministry integration that has happened is undertaken to aid in the achievement of the core objective and as a lesson learned rather than functioning as a ministry value. Most remain siloed.

Furthermore, the actual experience on the ground is far closer to that of a traditional missionary. Namely, one is sent to a specific place, they work hard to build relationships, learn the local culture and language, and slowly through much toil God brings about fruit. The picture that emerges

---

11. Wan, *Diaspora Missiology*, 98.
12. Wan, *Diaspora Missiology*, 98.

of the missionary work of the Việt Kiều is that ministry flourishing is a slow gradual process that impacts lasting transformation on an individual and community level. Ministry in Vietnam takes the investment in time. It is not a fast change, even for the returning diaspora. This held true in every region of the country and among respondents engaged in all three ministry platforms. As Kiet says, "you cannot rush it when it comes to work with the church in Vietnam. There are no shortcuts."

Second, the Việt Kiều that have returned are unanimous in the experience that returning to their natal homeland is a cross-cultural experience. A shared heritage does not equate with a serene homecoming experience. Reaching out to fellow kinsmen is just as much a cross-cultural exchange as reaching out to other ethnic groups in Vietnam. Returnees report making cultural blunders, various misunderstandings in ministry and life situations, and needing to devote energy and time to language and cultural learning. As one returnee put it, "in the US, we've worked with the Vietnamese church, but it's very different. Very different. That is Vietnamese-American. This is Vietnamese-Vietnamese. The culture is so different" (Nhân).

Even still, the shared heritage can be helpful in very practical ways as it pertains to cross-cultural adjustment. For instance, the language foundation that exists among the diaspora makes this aspect of adjustment smoother and faster than for the typical foreigner. Indeed, the average returnee in this project reported the equivalent of a third-grade language competency at the point of return to the homeland.[13] As such, it would be a mistake to assume Việt Kiều are bilingual, even as they typically have a significant head start in language acquisition. Moreover, language is fluid rather than fixed. Therefore, even Việt Kiều fluent in Vietnamese will discover some degree of learning is required to engage people in the homeland in Vietnamese. Vietnamese as spoken in Vietnam, has developed significantly since 1975.

Moreover, the act of migration has changed people and their relationship to their homeland people and places. The local Christian leaders are in alignment with this perspective, even as they are keen to welcome

---

13. The United States Department of State Foreign Language Training considers Vietnamese a Category III Language, or a "Hard language"—in this case referring to "Languages with significant linguistic and/or cultural differences from English." This means that one could become proficient in approximately 1,110 classroom hours of study or three years of daily one-hour classroom study (United States Department of State, "Foreign Language Training," paras. 27–28). Almost all returnees reported needing to study the language, but the learning process is significantly easier than it is for the typically monolingual native English speaker.

the diaspora back. Returnees are in their own category: neither foreign nor local. This can be an uncomfortable place to be for several reasons. Deep questions of identity surfaced for most returnees as part of the return journey. For internal harmony and ministry sustainability, one has to work through this dissonance and come to peace with their story, the roles that Việt Kiều can perform effectively, and the group limitations. The riddle of one's identity is not going to be easily solved by returning to the natal homeland. Going back only complicates the picture for most.

This identity riddle is a complex puzzle to solve. There is no one-size-fits-all easy answer. One research project can not presume to untangle all the implications. It can be nuanced and conditional. As this project discovered, there is great diversity within the group collectively labeled Việt Kiều. Simply put, who one is and one's journey cannot, nor should it be erased, as if social or cultural boundaries no longer exist in a globalized world. Ultimately, the dual/third culture, hybrid identity, is emphasized by both returnees and locals. Vietnamese-American, Vietnamese-German, etc. One of the respondents found comfort in her faith as she processed the journey. "He (God) gave me the scripture and He said, 'You know what, your citizenship is in heaven that's who you are.' So from then on, my identity got cleared. I don't define myself as Vietnamese or American, I'm a Vietnamese-American. This is where he's placed me and this is where I am. It's a pretty amazing discovery. Then I have this great sense of peace about it" (Nhân).

Viewing oneself as a bicultural, neither local nor the same as a foreigner can be liberating for the returnee and an essential variable in establishing healthy relationship patterns between the diaspora and local communities. It is part of the sometimes painful journey towards ministry flourishing. Locals expressed a desire for returnees who come to be ready to listen, learn, and collaborate rather than control. They are looking for returnees who return with a spirit of humility—one who does not think too highly of oneself or one's status, a learner's attitude, and are not quick to move towards judgment (particularly of the Church). Anh Dung describes the desired attitude well as he unpacks elements of his ministry ethos, "I want them to look at me as a foreigner, and that I'm not going to be here permanently. I just want to help, leave something here for the church here." He wants to serve and support the local church, not be seen as trying to gain a leadership role because he is not the same as the local leaders who never left. This journey forever marks him as different. He has the self-perception to know that he will not be in Vietnam forever, even as he is fully committed to the ministry in Vietnam in the present moment. From this position of identity self-understanding, he can better support existing ministries and leaders in partnership. The bicultural ministry platform can be powerful when returnees intentionally make it part of their ministry ethos. Humble collaboration, not control, is the preferred ministry model. In practice, this goes both ways. Project participants spoke of patronizing actions from actors on both sides. Self-awareness on the part of the returnee that they are not the same but have valuable things to offer is a good starting point for this cross-cultural ministry relationship. The awareness that returning "home" or ministering to a people that have a shared historical bond comes with its landmines to navigate might help potential missionaries be better aware of what they will be getting into as they embark on their journey. The study also highlights the need for more rigorous training (training in culture, society, communication, missiology, etc.) before returning to Vietnam. A returnee needs this rigorous preparation for the cross-cultural task.

Third, money and missions has long been a topic of keen concern for missiologists.[14] This implication goes beyond the standard breadth of the discussion due to long-established patterns of relating between diaspora and homeland being added into the mix. It is well documented that economic remittance has been a long-standing practice between the diaspora community in the West and family, friends, and others in the homeland. Current government policies further solidify and encourage this dynamic. This has not waned as the homeland has emerged from the crippling poverty of the early reunification years. Transnational relationship patterns are deeply entrenched on both sides.

Most returnees who participated in this project expressed a charitable or humanitarian motivation as a salient motivation to return. This is broadened beyond the micro level of helping immediate kin or personal friends. It is more of a motivational pull towards the people/homeland as a whole. As Ping states, "You saw the need of the country and that was my home country." Ping is speaking of Vietnam in the second decade of the twenty-first century. Vietnam is a rapidly developing emerging economy. Yet, the internalized perception of need in the homeland and a personal obligation to help make a difference is powerful. Nevertheless, the experience of living and working in Vietnam as it pertains to money and ministry and the expectations seemingly baked into the ministry equation is an area

---

14. E.g., Bonk, *Mission and Money*; Rowell, *To Give or Not*; Schwartz, *When Charity Destroys Dignity*; Lederleitner, *Cross-Cultural Partnerships*.

spoken of as one of the greatest frustrations by returnees and local leaders. There is often the perception of a transactional nature of relationships as returnees perceive a dynamic of paying for ministry access. At times returnees expressed perceptions of feeling personally devalued, and their ministry contributions as being devalued, as people are looking at them as an ATM for their livelihoods and personal ministry projects rather than as co-laborers in God's harvest field. The Việt Kiều desire genuine, not transactional relationships in which they perceive that they are chiefly valued for their potential financial remittance. They long to work together with Christians rather than feel as if they have to be on their guard to not be taken advantage of. On the other end, local partners are not always happy with the status quo either. Some expressed concerns of dependency that limits the ability of the Church to flourish, others spoke of the conflicts and various internal and external problems that have sometimes developed when outside money is injected into a community, yet others spoke of givers that are overly controlling so money might not be allocated most beneficially.

Discussions of money are simply unavoidable in cross-cultural missionary work. This case study demonstrated that it is even more complicated when you add long-established transnational remittance patterns into the equation. Future research would benefit from applying this research lens to other diaspora communities. Are there unique money patterns within a diaspora and homeland group that impact the practice of Christian missions? Before one goes back to the historic homeland, the questions of money and how money is conceptualized between homeland and diaspora are important to work through.

Fourth, as attested to in this research, returnees are contributing to the natal homeland in many spaces via the three primary ministry platforms. The data from this project from both the returnees and local partners is clear on this point. The diaspora returning is a meaningful variable contributing to the contours of Christianity in the homeland and measurable economic increase via BAM and various community development ventures. Moreover, returnees are engaging in creative ways often informed by their diaspora sojourn. They have gained valuable competencies through educational and life experiences in the West. They bring who they are back to the homeland in forms of social remittance that are making waves in the homeland. Remittances such as Western-based educational values, theological/discipleship resources, leadership models, and various business practices are forms of social remittance among other forms of remittance that are being brought back into the homeland. This is a case study demonstrating the Christian cross-cultural Christian missionary patterns of one diaspora group.

Yet, at the same time, a word of caution comes from this case study through the counsel of the local partners and is worth reiterating as an implication for those considering returning to their natal homeland. As Toan stated, "Right now, I have seen missionaries who come to Vietnam, make friends, and really are effective at building friendship and then discipleship. But their returns, as in their fruit, is very hard-earned. It could be four years or five years to eventually have a friend who become a Christian or is led to convert." He went on to say that

> the nature of ministry is hard. It's hard to keep giving, giving, giving, giving, and investing until finally it can come to fruition. A lot of people feel discouraged at first. Yeah. Working with returnees is good, but there is also for locals, it's sometimes a challenge. Or they don't realize that it takes a decade or more to invest in something like a country. It would take a lot longer for someone to say that okay, I'm committed to be in Vietnam, and it's going to be two or three decades before I can even start being influential.

This correlates with the narratives told by many of the returnees. Namely, that it is slow to build relationships. It is slow to start ministries. It is slow to establish thriving BAM enterprises. It is slow to disciple. It is slow to work in Vietnam and have an impact. Yet there is evidence of all these things happening. The diaspora is contributing to the homeland. Ministry goals are reported as being in the process of being accomplished, even if they are five or more years behind schedule as some returnees report. Several returnees have stayed well beyond their initial time commitment due largely to the slow and laborious pace of working and seeing change in Vietnam. Flashy events or economic remittances for a building project might produce numbers for a newsletter, but that is not the most meaningful way to build a lasting missionary impact. Count the cost because it is an investment to return and seek to serve in the natal homeland. Ministry to a displaced diaspora group that has recently found its way to an American city is a very different picture of missionary praxis than that which emerges of ministry by and beyond as undertaken by the Vietnamese diaspora. While good things are happening, the picture of excitement that permeates the diaspora missiology literature is not an apt descriptor of ministry though, and by and beyond for the Vietnamese diaspora that have returned to Vietnam in recent years.

Fifth, and finally, one who returns to Vietnam is returning to a Protestant Christian Church ecosystem that has continued to develop. The Protestant Church in Vietnam is exponentially more complex than it was at the time of the waves of Vietnamese emigration. Moreover, most returnees left as young children. As such, most would have only known their local church and related to the Church as a child. Over the years, the Church (Protestant denominations and leaders) have negotiated their place and performed ministry in the context of the Vietnamese State and secular society through decades of repression, turmoil, and changes that have shaped the contemporary sociocultural context. Moreover, as returnees attest, the Vietnamese church that they have returned to is noticeably different than their diaspora churches (even those that came directly from being members and/or leaders of Vietnamese immigrant churches in their diaspora homeland). In this regard, returnees are not returning to their homeland and church family of memory (either their own or the communities' collective memory). It is not just the diaspora that has changed over the years. Diaspora and homeland have grown apart over the years.

This dynamic suggests a need for suspension of judgment and working hard to gain mutual understanding and appreciation of each other. The current relationship could be improved upon. For instance, returnees articulated an overwhelming consensus regarding perceived spiritual maturity in the Vietnamese Church. This perception that the church is weak in maturity or discipleship is shared by workers in all regions of Vietnam. Moreover, returnees frequently used the word "politics" to describe the church and attempts to work with the church and various church networks. Attempting to work with the local church can be messy at times. The Việt Kiều returnees who attempt to work with the church must be prepared to navigate sensitive situations and build up the church rather than partaking. One cannot put oneself or the Vietnamese church up on a pedestal. The church has conflicts and its idiosyncrasies. Therefore, it goes to follow that Việt Kiều perceptions of a local church as lacking spiritual maturity or caught up in messy political in-fighting are received by local Christian leaders. The message, that you (local Vietnamese Christians) are lacking in some capacity, and I (returning Việt Kiều) am here to help, is being received, and is largely unwelcomed. Respondents articulated a sense of perceiving that the diaspora operates from a place of judgmental attitudes while not fully appreciating nor understanding the local sociocultural context.

One returns with a high status, but as a semi-outsider with potentially deep knowledge gaps. Perceptions among local Christians as receiving judgmental attitudes and exchanges that reveal gaps in social and cultural understanding in the cross-cultural missionary encounter are found in many places around the world and well documented in literature. Indeed, missions in a post-colonial world has engaged in a robust discussion of imperialism, paternalism, indigenous leadership, funding structures, and the relationship to Western sending churches for decades.[15] The discussion typically is concerned with "Western foreign missionaries" and "Western missionary organizations" and their relationship to local indigenous churches in the developing world. This study has demonstrated that some of these same concerns can be seen in the relationship between returning diaspora Vietnamese and the local Vietnamese Christian church. The shared heritage does not diminish this. If anything, it might contribute complexity to the relationship due to the hybrid identity. These discussions need to be brought into the space of diaspora missiology. A shared ethnic heritage does not erase the need to have these hard and serious conversations.

Recommendations for Further Research

This study proposes three recommendations for further research. First, this is one case study of one diaspora group presently engaging in missionary work. Similar research could be conducted among other diaspora groups that are engaged in missionary work in their natal homeland to explore their actual motivations and experiences, challenges, and unique opportunities. Gathering empirical data from additional diaspora groups would expand our understanding of the practice of missions in the context of migration in the twenty-first century. Cross-cultural missionary work in the twenty-first century will increasingly reflect the vision of from everywhere to everyone. This study demonstrates that who one is and one's unique journey is still relevant to this picture. If anything, it demands that the missiologist and practitioner think harder about what it means to be a representative of the Kingdom of God in the world in which we live. The Việt Kiều hold their own unique story of diaspora sojourn, motivation to return, ministry experiences, and lessons. Nonetheless, their story has implications for missions in the globalized world that reverberate beyond

---

15. E.g., Scherer, *Missionary, Go Home!*; Smith et al., *Evangelical Postcolonial Conversations*.

the boundaries of this specific diaspora community and their missionary work in Vietnam. Data from other diaspora communities will add to the research footprint as missiologists gain a clearer picture of the paradigm of twenty-first-century missions.

Second, this study was primarily concerned with the micro-level, the level of individuals and couples involved in transnational religious work. Further research could be conducted within the same diaspora group that explores the meso-level,[16] the level of religious institutions, to add texture to the context of contemporary missions work in Vietnam. Case studies could be done more directly with Vietnamese organizations in the West and their transnational religious partnerships in the homeland. For example, there are findings presented in this paper that come from interviews conducted with individuals at a drug rehab ministry center. This center has a robust partnership with an association of Vietnamese churches in the United States. This level of the transnational religious group partnership could be explored to aid the understanding of the practice of diaspora missiology. The various diaspora religious associations working to support ministries such as the drug rehab centers would enhance the picture of how this ministry and others like it have grown in recent years.

Third, this study focused on ethnically Viet Protestant Christians ministering in the natal homeland. The research lens could be expanded to explore three related avenues of research that were not explored in this project. Each of these avenues deserves empirical attention. Exploring these avenues of research would add further texture to the emerging picture of the phenomenon of ministry through the Vietnamese diaspora. First, Catholic Vietnamese, while making up the majority of Christians in Vietnam were not considered in this research. Are diaspora Catholics returning for similar reasons as the Protestants? If so, what are their transnational patterns and ministry outlets in the homeland? What are their challenges and contributions? Second, there are significant populations of Vietnamese ethnic minority groups that constitute diasporas and have settled and established belonging in the global West. This research could be replicated among groups such as the Hmong who have also returned to Vietnam with missionary intentions. Lastly, the study located diaspora ministry within the historic homeland. However, the scope of the Vietnamese Protestant Christian diaspora in ministry is not limited to the geographical boundaries of Vietnam. For instance, to enhance the comprehensive understanding

---

16. Biney, "Transnational Religious Networks," 286.

of ministry through the Vietnamese diaspora, one could explore ministry such as that which takes place to the displaced diaspora that settled in Cambodia. Vietnamese constitute approximately 4–5 percent of the population in Cambodia. Moreover, the experiences of the diaspora that has settled in the West and those that have remained in Cambodia are vastly different.[17] Would similar ministry platforms be discovered for ministry in that context? Examination along each of these three lines of research inquiry would aid in adding further texture to the understanding of diaspora ministry in our contemporary global village.

Conclusion

The many layers of implications of ministry to everyone from everywhere need to be teased out in the individual lives of those who are participating in this global current of movement. It is probable that the phenomenon of missions and migration will only increase as we move deeper into the twenty-first century. The inspirational statements circulated in the literature are perhaps acceptable starting points in the conversation that is attempting to rally a local church to action. However, as missiologists, we need to move beyond the current rhetoric to think harder and imagine the true opportunities and limitations that the phenomenon of mass migration places upon Christian missions. It is not enough to simply say that people are on the move. We can and ought to think harder about a theology of migration that contextually lands in the twenty-first century and speaks to the actual experiences of the people on the move, the communities that receive them, and those that they leave behind. This dissertation is one attempt to speak into the conversation. This study looked at one specific diaspora community from the global West that has returned to their natal homeland in recent years. For the Vietnamese, this is an ongoing movement as the diaspora and the homeland continue to progress. The story can continue to be followed as the next chapter(s) is written by the diaspora and Vietnamese in Vietnam.

---

17. Around 90 percent of ethnic Vietnamese do not have birth certificates and/or identity cards. They are Stateless. The Vietnamese often live in dire poverty faced with a history of genocide, persecution, forced displacement and discrimination by successive regimes and administrations. Minority Rights Group, "Ethnic Vietnamese in Cambodia."

Appendix 1
Table of Interviewees

Pseudonym	Vietnamese migration status classification	Primary ministry location	Core ministry classification	Specialized training	Immigration generation classification	Age range at the time of the interview
Dao	Việt Kiều Returnee	South	BAM	Graphic design college degree No cross-cultural or theological training	1st	30–35
Van	Việt Kiều Returnee	Central	Discipleship	Theological education	1st	45–50
Tuan	Việt Kiều Returnee	South	BAM	MBA	2nd (although he lived in Vietnam for four years as a youth)	30–35
Yên	Việt Kiều Returnee	Central	BAM		1st	
Cau	Việt Kiều Returnee	South	BAM	College business degree	1st	40–45
Kiet	Việt Kiều Transnational	South	Discipleship	Training from his church	1st	50–55

APPENDIX 1

Liêm	Việt Kiều Transnational	South	Discipleship	Pastor; BA Biblical studies	1st	55–60
Nhân	Việt Kiều Returnee	South	BAM	Education training	1st	45–50
Quyen	Việt Kiều Returnee	South	Discipleship and BAM	In-house church discipleship program; missionary practicum	1st	45–50
Mai	Việt Kiều Returnee	South	Community development	Education research degree; some seminars from her missions agency	2nd	30–35
Ha	Việt Kiều Returnee	South	Discipleship	Ministry experience and some training in seminary	1st	55–60
Bing	Việt Kiều Returnee	South	Discipleship	Business training; ministry experience and some training in seminary	1st	60–65
Lan	Việt Kiều Returnee	Central	Community development	Personal experience	1st	55–60
Hùng	Việt Kiều Returnee	North	Discipleship	Ordained pastor; degree from a Bible college	1st	45–50

TABLE OF INTERVIEWEES

Vy	Việt Kiều Transnational	South/Central	Community development	none	1st	60–65
Anh Dung	Việt Kiều Returnee	North	Discipleship	Master of Divinity; International worker with his missionary organization	1st	55–60
Diệu	Việt Kiều Returnee	North	Community development	International worker with her missionary organization	1st	
Ping	Việt Kiều Returnee	South	BAM	Social emotional counseling degree	1st	30–35
	Việt Kiều Returnee	Central	Discipleship	Three-year church-based Bible training program	1st	50–55
Bach	Việt Kiều Returnee	Central	Discipleship	Three-year church-based Bible training program	1st	55–60
Vien	Việt Kiều Transnational	South	Discipleship	Pastor; Bible and theology degree	1st	60–64
Thuc	Việt Kiều Returnee	North	Discipleship	Theological training	2nd	35–40

APPENDIX 1

Tai	Việt Kiều Returnee	North	Community development	none	1st	30–35
Sơn	Việt Kiều Returnee	North	Discipleship	None	2nd	25–30
Hieu	Vietnamese Local	South	Discipleship	Theological training		35–40
Thang	Vietnamese Local	Central	Discipleship			35–40
Hoa	Vietnamese Local	Central	Discipleship			35–40
Quy	Vietnamese Local	North	Discipleship			30–35
Toan	Vietnamese Local	South	Discipleship	Theological training		35–40
Hue	Vietnamese Local	North	Discipleship			25–30
Thi	Vietnamese Local	North	Discipleship			25–30

Appendix 2
Interview Protocol: Vietnamese Diaspora

1. Describe your journey in deciding to return to Vietnam. Tell me about why you decided to return and why you are returning at this time in your life.
2. What are some of the goals that you had as you returned? What keeps you coming back?
3. How do you describe that decision to your family and friends in the diaspora community? How did they respond as you discussed your plans to return to Vietnam?
4. Have you received any training or particular preparation for your ministry in Vietnam? If so please describe it. How does your organization train others for ministry in Vietnam? If you were leading a training session for new missionaries, what would you include in the session? Why?
5. Tell me the story of your first trip to Vietnam. What are you doing differently now?
6. Tell me about your approach to initiating ministry in Vietnam.
7. Describe how you decided who you will work with in ministry in Vietnam. Can you give an example?
8. Have people or ministries chosen not to work with you (or your organization) in partnerships? If so, why do you think that has happened? How was this communicated?
9. How are ministry decisions made? Tell me a story about this process.
10. What have been some of the highlights of your return experiences, particularly as they relate to ministry engagement?

11. Describe something that has been disappointing and/or unexpected in your return experience. Why do you think this happened? What lessons did it teach you?

12. What has surprised you about Vietnam as you have returned and engaged in life and ministry in Vietnam?

13. Describe your ministry. Who do you minister to? What does the rhythm of your ministry life look like?

14. What have been some ministry highlights? Tell me about some unexpected positives experience as it relates to life and ministry in Vietnam. Why are these highlights? Why do you think this happened?

15. What have been some hard challenges you have encountered in ministry? Tell me about some unexpected challenges to as it relates to life and ministry in Vietnam. How is this different than what you expected prior to return?

16. When you have faced challenges in life and ministry, how have you adapted? What are the most important lessons that you have learned?

17. Tell me about what you envisioned ministry to be like before you returned. How much of that has been realized?

18. How do you feel you have been received by the local Vietnamese? Is there a difference between Christian Vietnamese and non-Christian Vietnamese? Can you give an example?

19. Are you personally supported by individuals, churches, or organization in the West? If so, how do they support you? What have you observed?

20. Has financial assistance happened as you have served in ministry in Vietnam? If so, is this a one-time occurrence, or is this reoccurring? What have you observed?

21. What are a few things you know now that you wish you would have learned prior to your initial return?

22. Has there been any points of tension or misunderstanding while working with local churches and ministry networks? If so, how has conflict been addressed? Why do you think the tension happened?

Appendix 3
Interview Protocol: Vietnamese Local Leaders

1. Tell me some stories about the returning Christian diaspora.
2. What has been your experience working with the returnees? Can you give an example?
3. Tell me about some ministry highlights in working with Christian diaspora believers?
4. Tell me about some challenges in the open-door era in working with the Christian returnees?
5. Do you feel the returnees are helpful in the growth of the church in Vietnam? How so?
6. Have there been any points of tension or misunderstanding while working with diaspora believers? If so, how has conflict been addressed? Why do you think the tension happened?
7. Is your ministry receiving money from abroad? If so, what have you observed?
8. Describe how you decided who you will work with in ministry in Vietnam? Are there Christian returnees whom you opt not to work with? If so, why?
9. How do you decide what to do together?
10. Who typically leads ministry events? How was this decided upon?
11. What do you wish the Christian returnees knew about life and ministry in Vietnam? What can be done to improve this?
12. How has your church or ministry changed since you started working with the Christian returnees?

Appendix 4
Letter to Invite Project Participants

Dear _____,

I trust this letter finds you well. I am writing to invite you to participate in a research study exploring the experiences of Protestant Christian diaspora Vietnamese who have returned to Vietnam for ministry-related purposes among other reasons. I want to thank you in advance for considering being a study participant; your input is valuable and critical to this study. This study is being conducted by me, Bryan Woods. I am a PhD Intercultural Studies candidate at Trinity Evangelical Divinity School in Deerfield, IL. I am writing to you at the recommendation of _____.

The research study in which you are invited to participate is designed to explore the experience of Protestant Christian diaspora Vietnamese that have returned to Vietnam for ministry-related purposes among other reasons. I will be looking at motivation, transnational networks, experiences and challenges in ministry, places of impact, and contribution to the growth of the Church in Vietnam within the framework of diaspora missiology.

I will be conducting interviews in Vietnam with returnees this July and August 2019. I will be in Hanoi for interviews from July 12th through the 19th. I will be in traveling in the Central and Southern regions of Vietnam from July 20th to August 8th.

Perhaps you know someone who fits this criteria and would potentially be interested in participating in this project? You might know Việt Kiều residing in the States and/or Việt Kiều returnees who it would be great to connect with while I am in Vietnam. Please know that every reasonable precaution will be taken. No names, locations or other identifying details will be used as per the protocol.

Thank you for taking the time to consider this letter.

Please let me know if you have any questions about the nature of this project.

I look forward to hearing from you.

Grace & Peace,

Bryan Woods
Intercultural Studies, PhD Candidate
PhD Programs Coordinator
Academic Doctoral Office
Trinity Evangelical Divinity School

Appendix 5

Protestant Christian Diaspora Returnees Pre-Interview Questionnaire

Instructions: Thank you for your willingness to participate in this research project. The purpose of this research is to explore the experiences of the Protestant Christian diaspora Vietnamese who have returned to Vietnam for ministry-related purposes among other reasons. This is a short pre-interview questionnaire to help facilitate a productive interview discussion. Please answer the questions below in the "comments" box, save, and return the completed questionnaire to me via email at bmwoods@tiu.edu prior to our interview time.

1. I would describe myself as a member of the Vietnamese diaspora?
    a. Yes
    b. No
    c. [Comments]
2. What is your age? [Comments]
3. Did you become a believer in Vietnam or after arriving in the States?
    a. In Vietnam
    b. After arriving in the States
    c. [Comments]
4. When did you first return to Vietnam? [Comments]

5. How many trips have you taken to Vietnam?

    a. I have not taken any trips to Vietnam

    b. 2–4 trips

    c. 5–6 trips

    d. More than 7 trips

    e. [Comments]

6. Do you travel to Vietnam with an organization or church? If so, please list the name(s) of the organization/church. [Comments]

7. Do you work with organizations or churches in Vietnam? If so, please list the partner(s) you work with. [Comments]

Appendix 6
Letter of Informed Consent

Thank you for your willingness to participate in this research. My name is Bryan Woods. I am associated with Trinity International University, where I am a PhD candidate. I am conducting research with the purpose to investigate and understand the experiences of the returning Protestant Christian Việt Kiều to Vietnam. I am speaking with Vietnamese from the diaspora community who are returning to Vietnam for ministry-related purposes among other reasons. I would like to ask you to assist in this research by answering questions about your experiences.

Please understand that your participation in this research is totally voluntary. You do not have to meet with me if you do not want to. If at any time during our meeting you want to stop, you are free to stop without needing to give any reason. I will then delete your information and not use any of it my research. The discussion will be audio-recorded, which will be deleted after the research project is completed. You may also request that the recording be paused at any time.

I want you to know that information you provide is confidential. It will not be shared with others. It is only for the purpose of this study. Your name, associated ministries and locations will not be reported in my writing.

LETTER OF INFORMED CONSENT

Thank you once again for participating in this research.

"I acknowledge that I have been informed of, and understand, the nature and purpose of this study and I freely consent to participate."

Name: _____

Date: _____

Bibliography

Ajani, Ezekiel. "Migration and Mission: An Exploration of the Mission Understanding and Activities of the Redeemed Christian Church of God, Jesus House Chicago." PhD diss., Trinity International University, 2015.
Anh, Dang Nguyen. "Enhancing the Development Impact of Migrant Remittances and Diaspora: The Case of Viet Nam." *Asia-Pacific Population Journal* 20:3 (2005) 111–22.
Ashcroft, Bill, et al. "Introduction to Part Sixteen." In *The Post-Colonial Studies Reader*, edited by Bill Ashcroft et al., 425–28. 2nd ed. New York: Routledge, 2006.
Babbie, Earl R. *The Practice of Social Research*. 14th ed. Boston: Cengage Learning, 2016.
Bellofatto, Gina, and Todd Johnson. "Key Findings of Christianity in Its Global Context, 1970–2020." *International Bulletin of Missionary Research* 37:3 (2013) 157–64.
Bernard, H. Russell. *Research Methods in Anthropology: Qualitative and Quantitative Approaches*. 4th ed. Lanham, MD: AltaMira, 2006.
Biney, Moses. "Transnational Religious Networks: From Africa to America and Back to Africa." In *Christianities in Migration: The Global Perspective*, edited by Elaine Padilla and Peter Phan, 281–98. New York: Palgrave Macmillan, 2016.
Bonk, Jon. *Missions and Money: Affluence as a Missionary Problem—Revisited*. Rev. and exp. ed. Maryknoll, NY: Orbis, 2006.
Bouquet, Mathieu, "Vietnamese Party-State and Religious Pluralism since 1986: Building the Fatherland?" *Sojourn: Journal of Social Issues in Southeast Asia* 25:1 (2010) 90–108.
Bradley, Mark. *Vietnam at War*. New York: Oxford University Press, 2009.
Brinkmann, Svend, and Steinar Kvale. *Doing Interviews*. 2nd ed. Los Angeles: Sage, 2018.
Bui, Long T. *Returns of War: South Vietnam and the Price of Refugee Memory*. New York: New York University Press, 2018.
Caldwell, Larry. "Diaspora Ministry in the Book of Acts: Insights from Two Speeches of the Apostle Paul to Help Guide Diaspora Ministry Today." In *Diaspora Missions: Reflections on Reaching the Scattered Peoples of the World*, edited by Michael Pocock and Enoch Wan, 91–106. Pasadena, CA: William Carey Library, 2015.
Cannon, Alexander. "Introduction: Epic Directions for the Study of the Vietnamese Diaspora." *Journal of Vietnamese Studies* 7:3 (2012) 1–6.
Carroll, Daniel. "Biblical Perspectives on Migration and Mission: Contributions from the Old Testament." *Mission Studies* 30:1 (2013) 9–26.
Carruthers, Ashley. "Saigon from the Diaspora." *Singapore Journal of Tropical Geography* 29:1 (2008) 68–86.
Casino, Tereso. "Why People Move: A Prolegomenon to Diaspora Missiology." *Torch Trinity Journal* 13:1 (2010) 19–44.

BIBLIOGRAPHY

Castles, Stephen, and Mark Miller. *The Age of Migration: International Population Movements in the Modern World.* 4th ed. New York: Guilford, 2009.

Chan, Kwok Bun, and Kenneth Christie. "Past, Present and Future: The Indochinese Refugee Experience Twenty Years Later." *Journal of Refugee Studies* 8:1 (1995) 75–94.

Chan, Yuk Wah, and Thi Le Thu Tran. "Recycling Migration and Changing Nationalisms: The Vietnamese Return Diaspora and Reconstruction of Vietnamese Nationhood." *Journal of Ethnic and Migration Studies* 37:7 (2011) 1101–17.

Chan, Yuk Wah. "Hybrid Diaspora and Identity Laundering: A Study of the Return Overseas Chinese Vietnamese in Vietnam." *Asian Ethnicity* 14:4 (2013) 525–41.

Chapman, John. "The 2005 Pilgrimage and Return to Vietnam of the Exiled Zen Master Thich Nhat Hanh in Hoi An." In *Modernity and Re-Enchantment: Religion in Post-Revolutionary Vietnam*, edited by Philip Taylor, 297–341. Lanham, MD: Lexington, 2007.

Cohen, Robin. *Global Diasporas: An Introduction.* London: UCL Press Limited, 1997.

Cowles, Robert. *Operation Heartbeat.* Harrisburg, PA: Christian Publications, 1976.

Downes, Stan. "Mission by and beyond the Diaspora: Partnering with Diaspora Believers to Reach Other Immigrants and the Local People." In *Diaspora Missions: Reflections on Reaching the Scattered Peoples of the World*, edited by Michael Pocock and Enoch Wan, 77–88. Pasadena, CA: William Carey Library, 2015.

Ebaugh, Helen Rose, and Janet Saltzman Chafetz. *Religion across Borders: Transnational Immigrant Networks.* Walnut Creek, CA: AltaMira, 2002.

Eisner, Rivka Syd. *Performing Remembering: Women's Memories of War in Vietnam.* Cham, Switz.: Palgrave Macmillan, 2018.

Engelbert, Thomas, ed. *Vietnam's Ethnic and Religious Minorities: A Historical Perspective.* Frankfurt am Main, Germ.: Peter Lang, 2016

Faist, Thomas. "Diaspora and Transnationalism: What Kind of Dance Partners?" In *Diaspora and Transnationalism: Concepts, Theories and Methods*, edited by Rainer Bauböck and Thomas Faist, 9–34. Amsterdam, The Netherlands: Amsterdam University Press, 2010.

Feener, Michael R. "Official Religions, State Secularism, and the Structures of Religious Pluralism." In *Proselytizing and the Limits of Religious Pluralism in Contemporary Asia*, edited by Juliana Finucane and Michael R. Feener, 1–14. Singapore: National University of Singapore, 2014.

Freston, Paul. "Globalization, Religion, and Evangelical Christianity: A Sociological Meditation from the Third World." In *Interpreting Contemporary Christianity: Global Processes and Local Identities*, edited by Ogbu Kalu, 24–52. Grand Rapids, MI: Eerdmans, 2008.

———. "Globalization, Religion, and Evangelical Christianity: A Sociological Meditation from the Third World." In *Religion and Globalization: Critical Concepts in Social Studies*, edited by Veronique Altglas, 59–83. New York: Routledge, 2011.

George, Sam. "Diaspora: A Hidden Link to 'From Everywhere to Everywhere' Missiology." *Missiology* 39:1 (2011) 45–56.

Greenham, Ant. *Muslim Conversions to Christ: An Investigation of Palestinian Converts Living in the Holy Land.* Pasadena, CA: William Carey International University Press, 2011.

Hanciles, Jehu J. *Beyond Christendom: Globalization, African Migration, and the Transformation of the West.* Maryknoll, NY: Orbis, 2008.

Hannah, Joseph. "The Mutual Colonization of State and Civil Society Organizations." In *Vietnam in Local Organizations and Urban Governance in East and Southeast Asia*, edited by Benjamin Read and Robert Pekkanen, 84–100. New York: Routhledge, 2009.

Hansen, Peter. "The Vietnamese State, the Catholic Church and the Law." In *Asian Socialism and Legal Change: The Dynamics of Vietnamese and Chinese Reform*, edited by John Gillespie and Pip Nicholas, 310–34. Canberra, Australia: Australian National University E Press, 2005.

Ha, Thao. "Evolution of Remittances from Family to Faith: The Vietnamese Case." In *Religion Across Borders: Transnational Immigrant Networks*, edited by Helen Rose Ebaugh and Janet Saltzman Chafetz, 111–28. Walnut Creek, CA: Altamira, 2002.

Hoang, Chung Van. *New Religions and the State's Response to Religious Diversification in Contemporary Vietnam*. Cham, Switz.: Springer, 2017.

Hoke, Donald, ed. *The Church in Asia*. Chicago: Moody, 1975.

Hostetter, Doug. "After the Debris Is Cleared: The Church in Post-Revolutionary Vietnam and Cuba." *Sojourners* 7:9 (1978) 20–23.

Im, Chandler H., and Amos Yong, eds. *Global Diasporas and Mission*. Eugene, OR: Wipf & Stock, 2014.

Jellema, Kate. "Returning Home: Ancestor Veneration and the Nationalism of Doi Moi Vietnam." In *Modernity and Re-Enchantment: Religion in Post-Revolutionary Vietnam*, edited by Philip Taylor, 57–89. Lanham, MD: Lexington, 2007.

Kelly, Michael. *On the Edge: Religious Freedom and Persecution across Asia*. Hindmarsh, Australia: ATF Asia, 2016.

Koh, Priscilla. "You Can Come Home Again: Narratives of Home and Belonging among Second-Generation Viet Kieu in Vietnam." *SOJOURN: Journal of Social Issues in Southeast Asia* 30:1 (2015) 173–214.

Kort, Michael. *The Vietnam War Reexamined*. Cambridge: Cambridge University Press, 2018.

Krabill, Matthew, and Allison Norton. "New Wine in Old Wineskins: A Critical Appraisal of Diaspora Missiology." *Missiology* 43:4 (2015) 442–55.

Laderman, Scott, and Edwin A. Martini. *Four Decades On: Vietnam, the United States, and the Legacies of the Second Indochina War*. Durham, NC: Duke University Press, 2013.

Lam, Andrew. *Perfume Dreams: Reflections on the Vietnamese Diaspora*. Berkeley, CA: Heyday, 2005.

Lausanne Movement. "Business as Mission: Business for God's Glory, the Gospel, and the Common Good." https://lausanne.org/networks/issues/business-as-mission.

———. "Diasporas and International Students: The People Next Door." Lausanne Occasional Paper no. 55, 2005. https://lausanne.org/content/lop/diasporas-and-international-students-the-new-people-next-door-lop-55.

LCWE Diaspora Educators Consultation. "The Seoul Declaration on Diaspora Missiology." https://lausanne.org/content/statement/the-seoul-declaration-on-diaspora-missiology.

Lederleitner, Mary T. *Cross-Cultural Partnerships: Navigating the Complexities of Money and Mission*. Downers Grove, IL: InterVarsity, 2010.

Le, Dung Thien. "The Bamboo Cross: Toward a Vietnamese Theology and Christian Educational Ministry in Vietnam." DMin diss., School of Theology at Claremont, 1994.

Lee, Sue-Im. "We Are Not the World: Global Village, Universalism, and Karen Tei Yamashita's 'Tropic of Orange.'" *Modern Fiction Studies* 53:3 (2007) 501–27.

Lê, Phu Hoang. *A Short History of the Evangelical Church of Viet Nam (1911–1965)*. New York: New York University, 1972.

Le, Vince. "The Pentecostal Movement in Vietnam." In *Global Renewal Christianity: Spirit-Empowered Movements Past, Present, and Future: Vol. 1, Asia and Oceania*, edited by Vinson Synan and Amos Yong, 181–95. Lake Mary, FL: Charisma, 2016.

———. *Vietnamese Evangelicals and Pentecostalism: The Politics of Divine Intervention*. Boston: Brill, 2019.

Levitt, Peggy. "Religion on the Move: Mapping Global Cultural Production and Consumption." In *Religion on the Edge: De-Centering and Re-Centering the Sociology of Religion*, edited by Courtney Bender et al., 159–78. New York: Oxford University Press, 2013.

———. "Transnationalism." In *Diasporas: Concepts, Intersections, Identities*, edited by Kim Knott and Sean McLoughlin, 39–44. London: Bloomsbury Academic & Professional, 2010.

———. *The Transnational Villagers*. Los Angeles: University of California Press, 2001.

Lieu, Nhi. *The American Dream in Vietnamese*. Minneapolis: University of Minnesota Press, 2011.

Long, Lynellyn D. "Viet Kieu on a Fast Track Back?" In *Coming Home? Refugees, Migrants, and Those Who Stayed Behind*, edited by Lynellyn D. Long and Ellen Oxfeld, 65–89. Philadelphia: University of Pennsylvania Press, 2004.

Louis-Jacques, Dorais. "Defining the Overseas Vietnamese." *Diaspora: A Journal of Transnational Studies* 10:1 (2001) 3–27.

———. "Politics, Kinship, and Ancestors: Some Diasporic Dimensions of the Vietnamese Experience in North America." *Journal of Vietnamese Studies* 5:2 (2010) 91–132.

Maxwell, Joseph. *Qualitative Research Design: An Interactive Approach*. 3rd ed. Thousand Oaks, CA: Sage, 2013.

Merriam, Sharon, and Elizabeth Tisdell. *Qualitative Research: A Guide to Design and Implementation*. 4th ed. San Francisco: Jossey-Bass, 2016.

Minority Rights Group. "Ethnic Vietnamese in Cambodia." https://minorityrights.org/minorities/ethnic-vietnamese/?utm_campaign=shareaholic&utm_medium=printfriendly&utm_source=tool.

Ngo, Tam Thi Thanh. "Ethnic and Transnational Dimensions of Recent Protestant Conversion Among the Hmong in Northern Vietnam." *Social Compass* 57:3 (2010) 332–44.

———. *The New Way: Protestantism and the Hmong in Vietnam*. Seattle, WA: University of Washington Press, 2016.

Nguyen-Akbar, Mytoan. "Finding the American Dream Abroad? Narratives of Return Among 1.5 and Second Generation Vietnamese American Skilled Migrants in Vietnam." *Journal of Vietnamese Studies* 11:2 (2016) 96–121.

Nguyen, Nathalie Huynh Chau. *Memory Is Another Country: Women of the Vietnamese Diaspora*. Santa Barbara, CA: Praeger, 2009.

Nguyen, Tien. "Vietnam and Its Diaspora: An Evolving Relationship." In *Emigration and Diaspora Policies in the Age of Mobility*, edited by Agnieszka Weinar, 239–56. Cham, Switz.: Springer, 2017.

Nguyen, Van Thanh, and John Prior. *God's People on the Move: Biblical and Global Perspectives on Migration and Mission*. Eugene, OR: Pickwick, 2014.

BIBLIOGRAPHY

Nguyen, X. Vinh. "A Contextualized Model for Small Groups to Bring about Spiritual Renewal and Awakening in the Evangelical Church of Danang, Vietnam." DMin diss., Regent University, 2013.

Ott, Craig. "Diaspora and Relocation as Divine Impetus for Witness in the Early Church." In *Diaspora Missiology: Theory, Methodology, and Practice*, edited by Enoch Wan, 73–96. Portland, OR: Institute of Diaspora Studies, 2011.

Payne, Jervis David. *Strangers Next Door: Immigration, Migration and Mission*. Downers Grove, IL: InterVarsity, 2012.

Pham, Andrew T. "The Returning Diaspora: Analyzing Overseas Vietnamese (Viet Kieu) Contributions toward Vietnam's Economic Growth." https://depocen.org/wp-content/uploads/2022/07/VK-contributions-to-VN-growth_APham_DEPOCENWP.pdf.

Pham, Andrew X. *Catfish and Mandala: A Two-Wheeled Voyage through the Landscape and Memory of Vietnam*. 1st ed. New York: Farrar, Straus & Giroux, 1999.

Phan, Peter. "Christianity as an Institutional Migrant: Historical, Theological, and Ethical Perspectives." In *Christianities in Migration: The Global Perspective*, edited by Elaine Padilla and Peter Phan, 9–35. New York: Palgrave Macmillan, 2016.

———. "Christianity in Vietnam Today (1975–2013): Contemporary Challenges and Opportunities," *International Journal for the Study of the Christian Church* 14:1 (2014) 3–21.

———. "The Dragon and the Eagle: Toward a Vietnamese American Theology." In *Asian American Christianity Reader*, edited by Viji. Nakka-Cammauf and Timothy Tseng, 313–31. Castro Valley, CA: The Institute for the Study of Asian American Christianity, 2009.

———. "Vietnam, Cambodia, Laos, Thailand." In *Christianities in Asia*, edited by Peter C> Phan, 129–48. Malden, MA: Wiley-Blackwell, 2011.

Phuoc, Nghia Huynh. "Marketing in Vietnam." In *The Economy and Business Environment of Vietnam*, edited by Roderick Macdonald, 93–111. Cham, Switz.: Palgrave Macmillan, 2020.

Pocock, Michael. "Global Migration: Where Do We Stand?" In *Diaspora Missions: Reflections on Reaching the Scattered Peoples of the World*, edited by Michael Pocock and Enoch Wan, 3–20. Pasadena, CA: William Carey Library, 2015.

Reed-Danahay, Deborah. "'Like a Foreigner in My Own Homeland': Writing the Dilemmas of Return in the Vietnamese American Diaspora." *Identities* 22:5 (2015) 603–18.

Reimer, Reg. *Vietnam's Christians: A Century of Growth in Adversity*. Pasadena, CA: William Carey Library, 2011.

Roeck, Rene. "Vietnam, Cambodia and Laos: The Church at the Crossroads of Chaos." In *Christ and Crisis in Southeast Asia*, edited by Gerald H. Anderson, 55–80. New York: Friendship, 1968.

Rowell, John. *To Give or Not to Give? Rethinking Dependency, Restoring Generosity, & Redefining Sustainability*. Tyrone, GA: Authentic, 2006.

Rushdie, Salman. "Imaginary Homelands." In *The Post-Colonial Studies Reader*, edited by Bill Ashcroft et al., 428–34. 2nd ed. New York: Routledge, 2006.

Rutledge, Paul James. *The Vietnamese Experience in America*. Bloomington, IN: Indiana University Press, 1992.

Salemink, Oscar. "Is Protestant Conversion a Form of Protest? Urban and Upland Protestants in Southeast Asia." In *Christianity and the State in Asia: Complicity and*

Conflict, edited by Julius Bautista and Francis Khek Gee Lim, 36–58. New York: Routledge, 2009.

Santos, Narry. "Diaspora in the New Testament and Its Impact on Christian Mission." *Torch Trinity Journal* 13:1 (2010) 3–18.

———. "Exploring the Major Dispersion Terms and Realities in the Bible." In *Diaspora Missiology: Theory, Methodology, and Practice*, edited by Enoch Wan, 21–38. Portland, OR: Institute of Diaspora Studies, 2011.

Scherer, James. *Missionary, Go Home! A Reappraisal of the Christian World Mission*. Englewood Cliffs, NJ: Prentice-Hall, 1964.

Schlecker, Markus. "Apparitions of Sapiocracy: Vietnam's Emergent Welfare State and the Restless Dead of Thanh Ha." In *Southeast Asian Perspectives on Power*, edited by Liana Chua et al., 151–64. New York: Routledge, 2012.

Schwartz, Glenn. *When Charity Destroys Dignity: Overcoming Unhealthy Dependency in the Christian Movement*. Bloomington, IN: AuthorHouse, 2007.

Schwenkel, Christina. *The American War in Contemporary Vietnam: Transnational Remembrance and Representation*. Bloomington, IN: Indiana University Press, 2009.

Senior, Donald. "Beloved Aliens and Exiles: New Testament Perspectives on Migration." In *A Promised Land, a Perilous Journey: Theological Perspectives on Migration*, edited by Daniel Groody and Gioacchino Campese, 20–34. Notre Dame, IN: University of Notre Dame Press, 2008.

Small, Ivan. *Currencies of Imagination: Channeling Money and Chasing Mobility in Vietnam*. Ithaca, NY: Cornell University Press, 2018.

———. "Embodied Economies: Vietnamese Transnational Migration and Return Regimes." *SOJOURN: Journal of Social Issues in Southeast Asia* 27:2 (2012) 234–59.

———. "'Over There': Imaginative Displacements in Vietnamese Remittance Gift Economies." *Journal of Vietnamese Studies* 7:3 (2012) 157–83.

Smith, Kay Higuera, et al. *Evangelical Postcolonial Conversations: Global Awakenings in Theology and Praxis*. Downers Grove, IL: InterVarsity, 2014.

Stebbins, Irvin R., and Thomas Stebbins. *Pioneering with Christ in Viet Nam: A Personal Account of How Dedicated Missionaries Brought the Gospel to Vietnam*. Fort Lauderdale, FL: Wining, 2006.

Stemple, Charlotte. *My Vietnam: Stories of the War Years from the Inside Out*. LaVergne, TN: Xulon, 2010.

Stott, John. *Christian Mission in the Modern World*. Downers Grove, IL: InterVarsity, 1975.

Sunquist, Scott. *Explorations in Asian Christianity: History, Theology, and Mission*. Downers Grove, IL: InterVarsity, 2017.

———. *The Unexpected Christian Century: The Reversal and Transformation of Global Christianity, 1900–2000*. Grand Rapids: Baker, 2015.

Taylor, Philip. *Connected and Disconnected in Vietnam: Remaking Social Relations in a Post-Socialist Nation*. Acton, Australia: Australian National University Press, 2016.

———. *Goddess on the Rise: Pilgrimage and Popular Religion in Vietnam*. University of Hawaii Press, 2004.

———. *Modernity and Re-Enchantment: Religion in Post-Revolutionary Vietnam*. Singapore: Institute of Southeast Asian Studies, 2007.

Tira, Sadiri, and Tetsunao Yamamori, eds. *Scattered and Gathered: A Global Compendium of Diaspora Missiology*. Regnum Studies in Mission. Eugene, OR: Wipf & Stock, 2016.

BIBLIOGRAPHY

Tira, Sadiri. "Diaspora Missiology and the Lausanne Movement at the Dawn of the Twenty-First Century." In *Global Diasporas and Mission*, edited by Chandler Im and Amos Yong, 214–27. Eugene, OR: Wipf & Stock, 2014.

———. *Filipino Kingdom Workers: An Ethnographic Study in Diaspora Missiology*. EMS Dissertation Series. Pasadena, CA: William Carey International University Press, 2011.

———, ed. *Human Tidal Wave: Globalization, Migration, Megacities, Multiculturalism, Pluralism, Diaspora Missiology*. Philippines: Lifechange, 2013.

Thomas, Mandy. "Crossing Over: The Relationship between Overseas Vietnamese and Their Homeland." *Journal of Intercultural Studies* 18:2 (1997) 153–76.

———. *Dreams in the Shadows: Vietnamese-Australian Lives in Transition*. St. Leonards, Australia: Allen & Unwin, 1999.

———. "East Asian Cultural Traces in Post-Socialist Vietnam." In *Rogue Flows: Trans-Asian Cultural Traffic*, edited by Koichi Iwabuchi et al., 177–96. Hong Kong: Hong Kong University Press, 2004.

Thuy, Pham Van. "The Road to Doi Moi in Vietnam." In *The Economy and Business Environment of Vietnam*, edited by Roderick Macdonald, 25–45. Cham, Switz.: Palgrave Macmillan, 2020.

Tran, Jonathan. *The Vietnam War and Theologies of Memory*. Malden, MA: Blackwell, 2010.

Trinh Vo, Linda. "Vietnamese American Trajectories: Dimensions of Diaspora." *Amerasia Journal* 29:1 (2003) ix–xviii.

Truong, Tu Thien Van. "Mệnh Trời: Toward a Vietnamese Theology of Mission." PhD diss., Graduate Theological Union, 2009.

United States Department of State. "Foreign Language Training." https://www.state.gov/foreign-language-training/.

Valverde, Kieu-Linh Caroline. *Transnationalizing Viet Nam: Community, Culture, and Politics in the Diaspora*. Philadelphia: Temple University Press, 2012.

Van Engen, Charles. "Biblical Perspectives on the Role of Immigrants in God's Mission." *Evangelical Review of Theology* 34:1 (2010) 29–43.

Vertovec, Steven. *Transnationalism*. New York: Routledge, 2009.

Veteran Vietnam Observer. "Two Steps Back? Vietnam's Decree (On Religion) ND-92 Effective January 1, 2013." January 18, 2013. Unpublished article.

VietnamNet Global. "Vietnam Receives Record 13 Million Foreign Visitors in 2017." April 1, 2018. https://vietnamnet.vn/en/vietnam-receives-record-13-million-foreign-visitors-in-2017-E193237.html.

Vo, Nghia M. *The Viet Kieu in America: Personal Accounts of Postwar Immigrants from Vietnam*. Jefferson, NC: McFarland, 2009.

Walls, Andrew. *Crossing Cultural Frontiers: Studies in the History of World Christianity*. Maryknoll, NY: Orbis, 2017.

Wan, Enoch. *Diaspora Missiology: Theory, Methodology, and Practice*. Portland, OR: Institute of Diaspora Studies, 2011.

———. "The Phenomenon of Diaspora: Missiological Implications for Christian Missions." In *Scattered: The Filipino Global Presence*, edited by Luis Pantoja Jr et al., 103–21. Manila, Philippines: Lifechange, 2004.

Wan, Enoch, and Thanh Trung Le. *Mobilizing Vietnamese Diaspora for the Kingdom*. Portland, OR: Institute of Diaspora Studies, 2014.

Wan, Enoch, and Michael Pocock, eds. *Missions from the Majority World: Progress, Challenges and Case Studies*. Pasadena, CA: William Carey Library, 2009.

Wan, Enoch, and Sadiri Joy Tira. "Diaspora Missiology and Missions in the Context of the Twenty-First Century." *Torch Trinity Journal* 13:1 (2010) 45–56.

———. "Diaspora Missiology." In *Mission Practice in the 21st Century*, edited by Enoch Wan and Sadiri Joy Tira, 27–54. Pasadena, CA: William Carey International University Press, 2009.

Wang, Chih-ming. "Politics of Return: Homecoming Stories of the Vietnamese Diaspora." *Positions* 21:1 (2013) 161–87.

Wild-Wood, Emma. "Common Witness 'in Christ': Peregrinations through Mission and Migration." *Mission Studies* 30:1 (2013) 43–63.

The World Bank. "The World Bank in Viet Nam: Overview." https://web.archive.org/web/20210102082326/https://www.worldbank.org/en/country/vietnam/overview.

Ybarrola, Steven. "Anthropology, Diasporas, and Mission." *Mission Studies* 29:1 (2012) 79–94.

www.ingramcontent.com/pod-product-compliance
Lightning Source LLC
Chambersburg PA
CBHW062024220426
43662CB00010B/1468